Barcelona to Buckie Thistle

Exploring Football's Roads Less Travelled

MAT GUY

Luath Press Limited

EDINBURGH

www.luath.co.uk

First published 2019

ISBN: 978-1-913025-35-9

The paper used in this book is recyclable. It is made from low chlorine pulps produced in a low energy, low emission manner from renewable forests.

Printed and bound by Ashford Colour Press, Gosport

Typeset in 11 point Sabon by Lapiz

MAT GUY lives in Southampton with his wife Deb and cat Ellie. He has written about football for a number of magazines, including *Box to Box*, *The Goalden Times*, *Thin White Line* and *Late Tackle*. He published *Another Bloody Saturday: A Journey to the Heart and Soul of Football* in 2015 and *Minnows United* in 2017 with Luath Press. *Barcelona to Buckie Thistle* is his third book.

To Deb, for absolutely everything. And Ellie for being Huckleberry Finn to my Tom Sawyer

Contents

Introduction

This is all one man's fault. A man without a name, having only met him briefly on a single occasion – a book-signing.

Not any book-signing though, it was a *terrible* book-signing, on a cold and wet Saturday afternoon in the bar of a football club whose supporters had no idea why I, the writer, was there.

Four hours sat smiling hopefully at people as they wandered past, some pausing to try to understand what all the books, scarves, shirts and photographs neatly displayed across a table were all about. At best, there were some sympathetic nods towards me, an isolated man lost amid a sea of unsold books – a tacit support of someone clearly floundering in whatever endeavour they were attempting. At worst, there were looks of great suspicion, like this man ostracised from the rest on his own table was somehow here as punishment for some crime committed, literary or otherwise – a public humiliation enforced on some heinous offender. Either way, best steer clear.

I say it was a terrible signing, but two books sold is two more than none. Two opportunities for the people whom I met on my footballing travels to have their stories heard. Any connection made, in reality, is priceless, and well worth the daggered stares from elderly gents from behind their half-supped pints. And without this ego-sapping afternoon I wouldn't have met the man who gave me my direction for this book.

He stopped with his companion, two men past pensionable age, fresh drinks in hand, and pointed at the colourful red and yellow Partick Thistle scarf draped across the table.

'Partick Thistle!' he said in a broad Scots accent. I nodded and began in on my faltering spiel about my book containing football stories far from the bright lights.

'Do you go up to Scotland to watch football often?' he said.

I told him of a couple of trips to Firhill, home of the mighty Jags of Partick, along with visits to Celtic, Berwick Rangers, Hamilton Academicals, Arbroath and Cowdenbeath.

'So, where next?' he asked, picking up a copy of the book, flicking through it way too fast for there to be any information imparted to him.

I began in on a notion I had about exploring The Highland League, a semi-professional division that was a part of the fifth tier of Scottish football. My grandmother had come from the region, I explained, though I knew little about her life, and the fact that it was the most northerly and isolated senior league in the United Kingdom appealed to me.

He shook his head, dropping the book back on the pile. 'Don't bother. It's awful. Terrible. Not worth the trouble.' He took up his pint, nodded at the table. 'Good luck with all this,' he said, still unsure exactly what *this* was, before dissolving into the crowd of the bar, all steeling themselves for the miserable weather they were about to face. This left me stunned, alone, copies of the book that had attracted no bites that day strewn about me, my next idea dismissed so out of hand as terrible, not worth the trouble. What a day!

If I had to give it a name, my journey through football could very well be entitled 'a series of random and mainly inconsequential acts of defiance'. From a young age, I felt compelled to swim against the tide of popular footballing opinion in the school playground. My grandfather's love for the unknown, the mysterious, the hidden, as witnessed though hours of us both poring over his collection of old and ragged *National Geographic* maps detailing far-away places I'd never heard of, had a far more profound effect than even I realised at the time. Where he wondered at lost cities and temples, his excitement somehow translated in my mind into a wonder of another kind; of the unseen football grounds and kits, at club badges that may exist among these far-flung places. I loved the sport, and I wanted to explore it, but off the beaten track, just like my grandfather explored the world from his kitchen table in rural Wiltshire.

When my playground cohorts began falling in love with the FA Cup-winning Tottenham Hotspur side of 1981 and that stupendous Ricky Villa goal, or the all-conquering Liverpool, or their near neighbours, Everton, whose league win in 1985 made all the kids want that vibrant blue kit for Christmas, I found myself falling for non-league Salisbury, my grandfather's team, absorbing all its charm, warmth, meaning (at least to the few hundred souls that would join us on bitter winter afternoons) sat next to him in their dilapidated old stand. The drama and excitement of any match at Victoria Park felt as powerful to me; the passion from the stands and terraces as tangible as at The Dell, Southampton, where I witnessed the very best of the English professional game. I held them both in the same esteem. Both, for me, were as important and wonderful as the other. They both mattered. Christmas would be made by my nan hand-knitting me a Salisbury scarf, as Southern League teams didn't have the wherewithal or finances to produce replica kits and scarves of their own. I wore it with pride. I still do.

When the school playground came alive the glorious summer of 1982, with children trying to recreate masterful moves by Brazil at the World Cup in Spain, or Marco Tardelli's iconic goal celebration for Italy, when the Panini sticker-swapping frenzy for him and Socrates, Zico and the rest grew to fever pitch, I had other main targets. While I wanted them for my album too, my reverence also befell the little double stickers, where two players had to share one sticker, that were afforded the 'inferior' teams of El Salvador, Kuwait, and Cameroon. Obscure names, hometowns, club sides, all listed beneath each player's space in the album – they all fascinated me as I imagined what they looked like, the stadiums they played in, the kits they wore, all in a far-away land. In the pre-internet era, imagination was all I had to go on. But it was clear to me, even then, that they mattered. Just as Salisbury's players, home ground and results did to me.

Pride, passion, belonging, identity and hope were all entangled among those obscure names and teams, knitting a mythology together that people believed in. Countless tales of last-minute winners, cup final victories, league titles, heart-breaking relegation that has become legend over time. Unknown acts of dedication and self-sacrifice to make it into the stands on match day, to make it out onto the pitch. All swirling about the ether of these distant lands, just as it does about the vast stadiums that are home to the game's biggest names. And here they were, having seemingly achieved the impossible in reaching the World Cup finals, alongside the game's greats, their stickers rubbing shoulders with them in piles of swapsies in excitable children's schoolbags. They were to be revered in equal measure, by me at least. All this information, along with lists of qualifying matches against equally obscure countries was all archived safely in my album. I still have it. Obviously. It is footballing *National Geographic* treasure. It excites and inspires me still, nearly four decades on.

When I began my love affair with football programmes, when they were the only source of reliable information in a pre-internet age, it was those of the likes of Forfar Athletic, Tranmere Rovers, Newport County and, of course, Salisbury that began to fill up boxes under my bed. Invaluable resources revealing a rich and fascinating world among the lower leagues; their grainy images, pen pics and league tables were a window into an intoxicating world rarely troubled by television cameras or national newspapers.

Now, in later life, it is Accrington Stanley and the Faroe Islands that excite more than the Champions and Premier Leagues. A simple (and inconsequential) act of defiance in the face of overwhelming public interest in the latter. Popularity never has and never will dictate importance and meaning to any footballing institution. They matter, no matter to how few, in the way that Barcelona fans care for their team, roaring with such intent and fervour at another goal that the very walls of the mighty Camp Nou feel like they could reverberate apart.

It is a towering sporting cathedral, Camp Nou, that competes with La Sagrada Familia, its religious cousin across town, for the devotion of the Catalan people and the millions of tourists that flock to both every year. It is a sporting pilgrimage for football fans near and far, taking buses, taxis, and the metro before walking the last few hundred metres along sun-baked residential streets that cower beneath the towering façade of one of the world's most important sporting institutions.

Queues form outside the gift shop, while other lines snake patiently in the heat, waiting for their turn on the stadium tour. Hundreds of people – possibly thousands – pass the time, slack-jawed, staring up at the vast oval walls that rise up to the heavens. Visualising the steep nosebleed-inducing banks of claret and blue seats that defy gravity, clinging to these walls along with their 100,000 other brethren, one can only imagine the fervour, the swaying passion of a sold-out Camp Nou on match day. Because this isn't a match day. In fact, it isn't even in season. The throng of souls milling about the base of this great building are doing so in the full knowledge that there will be no magic from Messi today.

But still they come, so strong is the pull of this place. They wait patiently to experience walking in the shadows of giants; through changing rooms, a chapel, the players' tunnel and out into the blinding light pitch-side. A final stop – right at the very top of the main stand, looking down at the tiny dots milling about taking photos by the dugouts – hammers home the majesty of the place. No matter your footballing allegiances, you can't help but leave a little bit of your sporting heart behind in such an overwhelming tribute to the beautiful game.

The Highland League currently has 17 mini Camp Nous dotted about the Scottish Highlands, miniscule in stature by comparison but equal in meaning, spiritual and physical, to the weather-hardened souls that call them home. There may be no queues for stadium tours and non-existent gift shops but these 17 Highland grounds encompass history and community, belonging and meaning across scores of decades, just as the Camp Nou does. Trophy cabinets and pictures on clubhouse walls detail achievements, friendships and adversity overcome in the face of relative obscurity. Lovingly maintained stands (albeit some past their sell-by date), pitches, turnstiles and clubhouses suggest that there is something worth the trouble here, there, and wherever a small patch of ground devoted to the beautiful game is treated with similar reverence. They are all Camp Nou, in meaning if not stature, if only to those loyal few.

In truth, there was no way one person, though probably representing a great many more in opinion, was ever going to halt a lifetime of progress exploring football on the roads less travelled. Too many trips taken, people met, experiences absorbed and words written to prevent any doubts from lingering much past the car park and the journey home that cold, wet, book-laden winter's day.

The knowledge that 125 years of the Highland League could not be so easily dismissed, in my mind or others', fortified what had been a demoralised soul.

125 years in which two clubs – Clachnacuddin and Forres Mechanics – have remained ever present. Another two founding members, Inverness Thistle and Caledonian, merged to form Inverness Caledonian Thistle,

a team who have frequented the Scottish Premier League in recent times and have dispatched Celtic in cup glory in years gone by. Premier League Ross County and lower league Elgin City and Peterhead have also gone on to represent the Highlands within the professional ranks.

The league that is not worth the bother has also caused Scottish Cup upsets. In 1959, Fraserburgh dumped out top-flight Dundee, who fielded Scottish Internationals Bill Brown in goal and Doug Cowie on the wing, as well as another three players who would go on to represent their nation and to become the first ever Highland League team to achieve the feat. In 2018, it would take Rangers to stop 'The Broch', as Fraserburgh are known, in the fourth round. A hat-trick by Josh Windass, a player admired from the terraces when he wore the red of Accrington Stanley, saw off The Broch in front of a home crowd of 1,865.

Cove Rangers and Brora Rangers would go one round better the same year, equalling the Highland League record of reaching the fifth hurdle before being defeated by Falkirk and Kilmarnock respectively. Both Rangers, one from the far north, the other from the eastern extremities of the league, had also recently fallen at the final play-off hurdles to enter the professional leagues above, Cove being edged out by the odd goal in five in their attempt to replace Cowdenbeath in Scottish League Two a few months before my Highland adventure began.

Fortified with these statistics, and the knowledge that there is a wealth of stories, experiences and characters to explore, so begins the latest round of acts of footballing defiance, though they will by no means be restricted to just the Highland League. Other much maligned leagues completely dismissed out of hand have bolstered this Highland odyssey like the lower reaches of the UEFA Nations League via the Faroe Islands. The mini premier leagues of San Marino and Andorra, and the absence of any league at all in Liechtenstein due to insufficient numbers, will assist the Highland League in proving a point that the beautiful game instils just as much magic and passion among the lesser lights as it does at the very top.

This journey is not a two fingered salute to my book-signing friend, more an outstretched hand, an open invitation to explore an intoxicating, mysterious, passionate and ultimately soul-enriching road less travelled. And you never know, these little acts of defiance may become contagious to a precious few. Because we all need a little adventure in our lives. And where better to explore than the communities and clubs hidden among the folds of football's own vast *National Geographic* map? They may be leagues apart in some respects, but with their all-pervasive sense of community and belonging, their celebration of identity and meaning, those that populate them just might, in fact, be leagues ahead.

CHAPTER ONE

Operation Zero Points – Fort William

AN ENTRY LEVEL act of defiance this is not. More a Hail Mary pass of convictions that could just as easily end up in the long grass as in a glorious last-minute winner. There would be no trip to mid-table security, or safer yet, to table-topping hopefuls. No, the Scottish Highland Football League would live or die, in the first instance, on its perceived weakest links and a mid-week match among the Munros of the West Highlands. Home to one of the remotest and, in footballing terms, most forsaken outposts in the division, if not the country – Fort William.

In the nine seasons since Strathspey Thistle joined the Highland League, there have been only three teams to pick up the wooden spoon in Britain's most northerly senior division, the Strathy Jags being one of them. Rothes is another. Representing the town of the same name (population: 1,200), the football club stands on the banks of the River Spey deep inside whisky-distilling country. From there, a cluster of world-famous Scotch whisky producers stretching from the foothills of the Cairngorm mountains to the south, up to the storm-battered coastline in the north, manufacture their fiery magic.

The Speysiders, as they are known, suffered the fate of coming last in 2015 and 2016, before recovering and moving up into the lower reaches of mid-table, from where they had fallen. Strathspey Thistle, a 40-minute drive south past the mouth-watering Aberlour and Glenlivet, also sits on the River Spey. Their Highland League baptism of fire came in 2009, and a season with only three wins and a goal difference of -90 saw them come last out of 18. Two wins the following season and a goal deficit to the tune of -95 was, however, enough to see them climb off the bottom to 17th. Their perennial basement bedfellows, Fort William, propped up the league that year with two wins and -112 goals conceded. In their nine Highland League campaigns, the Strathy Jags have finished last twice, second-last four times, and third from bottom twice. Only in 2012/13 did they escape the bottom three, finishing fourth from last with five games won and 73 goals conceded. It is an unenviable record. Unless you are Fort William.

The Fort are an anomaly. Geographically they are not easily compatible with any league anywhere. Where most of the Highland League congregates along the northern coastline to the east of the Highland capital of Inverness, stretching south toward the Cairngorms and south-east to Aberdeen, they do not. The only contradictions to this general Highland League trend are Brora Rangers and Wick Academy, who can be found along the long and winding road that links Inverness to the most northerly points of the Scottish mainland, and the ferry to the Orkney Islands. Their relative isolation – Wick Academy needing a ten-hour round-trip to face Aberdeen-based Cove Rangers – means that a simple hour-long jaunt between the two results in some feisty derby matches.

For Fort William, overlooking Loch Linnhe on the west coast, it is not only their footballing pride that sits out on a limb. Known primarily for its proximity to Britain's largest mountain, Ben Nevis, where it is used as a base camp for most of the 100,000 who climb its slopes every year, Fort William is the epitome of isolation. Two and a half hours by car from Glasgow, and two hours from Inverness, Fort William is on the way to nowhere for most and is often bypassed in favour of the more picturesque Oban to the south. It is, however, the West Highlands' Mecca for climbers and hill-walkers, as it marks the beginning and end of the 96-mile long West Highland Way, which traverses spectacular scenery amid vast, looming Munros (mountains with a height over 3,000 feet), and rugged valley floors that wend their way between the town and Loch Lomond to the south. Fort William also hosts the start and finish of the Great Glen Way, which weaves north between equally beautiful landscape for 70 miles until it reaches Inverness via the banks of the infamous Loch Ness. For even hardier explorers, it is also the last staging post before the long road to Glenfinnan and the Western Isles beyond. Apart from these walkways and narrow roads, the odd village sheltering in the lee of a mountain pass, there is precious little else to suggest humanity ever ventured this way.

Such isolation meant that a significant settlement didn't manifest itself until 1654, when Cromwell had a wooden fort built there to house English troops in the region. Their aim being to pacify the Clan Cameron after the 12-year War of the Three Kingdoms between England, Scotland, and Ireland. In 1688, after the overthrow of King James II of England by William of Orange, the settlement was named Fort William in honour of the Dutch Prince who ruled not only the lowlands of what is now Holland, but also England, Scotland and Ireland until 1702. In 1745, Fort William was besieged for two weeks by Jacobites, a group following a political movement which aimed to restore a Roman Catholic King to power. But while regional neighbours Fort Augustus and Fort George fell, Fort William held firm.

Modern-day Fort William (An Gearasdan to the 700 or so Gaelic speakers that live here, the derivation of which is unclear, but most likely an approximation of the English 'Garrison') is home to some 10,000, who rely on tourism to fuel the economy, populate the shops on the high street, guest houses and camping grounds and fill sight-seeing boats and local fish restaurants supplied by the handful of fishing boats tied dockside. It is an idyllic setting for an antidote to modern living, but hard work for a football team competing in senior football.

Just as location is against Fort William's football team, so too is history. While Fort William FC were formed in 1974, playing friendly matches and cup games in the North of Scotland Cup and the Inverness Cup until 1983, when they joined the North Caledonian League, their main sporting competitor, shinty, had close to 2,000 years' head start.

Shinty is a game that was once popular the length and breadth of the United Kingdom. The Olympic sport of hockey is a more sedate variation of the Gaelic form that continues today in Ireland as hurling, and in Wales as bando, along with its Scottish cousin. Thought to originate from the Legend of Cùchulainn, a hero in Celtic mythology and son of the Celtic God Lugh, shinty has been ingrained in Highland tradition for millennia. No surprise then that Fort William's two shinty clubs, Kilmallie and a side named after the town itself, dominate sporting proceedings here. Even now, more than 30 years on, the thrill and wonder as a young boy catching a shinty match in Kingussie, a small town within the Cairngorm National Park, while on holiday with my family remains vivid. Flailing camans (sticks) creating a blur amongst players fearlessly facing them down, all in the pursuit of a small hard ball and a sight of goal. Blood curdling body checks, industrial-strength swings, a hurtling ball, all set to the familiar cries of sportspeople at war; it was intoxicating stuff, even for someone already committed to football. That an ambulance was already parked up pitch side, its driver sitting idly with the rear doors open waiting patiently for the almost inevitable call to action from the battleground, made it a memory that would last. The ferocity of play was worthy of the great tales I would tell on the playgrounds back home after the summer break, a new addition to the mythology of the sport that grew from Celtic Gods.

With such competition and history, it is a wonder that football managed to claim any kind of purchase at all. But it did, and enough to register three cup wins and a runner's up spot in Fort William's first season in the North Caledonian league. In the Fort's second and final season in the league, they won it, as well as managing to retain two of their cups from the year before.

After two years of success, Fort William were finally admitted into the Highland League, the competition they had been trying to enter, but had been rebuffed every time, since their formation. Highland League life began with a 1-0 home win over Clachnacuddin, their nearest rivals based two hours away in Inverness. The 1985/86 season continued to see Fort William break new ground with a record home game of 1,500 witnessing them play Stirling Albion in the second round of the Scottish Cup. A goalless draw meant that record crowd left Claggan Park happy, before a 6-0 defeat in the replay. A creditable 12th place finish in their debut season was followed by 11th the season after. But momentum began to stall, maybe as the club's novelty began to fade among the town's population, and more than 30 years of doldrums descended.

With a limited pool of players to choose from, the history and popularity of shinty and arduous away trips to the other side of Scotland to face established Highland League teams began to see results turn for the worse. This geographical isolation, coupled with the fact that Fort William has always worked within a non-existent budget (even today, players receive no more than a nominal fee per game to play), saw a set of statistics build that might crush a less hardy bunch. In their 33 seasons in the Highland League, the Fort have come last 17 times, and finished in the bottom three on a further 11 occasions. In the nine seasons since fellow strugglers Strathspey Thistle joined the Highland League ranks, Fort William have finished last five times, and second last another three times, the only respite being the heady campaign of 2014/15 when the Fort finished in 13th place, with eight wins to their name. Indeed, in 2008/09, the year before the Strathy Jags came on board, Fort William set another unwanted record, finishing the season with a solitary point, the worst tally in the league's 125-year history.

With cold hard statistics like this, and year on year of long, fruitless and often humiliating trips to play – and lose heavily – games far from home, it is a miracle of passion and perseverance that Fort William keep on doing what they do. However, as the 2017/18 season drew to a close, it was announced that all six Fort Directors would be stepping down, their energies having run their course. Very real doubts began to surface as to whether Fort William Football Club would, or could, keep on keeping on.

With no Board, it seemed more likely that a club so down on its uppers would simply call it a day and bring an end to more than three decades of struggle. Who on earth would want to take on what on the face of it looked like such a thankless and soul-destroying enterprise? Logic should have dictated that Fort William FC withered and died during the unseasonably hot summer of 2018, becoming a footnote in Scottish football, and the answer to numerous cruel pub-quiz questions on the worst football team in Britain. The odds of finding replacements in the few short weeks before league constitutions needed to be formed and confirmed seemed to have sealed the Fort's fate.

Seemed to. But didn't. Because from out of the shadows of the supporter's club bar, a few unlikely hands found themselves raised at one final meeting, being propelled up into the air by heart rather than head. And from those smattering of hands, a new Board was quickly formed before they could be lowered again, before the enormity and insanity of their task could sink in. They would be assisted by the old secretary and treasurer, who would stay on for a short while to show these novices the ropes. Or at least as many of them as they could.

And with that, remarkably, Fort William set off on a new chapter. A chapter that would, in the first instance be a slightly chaotic one, with the club being five or six weeks behind its Highland League colleagues in preparing for the season ahead. Fixture lists were released, and Fort William found themselves planning for an opening day away trip to Rothes on the last weekend in July, despite the attendance of the first training session being so low that they could not field a five-a-side team.

Regardless of their two poor seasons a few years ago, Rothes would not be Fort William's main rivals during the season ahead. Raising a side to face them would be the Fort's first major hurdle, and they managed it, just. With a side comprising four trialists and only two makeshift substitutes, just making it across the white line ready for that opening whistle in Mackessack Park was victory in itself for the new Board. Just as well, as the Fort fell to an 11-1 defeat, triallist Liam Taylor scoring the consolation goal for the new era Fort William.

Victories would remain of a similarly ethereal nature in the following weeks. A 16-0 hammering at the hands of a strong Inverness Caledonian Thistle side in the North of Scotland Cup would open proceedings at home. Hailing from the professional ranks of the Scottish Championship, the second tier of Scottish football, Caley Thistle were embarking on only their second season at that level for 13 years, having previously made themselves a fixture in the Premier League. It was a game the Fort were never meant to win, but with only one sub, and barely three days to recover from the trip to Rothes, it was a bruising experience.

Three further double digit defeats to Buckie Thistle, Turriff United and Inverurie Loco Works in August were interspersed with a 6-0 loss at Huntly, and an 8-2 defeat at home to Formartine United. Another triallist, Alan Kerr, scored the Fort's second and third goals of the campaign. Despite the tough start, there was no lack of passion, on or off the pitch. It was always going to be tough, having had six weeks less than everyone else to get the club back up and running and to get a team together. But what was lacking in expertise, this small band of football brothers made up with pride. A pride and passion that sometimes got a little carried away with itself, as witnessed through Fort player Ryan Henderson, who found himself red carded against Formartine for a late challenge. So incensed was he that a string of expletives aimed at the referee as he trudged toward the changing rooms resulted in him being sent off, again, for abusive language. A second red before he had even left the pitch! Not exemplary behaviour, for sure, but an indicator that Fort William was an institution worth fighting for.

And just as Henderson displayed it on the pitch, so too did the paying faithful who parted with their seven pounds, week in and week out. Regularly amassing well into three figures, they populated the touchline, cheering on their team even in the face of a certain battering. Moral victories sustained all concerned, given how close they were to having no team to support come 3.00pm on Saturday.

But when it came to tangible victories, victories that could be registered on a league table that could chunter through a vidi-printer and into homes up and down the country, it would be Strathspey Thistle that Fort William would aim for, just as they had done for close to a decade. With the fixture computer throwing up a mid-week home tie against the Strathy Jags for matchday seven among the last days of August, both teams knew that, for them, this would be the true beginning of the Highland League season.

Like their basement rivals, Strathspey Thistle's record that season had been 'played six, lost six' though defeats had only come by five or six goals instead of by double figures. A couple of consolation goals and a 2-0 defeat to Rothes was as good as it had got thus far. Indeed, looking at both teams' results in the nine seasons since Strathspey joined the league, there was little to separate them. While Fort William had won just 27 of the 306 league fixtures in that time, racking up a goal difference of -852, the Jags had won 31 and conceded 780 times more than they had scored. Despite the season being barely two months old, and the year not even out of the summer months, there was no doubt that this fixture between the two would probably go a long way to deciding who finished up bottom of the pile come May. Or it would have, had a bombshell not been dropped just a few days before...

There is kicking someone when they are down, and then there is booting them in the head over and over. And for a lesser team, for a lesser collective of proud souls, this could well have killed a club dead in its tracks. For any team, a points deduction is a crippling blow to a season. For a team who managed just five the season before, it is catastrophic. And in the days leading up to the Strathspey Thistle fixture, days that had been for Fort William a real tonic – with the feeling that a corner had been turned with a better performance against one of the leagues strongest sides in Formartine, notice came down from the Highland League:

> The matter of Fort William FC fielding an ineligible player on three occasions was considered by the League Management Committee at its meeting yesterday evening.
>
> In forming its conclusion, the League Management Committee took into account the fact that the club had agreed that this amounted to a breach of Rule 8.9.4 and that the terms of clause 8.9.13 provided for a mandatory penalty.
>
> Consequently, the meeting decided that Fort William FC be fined a total of one hundred and fifty pounds and deducted nine points with immediate effect.

When it came to regulations, there could be no wriggle room, no matter the unanimous sympathy from across the league. With everyone aware that a small band of new volunteers, with little to no experience of running a football club, had kept one of their own afloat, this felt like overkill. But the integrity of the competition had to be maintained. Rules are rules.

For Fort William, the mountain to climb in being competitive for the season had grown to monstrous proportions. Just as Ben Nevis loomed over their Claggan Park home, so too would that misplaced envelope with a player registration form dominate the next eight months, and beyond. Already holding the unwanted record of lowest ever points tally in the league, the Fort faithful found themselves looking down the barrel of becoming another pub quiz statistic: Who are the only senior team in Britain to have ever finished a season on minus points?

It would take unbelievable resources of courage, determination and pride to face down a plight many would describe as hopeless, pointless, terminal, and a league table in the local and national papers that read: Fort William, last, played six, goals scored, four, conceded 56, minus nine points. A laughing stock to all except those within the Highland League, surely you would check your plans to undertake a thousand mile round-trip for this now sub-basement match against the nine-points-clear Strathy Jags?

The road from Glasgow wound along an ever-narrowing path north to the banks of Loch Lomond. There was a chill on the air, thick with the smell of pine from the forests that choked the shoreline, rolled in off the vast, still, slate-grey waters. Rain cloud drifted, snagged among the dark mountains beyond. As the Highlands opened up, the road crept among scenes more breathtaking than the last. From the Bridge of Orchy, the peaks of Black Mount and Meall a' Bhùiridh rose up. Up and on toward the pass of Glencoe and the Munros – though that word doesn't seem to possess the awe needed to evoke their vast, staggering beauty – that began to rise and close in on the ribbon of road threading its way across valley floors, which shrank beneath the sheer, bleak rock faces of Stob Coire Sgreamhach and Meall Dearg, forcing cars to slow, sometimes stop dead on the road, their drivers lost in wonder at their timeless awe.

Small patches of scree at the side of the road played host to cars and people, halted and staring up, watching mountains fade and drift among banks of mist and cloud, breathing in the sharp air. The spectacle is topped out with the black walls of the Three Sisters: Gearr Aonach, Aonach Dubh and Beinn Fhada, all well over 3,000 feet in height, all menacing the road enough to send chills down the spine.

The bridge connecting Ballachulish and North Ballachulish traversed a boiling mass of water. The calm of Loch Leven to the right met the chop and current of Loch Linnhe to the left – a vast body of water emanating from the Firth of Lorn and the Sound of Mull, the fathomless Atlantic Ocean beyond. The result was a near perfect line separating the two, where the swell and chaos of one attempted to swamp the benign lulling of the other. A protective loch bank, acting as a natural harbour kept eternal parity. The road went on, snaking the contours of the Loch's edge, until finally Fort William began to appear.

Sat among such rugged countryside, the town almost looks a disappointment, especially if tourists have just come from the picture-postcard Oban to the south. But unlike its cousin, Fort William can't afford to be anything other than multi-purpose. Yes, there are enough old buildings, tea rooms and shops selling souvenirs to keep the day-tripper happy, but there is also a workmanlike edge to the town. It feels like a staging post, a base for some significant endeavour. Groups of climbers, hillwalkers and other expeditionary forces decked out in some serious gear stock up on food, maps and other bits among gaggles of coach-tripping pensioners and foreign school children. Whether heading west to Glenfinnan, out on the walkways to the north and south or straight off the beaten track and up into the Munros, serious outdoor pursuit shops supply all manner of kit that could save someone's life out among the wilds beyond.

One complex at the far end of the high street seems to have got the town's multi-faceted persona down to a tee. Wooden steps lead up to a tea shop, postcards, cuddly Nessie toys and shortbread. Turn a corner and there are serious-looking maps and equipment, crampons and survival rations. A narrow staircase leads down to toilets and the entrance to a dark pub littered with regulars tired of watching lost sightseers stumbling upon their refuge. Beyond, a large bus station and connecting train station bustles to the warning horns of reversing vehicles and conductors' whistles. Among it all, a lone bagpiper brings the high street to a hush as a funeral cortege pulls up outside the church, a reminder that Fort William is also just a place where people live, and die, and have done so for more than 350 years.

Sat in pride of place just off the high street behind the bus station is Fort William Shinty Club. Overlooking the loch beyond, the pitch is a pristine, manicured swathe of emerald green. Hours of painstaking devotion are needed to create such a billiard table out of grass. Lining it, a stand of immaculate benches that could seat 500 waits patiently for the next match, and another chapter in the battle to gain promotion back into shinty's top-flight, the Marine Harvest Premiership. With little to separate local rivals Kilmallie and Fort William at the top, it would be an exciting end to the season for the town. If ever there was needed a physical manifestation of what shinty means to the Highlands and Fort William, the care and attention to this ground is it. A sport so ingrained by millennia deserves such immaculate shrines.

Fort William Football Club, however, being the new team on the block, doesn't enjoy a similarly prominent outlook to their caman-wielding cousins. The turning to Claggan Park is easy to miss on the Inverness road out of town. A sharp right sends you weaving between a small estate of council houses and a run of industrial units huddled along an ever-narrowing tongue of macadam. The ground is on you before you realise, first time travellers often having to double back past the brutalist back wall of a concrete stand fighting for prominence amongst a row of large, clawing fir trees.

It seems like Claggan Park is on a road to nowhere; fitting for a club with the eternal struggles of the Fort. However, just as this road deceives – thinning out among rough-hewn stone walls and steep sheep pastures, eventually ending in a small, exposed car park, and an Inn to fuel those wanting to take the hikers tracks across the spectacular foothills and valleys of the Nevis mountain range beyond – so too does the home of Fort William FC.

The thick wall of firs that encircles the ground looks like it was planted in the early 1970s when the club moved here. Too tall now to be topped out without the aid of a significant cherry-picker, they screen the club from the rest of the world, save for a small break and a sliver of a view rarely beaten by any other sporting venue the length and breadth of the country. At the foot of this break, a Narnia-esque entrance beckons. Between the branches, a narrow gate, a little hut, and then the Nevis mountain range rearing up behind the far goal: a silent Holt End, The Kop, Gallowgate End. It takes a moment to sink in. Thankfully there isn't a queue. A mountain range is an impressive natural 12th man. This awe-inspiring view must have drawn an error or two from a visiting keeper, not through intimidation like its constructed brethren of Birmingham, Liverpool and Newcastle, but through a simple distraction and wonder as clouds ripple and dapple, changing complexion and contour like a geological chameleon.

Cut adrift to the right, that concrete stand beckons. Dislocated from the dimensions of the pitch when the white lines were rotated 90 degrees a few years ago to try and aid drainage (Claggan Park often falls foul of waterlogging) it now stands a forlorn figure. Too full of memories to simply tear down, this smaller version of the one at the Shinty Club, and no less loved in its time, now slips into dereliction. Fenced off to prevent the failing roof from falling in on similar lovers of sporting architecture, it and the ghosts of crowds gone by crane from afar to view modern-day matches. Where it was once centre stage, distance and unkempt weeds and shrubs now obscure its view. Saplings and bushes replacing supporters on the crumbling terracing, commemorating favourite spots, regular haunts among friends. With failing rafters once reverberating with the roar of that famous cup game against Stirling Albion, an inaugural Highland League win over Clachnacuddin, it now cuts a sorry sight, although at least it remains, of sorts, a memorial to the past, looking on jealously at the two small pre-fab stands either side of the reconstituted halfway line, beginning to come to life as game night begins.

As floodlights splutter to life, slowly growing stronger, deepening shadows among the firs and the recesses of this derelict temple, Sam Lees, dressed smartly in a shirt and club tie, walks proudly to the little hut by the entrance. Setting out his tin for the gate money, he stands patiently, expectantly, peering out into the car park for any signs of activity while the Fort keeper and trainer amble out onto the pitch to begin their pre-match rituals.

Cutting a diminutive figure, Lees looks younger than your average community club committee member – much younger. Indeed, you would assume that the club, only 44, had a good few years on one of its latest custodians. Traditionally the preserve of pensionable men, his infectious smile is almost disarming, so used to the weather-beaten gruff of old-timers who had seen more seasons than they cared to mention from their little ticket booth. Being one of the few who found himself raising a hand to save his club in the summer, you would have maybe thought that the baptism of fire he had recently endured might have dented that smile. But none of it. Perspective saw to that.

'I really thought, leaving one meeting, that that was that last season. That the club was gone.' He shook his head. 'It was terrible. But here we are.' He beamed with impeccable timing as his pride and joy – the rest of the Fort William squad – jogged out onto the pitch to join their keeper. 'I'd never done anything like this before, but when it came to it, I had to step forward, to keep our club going. It has been a steep learning curve, and we are still learning all the time.'

Case in hand manifested itself when one of the Highland League Committee peered their heads round the line of firs – a jolly old man with a broad Aberdeenshire burr. 'Is it safe to come in?' he only half joked, having been one of the decision makers on the Fort's nine-point deduction a few days earlier. 'It is unfortunate, certainly, but we are right behind these lads.' Nodding at Sam, he added, 'and the club. They are one of our own and we are happy to have them. Now, where is that tea hut? I am parched.' And with that, the Highland League set off, shaking hands warmly with anyone and everyone in his path.

'We thought we had done everything our end,' Sam said as we watched him on his way. 'We thought we had the player registration in the post in good time. But it never arrived at the league's office.' He shrugged. 'We should have checked I guess, but with so much going on, we didn't. And here we are, on minus nine!'

'No matter. The club is here and in the long run that is all that matters. Points and results aside, just seeing a Fort William team cross the white line on match day is victory in itself for us, given how close it was to never happening again, and how little time we had to get everything ready once the decision was made.

'Even with the decision to take it on confirmed, we didn't know where to take it,' he said as I offered him the admission fee and he rummaged about the tin for change. 'The club had already indicated that they would be leaving the Highland League toward the end of last season and dropping down into the amateur ranks of the North Caledonian League. We weren't sure if, one, that could be undone, and two, if there was an appetite to stay.

'But at one meeting there were some home-truths spoken about the struggles to maintain senior football in the town over the years. How we couldn't take the easy route, and just give up. It would be as good as not keeping the club afloat in the first place.'

Sam spoke with passion, and a certainty that the right path had been taken. 'We are the only side offering senior football in the West Highlands. And that means something. Those that really want to test themselves at the highest level, they come here. It gives the kids in the junior teams something to strive for. Not having that would have killed football in the town. And, to be honest, dropping into the North Caledonian League wouldn't have solved any of our problems. It would have compounded them.

'We would still have been a good two hours from our nearest rivals in Inverness Athletic and would still have had to travel vast distances to face Thurso and the Orkneys. No, we knew that we had to stick with where we were, even though we knew it would be a rocky start.' Sam alluded to the early season results. 'We were a good six weeks behind every other club in preparing for the season. All the uncertainty about what league we would be in, and if we would be in any at all meant that we only had four players to our first pre-season training, and no manager!

'Getting to that first league match at Rothes with a team and a boss was such an achievement, and it continues to be every single match. Even getting beat 16-0 by Caley Thistle in the cup had to be taken with a pinch of reality: we only had one sub, and they had a full-strength professional 11 that had recently been playing Celtic in the Premier League. Sometimes results on the pitch aren't everything. We are just glad that the community have their club still.'

As he spoke, that same community began to trickle through the gates, depositing their seven pounds into Sam's tin before either heading for a pint in the lovingly tended clubhouse, or joining the cheery Highland League committee man at the tea hut. Kids take up a spare ball to have a kickabout adjacent to the pitch and the limbering Fort squad. A quintessential image of a community club.

'They all know the score,' he said, nodding at the club's stalwarts, young and old, coming through the gate; fading Fort scarves that had whipped in the winds of many winter storms laying limp across their shoulders. 'They all know that our players do this for the love of it. They all know that our lads get 15 pounds a week, while they are facing sides some of whom are paying their players hundreds of pounds every game.

'It is a semi-professional league but some are more so than others, which means there are really three leagues within our league. You have those that are punting for the title, that want promotion up into League Two. You have those that want to be competitive, and you have about five or six of us at the bottom who can't afford that, but who aim to be as competitive as everyone else. Sometimes it works. Sometimes not!

'It's not easy for them,' he said, nodding at the team continuing with their stretches beneath floodlights that had attracted clouds of midges, moths and other bugs to their strengthening beams. 'We all have a pride in what we do, and they are in the firing line, week in, week out. It is their names on the team-sheets, their bodies on the line. I get how being beaten badly can hurt. The ribbing at work, on social media.

'There is a new junior team that has been formed in the town, playing winnable matches in a winnable league. It must be tempting for some. But it isn't senior football. There isn't the same buzz as testing yourself against the best. And if we can continue to encourage, then hopefully we can build on what we have here,' he said, pointing at the pitch, 'by bringing in our young players from the youth teams. A community team, a senior community team, for and by the community. The players get it. They want to be part of it, even if it hurts some weeks.'

That a smattering of hands, inexperienced but willing, had pulled this scene of limbering players, milling supporters, old friends meeting up in slowly filling stands, children playing at the edges of the flood-lights, reach all together seemed victory enough somehow. But now that the club was up and running and moral victories had been scored and collected, Sam had ideas on more tangible results, that would begin to affect the cold hard black and white statistics of the Highland League table.

'Saturday's match against Formartine United felt like we had turned a corner on the pitch. Even though it was match six in the league, it felt like the end of pre-season for us, and the beginning of the rest of the year. Things felt like they were beginning to come together, and against one of the favourites for the title at that.

'We still have trialists in the team, but we are starting to see the body of a squad emerging. And tonight's match against Strathspey Thistle feels like the beginning of something.'

When asked if that night might be the night that the Fort began to make a dent on those minus nine points, he nodded. 'Could be, though it depends on which Strathspey Thistle turns up.' It was unintended serendipity, but as he uttered those words, Strathspey Thistle turned up in dribs and drabs, as the convoy of cars that had transported them from the Cairngorms began to pull into the car park.

'They can be very good, but they can also not travel well,' he said, diplomatically waiting until the straggle of threes and fours had strayed beyond earshot before passing judgement. 'They are one of the clubs like us with no money. These guys play and travel for the love of it, just like our guys do. And sometimes work commitments, family commitments, life gets in the way of a Saturday afternoon's football. It's not so easy to field a steady team, especially on those long away trips. They are one of the teams we will try to keep pace with, in our own mini league at the bottom. We will see,' he said, smiling as they passed by.

With the arrival of the opposition, the bodies queuing at the gate began to thicken. As if satisfied that their admission fee wouldn't go to waste now that the Strathy Jags were on the scene, they began to come in.

31

Sam nodded, waved, then disappeared into his hut, setting off with his cash tin on numerous random acts of arithmetic: 'One adult, a pensioner and a child? Not a problem. Would you like a team sheet?'

Complementing the hardcore Fort supporters snaking a queue away from the tea hut were a good number of first-time visitors. Families from the campsites that littered the outskirts of town batted away excitable questions from their eternally energetic children. 'No, I don't know if that is their centre forward' came one tired response to a pointed finger in the direction of the track-suited players warming up. 'Look, I don't think they do bottles of Tango here, you can have Sprite?' A sigh, as an oh so familiar whine began to grow in the throat of their offspring. He cut it off before it can blossom into a full-grown grumble. 'It's that or nothing, Liam, what'll it be?'

Warm-ups complete, the players made for the dressing rooms for one last pep talk, culminating in a collective roar and the banging of walls that reverberated out into the darkening summer night. As kick-off approached, supporters drained away from the clubhouse and tea hut, drawn to the perimeter of the emerald green floodlight pitch like the moths flitting about the lights high above.

There can be no better physical manifestation of the magic of football – this floodlit scene on a late summer's evening; the hopes and dreams of a season laid bare on a pristine canvas; a pitch isolated, elevated that much higher in a supporter's reverence, cleansed by the light from any prior disappointments. Like a nine-point deduction.

Chains were erected between changing room and pitch to enable the players an unhindered entrance. The pops and scratches of stud on concrete from within the changing room complex, like some distant outbreak of firecrackers, signalled that the players were on their way. Applause and shouts of 'Mon the Fort' broke out as the two worst teams in the Highland League ran out with purpose beneath the shadow of Ben Nevis.

Fort William looked serious, chests puffed out, menacing in their changed strip of all black that seemed to give them an extra few inches on their opponents. A psychological masterstroke, or a by-product of not enough time and hands to get their traditional gold home kit washed after Saturday's match? Given the passion and paucity of committee members, both were plausible.

The match began at a frenetic pace. Precise passing, surging runs, wicked crosses by winger Jamie Wilmshurst into the path of Saturday's two-goal hero Alan Kerr had the Strathy Jags on the backfoot. With midfield lynchpin Scott Hunter shouting himself hoarse and almost single-handedly keeping the formation tight with his constant direction, Fort William looked every bit a team and club worth fighting for. They played neat, exciting football. Football that could make a community proud, that could make you want to belong, that could make you raise your hand when the club needed you most.

And lo, it was ever thus: from Barcelona to Buckie Thistle – the simple beauty and passion of a simple sport igniting the souls that populate it, elevating them, inspiring them, nourishing them. Given all that had gone before, even a first-time visitor to Claggan Park couldn't help but become caught up in the thrill of such a passionate display.

But it was a display that was far from one-sided, as Strathspey Thistle slowly grew into the match. They, too, clearly possessed players that could play as the game turned into a ding-dong end to end affair. Shaking off stiff legs from a cramped two plus hour car journey, The Strathy Jags did nothing to suggest that the poorer cousins of the Highland League were anything other than well worth the respect of the wider football community.

As the game grew edgier the clearer it became that, for one side, this would be a morale-boosting result that could set up the rest of the season, and a set of young Fort ultras decided to employ some dark arts from the side-lines in the hope of upsetting the balance. Already decamped in the small stand nearest the away dugout, this group of five pre- or barely teens began to harass the opposition with shouts of 'You are shite' whenever a Strathy Jag strayed too close, 'Sit down' every time the opposition manager stood up and a barrage of wolf-whistles whenever a misplaced pass found touch.

Whether they had any effect on the opening goal, maybe we will never know. But when defender David McGurk hooked the ball past Michael MacCallum to give the Fort the lead, they banged the back panelling of their little prefab stand as if they knew for sure. How far the cheers of this 150 plus crowd reached into the mountains beyond the goal, or the nearby estate and campsites is uncertain, if they even reached them at all. But standing pitch-side, the joy in Fort William's fifth goal of the season and the first that had put them into the lead in a match was tangible.

A lot of blood, sweat, and tears had been shed to get to this point, and those that knew let their emotions show. This was much more than celebrating one scrambled goal. It was affirmation that their convictions had been right, that Fort William both deserved and needed to be right here, right now. It was a euphoria that reached half-time, and a breathless set of Fort diehards found themselves heading back to the clubhouse and tea hut with a skip in their step. Children set back out with their found ball to re-enact the first 45, but not the ultras. Fighting the urge, they sat back and rested up in preparation for another half of (possibly ineffective) disruption.

After all the exertion, passion, and sheer bloody-minded determination of the first half, Fort William began the second with a lethargy that suggested that the six weeks pre-season missed was starting to catch up with them. The influential Scott Hunter, who seemed to have carried an injury through the last few minutes of the first half, found himself benched with that same injury for the second. Wing play was failing on tiring trialist legs and a blue Strathy Jag wave pushed the Fort deeper and deeper. Just as the mountains beyond the goal Fort William were defending seemed to grow and loom with more menacing intent as shadow and darkness bolstered them, a similarly ominous atmosphere began to spread through the Fort faithful. Though it didn't stop them from spurring their side on.

Further substitutions for the tiring David McGurk and Jamie Wilmshurst brought the Fort to the bare bones. And when a rare Fort attack resulted in the Jags last man fouling Alan Kerr for an inevitable red card, it brought little respite. Despite being down to ten, Strathspey Thistle smelt blood, and no one was surprised when the equaliser came. A second, and a cruel defeat for the Fort seemed to be just a matter of moments away, every moment.

A rattled crossbar, shots rasping past the post, frantic scuffed clearances and scrabbled saves somehow kept the visitors at bay. When the Fort did get the ball, a narrowed pitch without the attacking wingers left Alan Kerr up front and isolated, but it didn't stop him chasing every lost cause, over-hit pass or hoofed clearance. As the 90 minutes drew to a close, one last lost cause saw him capitalise on a defensive mistake, driving forward as far as he could on heavy legs before a speculative shot from distance looped up and over the keeper, cannoning off the bar and to safety. It seemed as if all of Claggan Park, all the supporters lining the touchline, sank to their knees, just as Kerr did, exhausted from the possibilities of a fairy-tale ending that had been a coat of paint away.

There was still the fight to dream, the will to hope among the Fort William supporters. It is what so many clubs are held together with. And as the final whistle echoed up into the night sky, they had seen more than enough of both to fortify them for the season ahead. It was a point, lifting them to minus eight, and an immediate reaction sent to the league that they might be down, but they were not out.

Sam Lees, beaming with pride, manned the chains and hugged the Fort players and management as they trudged off toward the changing rooms. One moment of joy that no doubt made all the hard work and self-sacrifice that had gone before more than worth it. Risen from the dead, the Fort had their first (minus) point and their first (positive) result. With a healthy crowd watching and a team of triers you could believe in, Fort William had proven itself to be a precious football institution to those that called Claggan Park their second home. Even to the occasional visitor, the magic under the lights was palpable that lingered long after leaving Sam, the players and supporters having a celebratory drink in the clubhouse behind, floodlights dissolving away to nothing after a few kinks in the road.

In the weeks that followed, two things happened: the Fort's point against Strathspey Thistle grew in stature as the Strathy Jags went on to draw with the much fancied and big spending Formartine United, before a narrow 3-2 defeat at league champions Cove Rangers and a 2-0 win over Keith. At the same time, Fort William lost to Cove 11-0, 4-1 to Keith and 9-0 to Brora Rangers. Sam and the team knew that there was still a long way to go in Fort William's recovery, and that Strathspey Thistle had realistically moved too far ahead of the Fort to be meaningful foe in the battle to avoid the Highland League wooden spoon. For that they needed to switch focus north of the Cairngorms, to a small town on the coastal road between Inverness and Aberdeen, and the only team yet to register a point...

Lossiemouth Football Club has lived a largely anonymous life outside of its immediate community. Forming in 1939, at a time when many clubs were going into enforced hibernation due to World War II, Lossiemouth's only league title came that first season, winning the four game-long Central Highland Emergency War League over Rothes, Elgin City, an Army XI and a side from RAF Kinloss.

Joining the Highland League when it reconvened in 1946, Lossiemouth spent decades in lower mid-table before a seven-year nadir at the foot of the league between 1979 and 1985, coming last all but one season when they ended up above Forres Mechanics on goal difference. A short boon in the '90s saw third place finishes in 1993 and 1996, followed by a Highland League Cup win in 1997. But since then, 12 has seemed to be their number, finishing in that spot more years than not. Ten straight defeats come the end of September 2018 had left Lossiemouth eight points clear of Fort William, and a date at Claggan Park with huge significance for both sides.

There is nothing in life at the foot of the Highland League that comes easy, so it was no surprise that this game was torturous for both teams. The Fort went one up. Lossiemouth equalised. The Fort scored to make it 2-1 by half-time. In the second half, Lossiemouth equalised again. The Fort's Stephen Lopez was sent off at 70 minutes. Shortly after that, Lossiemouth went ahead for the first time. Somehow the Fort came back with ten men and equalised to make it 3-3 in the 88th minute, before a 90th minute Lossiemouth winner sealed a 4-3 debut victory that took them 11 points clear of Fort William.

Despite the stark realities of the Highland League table, the players, supporters and committee members of Claggan Park have enough perspective to mitigate it. From keeping the club alive, to getting 11 players across the white line for the league opener, to that point against Strathspey Thistle, they all know that they are building for the future. That future can be bright. But for now: small goals.

Clachnacuddin are having a tough year and are only one point ahead of Lossiemouth. With two games against their closest neighbours from Inverness still to come, and the reverse fixtures against Lossiemouth, the Strathy Jags, Keith and Nairn County who they have already run close featuring in the second half of the season, operation zero points is in full swing.

And if they don't make it, they do become the first senior team in British football to finish a season on minus points. If they do become that pub quiz question, it will hurt, but it won't dent their passion one bit. Because the alternative for those that care for this little team in the mountains is, and always will be, unthinkable. With a proud community, with people like Sam Lees and players so passionate they get themselves sent off twice during the same game, you can be sure that Fort William will be writing more positive chapters in their history books before too long. If Fort William are the worst that the Highland League has to offer, then the notion that the division is 'Awful, terrible. Not worth the bother' is already way off base. Bottom by some way, they may be. But not worth the bother, they most certainly are not. And that pride, that sense of belonging, that desire, against all the odds, is infectious, precious, and it will sustain them. It will also have even the most docile of first-time visitors to this small outpost of Scottish football howling from the touchline up into the mountain air, ''MON THE FORT!'

'Mon the Fort indeed.

CHAPTER TWO

The League of Nations – the Faroe Islands, Azerbaijan, Kosovo

IT IS ONE thing for a person to dismiss an entire football league to another over a pint at a book-signing. An anonymous conversation between two people, overheard by a third, the only effect of which being the fortification of one writer's future direction. It is another thing entirely to dismiss an entire country, or countries, on national television and in the press; claiming that they are wasting the time of larger, more successful footballing nations when forced to face them in European or World Cup qualifying campaigns. It is offensive and humiliating.

Every qualifying cycle it is the same. Whenever England are drawn in the same group as Andorra, San Marino, Liechtenstein or any of the other sides at the foot of the FIFA world rankings, the calls for pre-qualifying ring out. Citing an already congested fixture list, a one-sided game with an inevitable outcome and the inconvenience of dragging the best of England's Premier League stars to provincial stadiums in micro-states (not to mention the vast travelling circus of print, television, radio and online media that cover each game), the demands grow louder for these 'lesser' footballing lights to have a pre-qualifying tournament among themselves, whereby only the very best of the worst get to bother England.

It is the single most perverse and upsetting aspect of the modern game of football: the desire for the lesser lights of the beautiful game to cede their right to a level playing field, to enable the ever-bloating Champions League and Europa League to expand the fixture lists, pockets and trophy cabinets of the game's elite. It is a certain marker that football at the highest level is more of a business now than a reflection of what the sport means to the people that love it. People who, by and large, don't buy into this rhetoric one bit. People who understand that its universal appeal remains, well, universal, because it is a sport that belongs to us all.

A ball, a scrap of land and the ability to dream, to let your heart sing with that ball at your feet is how virtually every single soul that loves and lives the game world-wide became enthralled. A game for all, for all time.

At the most basic level, the world's governing bodies of the sport understand this intrinsic base value. When it comes to voting on World Cup hosts, or other issues, each member state has one vote of equal value. Be it American Samoa (holders of the world's heaviest FIFA-sanctioned international defeat when they lost 31-0 to Australia in April 2001) or serial World Cup winners Brazil.

It is a fundamental notion that the game really is everyone's and everyone is equal. It is how the game remains vibrant, relevant and captivating, because it feels like it belongs to you, me, anyone, not just the multi-millionaires at the top.

This is an idealised mission-statement view of how the game is run. We all know that there can be corruption, coercion and other methods of foul play that can skew these fundamentals. But, ultimately, this is how the sport has surpassed all others in the hearts and minds of the world. The fans understand this. The die-hard Tartan Army will spend their hard-earned money visiting Kazakhstan, Malta, wherever, with as much passion as trips to face Germany or Brazil. Because it is a celebration of identity, belonging, history, meaning, all through the sport that runs through our veins, that is an integral part of our spiritual DNA. They are acutely aware that if they feel like this, then so do the fans, the players of the opposition, no matter their status in the world rankings. It is a passion handed down to them when taken to their first matches by their parents, who were taken by their parents, who were taken by theirs, be it in Brazil, England, or San Marino.

In the 21st century, there is a fundamental respect between two nations facing each other on the football field, whereby anthems of the opposing side are observed with a hushed reverence, their end met with applause. So if yours can bring you to tears just by singing it, if the emotion of embracing your identity can do this to you, then why not a micro-state nation with a fraction of the talent on display?

The fans ultimately understand the meaning and the necessity of 'mismatches', despite the predictable grumblings from the same predictable culprits across the airwaves and back pages that can sway the armchair supporter to phone or write in to concur. They are mismatches in ability only, nothing else. Every one of the 55 UEFA member nations are equals when it comes to passion and the meaning forged from representing or supporting your country, your home. And when it comes to qualifying for the European Championships or the World Cup, the sanctity of the game demands that they start out as equals, these part-timers that will face down world-beaters. Because these nations *are* equal. That they can be drawn together is a unifying bond – a magical wonder of the footballing world, a necessity in order to maintain football's status as meaning all things to all people.

Surely a pre-qualifying tournament will offer smaller nations the chance to win, to gain confidence and, at the very least, to only lose by the odd goal or two? The continental bodies governing Asia, Central and Northern America and Oceania use pre-qualifying for the World Cup and their regional tournaments, so why not Europe?

Fundamentally, pre-qualifying isn't used for these idealistic goals. For the isolated Polynesian nations that make up a vast swath of Oceania's footballing population, it is too expensive, too time consuming to travel home and away across a qualifying group of five or six teams as their European cousins do. If it had to be done like that, only a handful of nations could afford to compete. The same is true of the Asian Confederation and Concacaf, who service the Caribbean islands as well as the likes of Mexico and the USA. Indeed, Bhutan, of the Asian Confederation, a country hidden deep within the Himalayas, only played their first World Cup Qualifier in 2015 thanks to a grant from FIFA, despite joining the world governing body 15 years earlier.

Pre-qualifying tournaments, where five or six nations meet at one venue and compete over a week for one qualifying spot enable the likes of American Samoa, the Cook Islands and Tonga to play the game they love, represent the nation they love and take part in the world's biggest sporting event. Yes, it is over in seven or ten days, leaving national teams dormant for years until the next one. No, there can be no development on such frugal opportunity. But where the alternative is no opportunity at all, it is gladly accepted.

Concacaf have used a home and away pre-qualifying fixture, meaning the likes of Montserrat, Aruba and the British Virgin Islands, barring an unlikely victory, have had two World Cup games to look forward to every four years. It is necessity, not design, that pre-qualifying is used in the remotest parts of the footballing world.

In Europe, where all 55 member nations have the finances and infrastructure to host any of the others (Gibraltar's Victoria Stadium being the last to pass UEFA's criteria in early 2018, enabling them to host internationals on home soil for the first time since they joined the international ranks in 2013), the only call for pre-qualifying is on the grounds of fixture congestion and one-sided score-lines.

It is true that facing down world champions, Ballon d'Or winners and household names can be a daunting proposition for those at the foot of the world rankings, especially if it is a new experience. Prior to 2013, Gibraltar's only competitive fixtures came via the Island Games. Admission into UEFA meant a swift re-calibration, swapping the likes of the Falklands, Jersey and the Shetlands for Germany, France and Italy. But having taken decades to finally gain admission into football's top table (Spain having been the stumbling block, asserting a claim to the territory), this footballing culture shock is one that they and every other nation down there among the high numbers embrace.

It was also a culture shock alleviated somewhat by UEFA's announcement of a new Nations League competition for 2018. While UEFA have resisted the urge to introduce pre-qualifying, appreciating that each one of their 55 members are equal, and deserve to be treated as such, they also understood their remit to offer equal opportunities for development to all nations. While upholding their inalienable right to be equal, UEFA also appreciated that for the likes of Andorra, San Marino and Liechtenstein, the opportunity to face teams of a similar stature, to take part in games they had a chance of winning, was very rare.

With all qualifying groups for the World Cup and European Championships drawn on a seeded basis, so as one group didn't include the top five or six nations, positive results for Europe's minnows could sometimes be recorded as simply keeping the score down. The odd goal against one of the big boys was a source of national pride. A draw or, even better, three points was a once in a generation affair, creating legends for all time.

The Nations League offers the best of both worlds, preserving UEFA's mantra (and tagline for their new competition) of 'Equal Game' for everyone by maintaining the status quo in qualifying for the big two tournaments. Meanwhile, this new competition is drawn based solely on ability across four bands. Within those four ability groups are four mini leagues of four teams each who play each other, home and away. The winners from each group in each of the four levels (A, B, C, D) will then have a play-off for the prize of a spot in the next European Championships: a unique opportunity for those in bands C and D.

A successful Nations League campaign can provide, at the most basic level, six games in a three-month period where, before, there could have been none. Many of the smaller nations struggle to find friendly fixtures outside of the qualifying groups, either through financial restrictions, or simply a lack of offers. Among those six Nations League fixtures, there is the opportunity for a team that doesn't meet up too often to really develop, for more competitive matches, possibly victories to celebrate. More games and more training can only be a good thing when it comes to other qualifying campaigns as well; a result of greater opportunity being improving standards, and possibly reducing the gulf in abilities by margins measurable in closer score-lines with the continent's giants. Beyond that, topping a Nations League group means promotion to the band above, and a play-off spot that could yield a place at football's top table.

It is a win-win situation for all, the tournament replacing 'meaningless' international friendly weeks with a competitive edge for the fixture-congested elite. For the rest, it's a wonderful opportunity. But a greater by-product than that, than anything that could happen within any given 90 minutes across any of the 55 continental national stadiums stretching from Reykjavik in Iceland to Astana in Kazakhstan, is the opportunity to be something more than just a whipping boy, an inconvenience. It's an opportunity to celebrate a national identity for a people so often dismissed out of hand by the media of Europe's elite footballing sons, without the tag of pointless underdog or the weight of ridicule and disrespect (should they ever read/see it) hanging over them. It is something we cannot fully comprehend because for us, identity, meaning and belonging comes easily. It is a given.

The further down the international rankings you go, identity, nationhood, recognition and respect can be hard-fought, hard-found and, in some instances, ongoing and precarious (and we haven't even touched upon those who fall outside the remit of football's governing bodies – those unrecognised by the UN, and therefore UEFA and FIFA. But that is another story...). It is an even greater reason why we – and by 'we' read 'our media' – should proffer respect rather than disdain to football cousins from far-flung places.

They may make great headlines, but they do not recognise the struggles some have faced to maintain that which we take as a given. For some, it has been a long hard road to preserve an identity, one of war, shifting political landscapes, religious divides, cultural imperialism imposed over decades, centuries, indifference and ridicule. For some, standing beneath the flag of your birth in an obscure venue in a capital way off the beaten path will probably mean a greater, and if not greater then at least the very same, rush of pride and emotion, that sense of belonging, passed down through generation after generation, than we feel at the likes of Hampden, Wembley or the Millennium Stadium.

And over four days on a cluster of remote, storm-battered islands facing down winter in the Atlantic, among the rarefied air of League D, group three of this new Nations League came to be, courtesy of the fearless footballers of the Faroe Islands.

The Faroe Islands is an archipelago of 18 islands roughly equidistant between Shetland and Iceland in the North Atlantic. Formed some 55 million years ago, they are the eroded remnants of a prehistoric volcanic plateau. During the last ice age, a vast ice sheet covered the Faroes and sculpted the breathtaking basalt mountains and cliffs that dominate this rugged outpost.

The first settlers on the islands arrived with the Irish abbott St Brendan in 560 AD, though it wasn't until the 9th century that the Vikings developed life on Føroyar (translated as Sheep Islands). However, these early inhabitants (led by Grìmur Kamban, as detailed in the 1200 AD text *The Saga of the Faroe Islands*) were not the typical Vikings of popular history, but farmers and peasants in search of a new life, having been forced to flee to avoid religious persecution at the hands of Norwegian King Harald Fairhair.

Despite their initial aims, the Faroes fell under the control of Norway around the same time as *The Saga* was written, before coming under the influence of Denmark in 1380. During the late 19th century, the first calls for independence came for the Faroes, fuelled by concerns that Denmark was suffocating the language and culture of the islands. Faroese, introduced by its early settlers 1,000 years earlier, is a variant of the old Norse exported by the Vikings, and remains as a living language in the Faroes and Iceland only. But under Danish rule it was seen as a peasant dialect, and wasn't taught in schools, Danish being the official language of the islands until 1948.

Yet, somehow the language (and the history, culture and stories of the Faroes within) survived. Passed down through folk songs that sometimes stretch into dozens of verses, the tales of the Faroes persisted. Just as well, as the first published text in Faroese came off the presses as late as 1823 in a translation of the Gospel of St Matthew. It was a controversial move, as even the Faroese, after centuries of having their language supressed and denigrated, didn't believe it worthy of the word of God. To quell calls for independence, Denmark finally introduced oral Faroese into the school curriculum in 1912, with the written form taught from 1920.

During World War II, with Denmark falling to Nazi Germany, the Faroe Islands came under British protection. The islands' fishing fleet helped feed Britain, while the Navy considered them a vital strategic point in keeping the Atlantic trade routes open. That period of home rule bolstered a second call for independence, and in peacetime a referendum was won. However, Denmark failed to honour the vote, instead offering a greater self-rule in 1948, including Faroese becoming the islands' official language. Despite this greater autonomy, centuries of cultural repression meant that progress with the written word was slow, with the first Faroese Bible published in 1962 and the first Faroese dictionary in 1998. The folk songs of the islands, which helped protect history, myths and tales for centuries, remained deep rooted into the islanders' psyche.

If the written word took a while to emerge, so too did a national football team. Despite club football emerging on the islands as early as 1892 with the formation of TB Tvøroyrar Bóltfelag on the southernmost island of Suðuroy, a national team took a lot longer to develop. Largely due to the political climate at the turn of the 20th century, where island identity was seen as being suffocated by Danish rule, a football team representing the islands alone was maybe a provocation too far. However, in 1930, the first Faroe Islands national team began to play a series of friendly matches against island neighbours Iceland, Shetland and the Orkneys, as well as a little further afield against Greenland and the Danish under-21 team. This would be the islanders' footballing lot until 1988 when the Faroes would affiliate with UEFA and FIFA, recording a famous 1-0 victory in their first ever competitive fixture against Austria in September 1990.

Since then it has been a largely anonymous life for the national team, often recording respectable results against countries with populations far greater than the 50,000 or so souls that call these islands in the middle of the storm-tossed Atlantic home. However, the psychological shadow of centuries of Danish rule and the rail-roading of the islanders' culture, dismissing it as no more than that of peasant stock for so long, did stunt the progress of the national team.

As late as 2006, supporters of the Faroes national team complained that their side was being hamstrung by club sides from Denmark, Norway and other countries who had cherry-picked the best talent from the islands. With the opportunity to make a living out of football on the islands limited and most of the club sides in the top-flight of the Faroes football league being part-time, it was standard for the best football talent to head to Denmark. Indeed, much of the island's youth find themselves spending time on the mainland for university or other studies at one time or another. However, it was also common practice for clubs to put pressure on Faroese players to feign injury, or retire from international football altogether, not wanting them to travel across Europe for what they believed to be meaningless, second class fixtures and risk actual injury. This was pressure on them to focus on their club career and respect the hand that fed them.

Not even this modern-day colonial subjugation, however, could prevent the Faroe Islands national team from slowly improving. The meaning of representing your family and your country beneath the flag of your people, especially with the weight of a history of cultural repression puffing your chest out, meant that the national team thrived – in its importance at the very least.

To this day, Europe's elite continue to travel via the windswept Vágar Airport, then wind between ominous, sheer basalt mountains, to play at Svangaskarð or Tórsvøllur stadiums, both exposed to the very worst that Atlantic storms can offer. There they meet this passion of meaning and identity head-on; even the world's best often failing to come away with anything more than a narrow victory. And with better facilities and better coaching, that gap continues to narrow, belying their status as the fifth smallest nation in UEFA.

It is probably only when that passion, that pride is removed that you can quantify just how far it can take you. Step forward the unfortunate tale of Pál Joensen, the greatest swimmer the Faroe Islands has ever produced. The Olympic Games is the pinnacle for any swimmer, the high-water mark (pardon the pun) in any athlete's career and is only matched by the World Championships. However, unlike the World Championships, where Pál could represent the Faroe Islands, The Olympics only recognises the totality of a territory (hence England, Scotland, Wales and Northern Ireland can compete as individual nations in FIFA-sanctioned competition, but could only do so as Great Britain and Northern Ireland at the 2012 Olympic football tournament). Pál and his fellow countrymen and women have to represent Denmark if they want to compete in the greatest show on earth.

Even though modern-day relations between the Faroes and Denmark are warm and amicable, and have been for some time, to the point that the Danes have said they would have no problem in the Faroes competing at the Olympics under their own flag, the International Olympic Committee disagrees. They are the rules. So, in 2012 Pál had to wear the red of Denmark, though he was born and had always lived in another country. And despite being a favourite to reach the podium in London in his preferred event, the 1,500 metres freestyle, he finished 17th. Training had gone well, there were no injuries or illnesses. He just came 17th, with a nagging feeling that something had been missing. This was compounded when he won bronze at the World Championships in the 1,500 metres a few months later. Fast-forward four years and after more heroics representing the Faroes by winning silver medals in the 1,500 metres in successive European

Championships, he arrived at the Rio Olympics at the top of his game, again wearing the red of Denmark. He came 30th.

Belief and pride can take you a long way, can make you achieve great things. It can help you face down the world's best and sometimes, like Pál, become one of them. But without it, we can become lost, a little rudderless. And as the fasten seatbelt signs came on, the plane from Copenhagen descending into the storm cloud below, shuddering as the wilds of an Atlantic October buffeted on all sides, I couldn't help but think of Pál. This was not Denmark we were heading for. This was something else. Something very different. This was the Faroe Islands.

Myriad waterfalls cascade from out of the thick cloud. Looming mountains tumble among the gloom; their ebbing and flowing shadow menacing the winding road. Occasional breaks reveal sheer, jagged basalt walls, slick and black. Away from the cascades, moss and grass cling and persevere in the failing light. Gravity-defying sheep somehow wander and graze. How vast these primordial volcanic mountains are, lost among the cloud, a first-time visitor can only wonder.

Having been some 12 years earlier, huge cliff faces, breakers smashing upon them with a relentless violence grew in my mind's eye. Villages huddled in the lee of vast geological wonders, overlooking stunning fjords, fishing boats safely home in small harbours. Turn after turn of breathtaking mountain scenery, all lost beneath an oppressive fog of cloud that often smothers the islands. Tunnels, roughly hewn through mountainsides, snaking for kilometres beneath the wild sea connect the villages and islands of the Faroes together. They are heavy and oppressive, feeling like you have descended into some fathomless mine. The air is damp and stifling, thick with subterranean pressures. Yet, somehow, they are comforting. The lights suspended from the ceiling are a reminder that human endeavour comes this way. Headlights from other cars on the road, no longer dimmed by fog and cloud, are welcoming, a sign that you are not alone in this supernatural landscape that you can only see a hint of among the ever-thickening pall that has snagged across the islands.

Faroese folk tales that read like extracts from some lost Tolkien story on the flight from Denmark took on a more believable tone once isolated from the home comforts of these man-made tunnels. Among the mist, cloud and the looming shadows, it seemed believable that early road construction across the islands had been altered so as not to disturb the Huldufólk (the hidden people). These grey, elf-like people who live in stones were 'Large in build, their clothes all grey. Black hair'. Their dislike for crosses and churches give them a sinister edge. The decision to avoid damaging rocks that they were believed to inhabit seemed a sound plan as the car edged further on, in failing light, across this land of cloud and menace.

Tórshavn, the islands' capital was completely lost beneath the fog as I approached. Visibility was close to zero as darkness descended. The streets were deserted. 20,000 people call Tórshavn home, more than a third of the Faroes' entire population. All were missing, which only exacerbated the feeling that a wrong turn somewhere had somehow resulted in driving into a silent horror movie. Reaching the nation's capital had been an experience in itself, trusting the signposts that had ghosted out of the gloom on the road from Vágar Airport. And then there it was: a close-knit weave of brightly coloured Nordic style houses hugging narrow streets; a church spire dissolving to nothing in the gloom; dulled shop fronts stretching up and away from the shimmering lights of the ferries in the harbour, a port that linked the more distant islands together. It was all lost, consumed, deserted. It was a disorientating experience.

The Faroese language has 34 different words for fog, and it felt like all had been experienced within minutes of weaving between the narrow streets of the Tórshavn. As night fell, *Kolampjórki* – an extremely dense fog had rendered all maps and distinguishing features useless. *Skuhur* – a threatening fog – had turned every narrow residential street into a seemingly identical set of neat, compact homes. External walls painted pastel colours dulled to monochrome, and every turn led to the sinking feeling that I was only getting more lost. The chime of a bell from the harbour rang tantalisingly close but not close enough to locate. A church spire ghosted in and out of view. Finally, having dropped the car off and attempted to walk into the town centre, *Regonskadda* – a rainy, wet fog – began to sap the spirit. All felt lost. Or at least, I knew I was. Could it really be that, after two flights, and one treacherous drive, having finally reached one of Europe's most isolated and smallest capitals, these various and ever-changing combinations of fog would prevent me from finding Tórsvøllur stadium, and a first taste of Nations League, Group D football? Very nearly.

Somehow, a mixture of good luck and Google Maps finally brought the vast Soviet era-looking floodlights of the National Stadium into view. Usually a landmark and footballing beacon that could be seen from every part of Tórshavn, these imposing, brutalist but beautifully designed stanchions only gave themselves up that night when virtually on top of them, so *Kolampjórki* was the weather. The powerful clutch of bulbs in each corner of the ground could only diffuse the fog for 50 metres or so. Just enough to illuminate all points of the pitch. But beyond that...

'It happens a lot in the Faroes,' said the man behind the bar, nodding at the fog, as I explained how long it had taken me to find the stadium. 'There is a saying here that if you don't like the weather, wait 15 minutes! It changes so much. Though I don't think that would have helped you tonight. It looks like it is here to stay.'

The Faroes sit in a belt of the Atlantic that attracts the worst of the storms. Fuelled by deep waters and trade winds, if there is weather to be had, it will find its way to the islands. And with the Faroe archipelago being the only land mass in this stretch of ocean, the fluctuation in temperature between sea and volcanic rock attracts cloud. Lots of it. That often swallows them whole, shrouding them from the outside world. They are real life 'lost islands', as if plucked from the pages of an adventure story and dropped into reality.

As with the deserted streets of the capital outside, shuttered windows of homely dwellings spilling slivers of warmth and light across yards that were no doubt bustling with play during the summer months (or rather, the more temperate months of a mid-Atlantic Faroese summer), Tórsvøllur stadium had a feeling that things were beginning to close down in preparation for winter. A community battening down the hatches in preparation for the wild dark that would dominate well into the following year. With daylight hours dwindling and winter storms upon them, the domestic football season only had two more weeks to play. When done, the nation's favourite sport would go into hibernation, riding out winter before re-emerging the following March. Indeed, this four-day home Nations League double-header against Azerbaijan and Kosovo had been pencilled in in October, because asking a visiting side to come across during the last round of matches in mid-November could well be pushing the limits of both sporting endeavour and sanity.

Couples, families, groups of friends, swaddled in all-weather gear that looked well suited to arctic exploration, began to congregate on the concourse and welcome one another. In a country of 50,000 and a capital of 20,000, being a stranger was an abstract concept. Groups of children ran and weaved excitedly between adults carefully carrying multiple beers back to their friends, picking up handfuls of inflatable clapper sticks that were being given away free, playfully hitting each other or playing 'tag' with them.

As the main stand began to fill (a wall of fog opposite marked out where an identical one would be built, construction beginning after these last two matches – winter not being able to halt this hardy people entirely), so too did a block in a smaller stand behind the left-hand goal. The Skansin Ultras, the most vociferous, colourful and dedicated fans of the Faroe Islands national team (named after the fort that overlooks Tórshavn harbour, protecting the capital from invasion) took to their positions decked out in shirts, face paint and flags. This was a white, blue and red wall that would sing, perform choreographed dances and roar on their team for 90 minutes, no matter whether they were playing Portugal or Azerbaijan. This was all about their country, their people and an expression of their pride in being Faroese. It didn't matter that they numbered no more than 150, or if they were being drowned out by a far greater number in opposition, as was often the case. The Skansin would do their thing and do it well. Not that it would take too much to drown out the support from Azerbaijan on that cold, surreal evening.

That there were any supporters from Azerbaijan seemed a miracle in itself, all the way out here in the mid-Atlantic. But there they were, a handful wrapped in their own flag of blue, red and green. Whether they had undertaken a 5,500-mile round trip from their capital Baku, a city on the Caspian Sea, or travelled from elsewhere, it was an impressive act of dedication, no matter their point of origin.

Like the Faroes, Azerbaijan are relative newcomers to the international scene. Breaking away from a disintegrating Soviet Union in 1991, the Republic of Azerbaijan found itself born into a politically volatile region. With Iran bordering its southernmost territory, and fellow post-Soviet Armenia and Georgia to the west and north respectively, it was a country founded on shifting political sands. No sooner had independence been gained, war was upon them, with a bloody conflict with Armenia over the mountainous Nagorno-Karabakh region that sat between the two. The majority ethnic Armenian population of Nagorno-Karabakh wanted to be independent from Azerbaijan, with close ties to Armenia, despite it always sitting within Azerbaijani borders. Azerbaijan refused to give it up, and a conflict that had been rumbling since 1988 grew vicious and unforgiving. Amid claims of ethnic cleansing on both sides, and fierce fighting that razed entire towns to dust, displacing hundreds of thousands of people (it is estimated that 700,000 Azerbaijanis fled Armenia and Nagorno-Karabakh, while 500,000 Armenians escaped to the west, some 40,000 soldiers lost their lives, and untold numbers of civilians). What was once a region in which ethnic Armenians and Azerbaijanis lived side by side had been turned into a battlefield. Life-long friends found themselves on opposing armies, and friends on the football pitch did too.

For as long as could be remembered there had been a healthy sporting rivalry between FK Stepanakert, from the majority ethnic Armenian town of the same name, and FK Qarabag, or Agdam Qarabag as they were known then, a predominantly Azerbaijani town of some 28,000 people. Less than 30 miles separated the two within Nagorno-Karabakh and fixtures between the two teams were eagerly anticipated in the region. With the war, all that ceased. Stepanakert was disbanded, the players joining the army, while FK Agdam Qarabag played on, right up until days before the fall of Agdam.

As the Armenian army drew closer, even the football team had to flee their town that was levelled in the shelling. Fleeing into Azerbaijan, the people of Agdam have never returned, the war won by Armenia in 1994. Their former home a ghost town, razed to the ground and derelict beyond repair, many remain in makeshift refugee settlements near the border, on occasion falling victim to sniper fire that threatens to enflame the uneasy peace.

In the eyes of the international community, Nagorno-Karabakh remains a part of Azerbaijan, seized by Armenia. And as such, the team from Stepanakert now exists within a country unrecognised by the United Nations. Players must move to Yerevan, the capital of Armenia, to continue their football careers. Failing that, the odd game for a Nagorno-Karabakh representative side against fellow unrecognised states in the region like Abkhazia is all that there is to look forward to.

For the homeless players and supporters of FK Agdam Qarabag, however, football lived on. Moving to the capital, Baku, Qarabag moved into the Azerbaijani League with much success in recent years, representing the country in both the Europa and Champions League. Despite the distance from the Nagorno-Karabakh border, supporters from those embattled settlements still make the ten-hour, 600 kilo-metre round-trip to the capital to see their team play (now known simply as FK Qarabag). Whether any of the handful of Azerbaijan supporters, shivering in the corner of this fog-bound stadium so far from home, were once from Agdam, we will never know. Whether they felt compelled, through the continued grief of their lost town, their beloved stadium, to travel to support the seven Qarabag players in this Azerbaijani squad, it is, again, unknown. The passion football evokes means you certainly shouldn't bet against it.

Despite the history they represent, most of the seven Qarabag players, wrapped up in hats and gloves as they came out to begin their warm-ups, were not old enough to have been born in Agdam. All would most certainly have been far too young to remember anything about the war that displaced the club they now played for. However, the fact that Armenia and Azerbaijan are kept apart in all qualifying competitions suggests that memories run deep via history books and stories handed down through generations. The benign rivalry between Stepanakert and Agdam has been lost forever. The bitter memories of lost homes and loved ones have ensured it will not return any time soon.

Theirs may be a national team that lives, to much of the world, in obscurity (from an all-time low FIFA world ranking of 174 in 1994, to a position 20 years later some 100 places higher, Azerbaijan currently sit alongside the Faroes around the 100 mark in mid-table), but it is a national team of a country that was hard-fought, and remains frac-tured due to the fragile ceasefire on its western borders.

No wonder, then, the passion on display during the national anthem. Arms locked around the player next to them, eyes fixed on some point way beyond the confines of the stadium. It mattered not a jot that the vast majority of the 3,000 crowd couldn't understand a word of what was being sung. They could appreciate their importance, if not meaning, unlike the smattering of souls in the far corner, witnesses on this far-flung island. Despite not understanding, the power of Azerbaijan's anthem wasn't lost on the respectful Faroese crowd, who, when it was time for them to sing their own, performed a similarly emotional and passionate rendition. Born not out of war but out of a pride for a language and culture that had been stifled for so long but never would be again.

As the two teams huddled on either side of the centre circle, a last few words of encouragement orchestrated by the captains and accompanied by pumping fists, the Skansin Ultras began a tireless, choreographed encouragement of their own. Singing, bouncing and Viking thunderclaps undulated beneath a sea of face paint, draped flags and replica shirts. A constant while their team was on the field, and only pausing at half-time to get a beer or two, some appearing to have had a few too many, as witnessed by a few ultras bouncing out of time and in the wrong direction for the majority in the second half.

And while the ultras encouraged, the team did plenty to fuel it. Beneath a canopy of tumbling fog, rolling out over the top of the ultras' stand and across to the sports complex behind the far goal, the Faroes dominated play, pushing Azerbaijan back, their fast wing-play and probing passing into willing strikers threatened an opening goal. A screamer from Gilli Rólantsson Sørensen grazed the bar, and a string of devilish crosses somehow evaded the desperate lunges of Faroese players, where any connection would have turned it in.

After such open and comprehensive play, the first goal came as a sucker punch to the hosts, who proved to be the masters of their own downfall. A misplaced pass, then a missed tackle gave Azerbaijan the chance to bear down on goal. A decent strike seemed to have resulted in a decent save by one-time Manchester City keeper, Gunnar Nielsen. However, the ball spilled from his grasp and rolled out to Richard Almeida. Brazilian by birth, playing for Astana in Kazakhstan, but a naturalised Azerbaijani after six years playing for Qarabag, Almeida fired his adopted country into the lead.

After only a handful of games for Santo André in São Paulo, then a two-year loan to Gil Vicente in Portugal, Almeida tried his luck further afield and found regular football and a new home in Baku, prompting him to switch nationalities in order to play international football. His goal was only his second in 11 matches for his new country, and the way he ran the length of the pitch to celebrate with the bench and the handful of delirious flag-waving supporters beyond spoke volumes as to the belonging he had found, far from home.

The goal deflated the stadium, for a second, maybe two, then the Skansin began in on another round of choreographed bouncing and chanting. Well used to seeing their side concede, the ultras, and indeed all supporters of the Faroese team, gauge effort and passion as a better reflection of the success of any match. And on that front, there could only be one winner, with the home side pressing even harder into the second half to find what would be a deserved equaliser. Sweeping forward at every occasion it is possible they were trying too hard, unused to having so much possession, they often rushed their lines when it mattered most.

Despite the guttural, near instinctive cries of anguish from the stands at a missed opportunity, or misplaced pass, there were no howls of derision. Everyone in the stands, on the bench and on the pitch knew the odds were forever stacked against them. An island nation of 50,000 people shouldn't stand a chance against a country the size of Azerbaijan, with a population of 10,000,000 potential footballers to choose from, let alone any of the sport's leading lights. As such, the support didn't waver, didn't slip away into the clawing fog as Azerbaijan scored a second on the counterattack, then a third from the penalty spot in the dying seconds; Almeida scoring his third goal for his new homeland. Instead, as time added on ebbed away, the Skansin began in on a rendition of the national anthem that quickly took hold across the main stand. The passion on the pitch, a display worthy of victory on any other day but somehow facing down a 3-0 defeat, was replicated through the rows of seats flipping up as people stood to sing the song of their homeland.

Players sank on their haunches at the final whistle, knowing an opportunity to add to their Nations League points haul, which stood at three thanks to victory over Malta in the first round of fixtures, had been lost. The rare opportunity to be the team on the front foot had led to gaps at the back that a decent Azerbaijan team exploited; the entire squad celebrating victory in front of their handful of supporters in the far corner of a rapidly emptying main stand. It had been, however, the kind of game that the Nations League had been designed to create: to offer an opportunity for all national teams to develop, to express oneself as the Faroes' team had; to head into games with the chance of victory, or at the very least the chance to put in a decent, attacking display, rather than the rear-guard actions needed to keep the score down against the best sides.

It was this new game plan, in which the Faroes could take a match to their opposition that saw a little bit of attacking naivety exposed; leaving gaps that could be used against them. But thanks to the Nations League, the opportunity to experience and learn from such a match could surely only benefit the team going forwards. This positivity of opportunity seemed to be the overlying emotion among the supporters as they dissolved into the fog and a cold Tórshavn night; enthusiastic conversations on an exciting performance over-riding any doom and gloom at a 3-0 loss.

It was still evident the following lunchtime as Hannis Egholm sipped a beer in a café overlooking the harbour, now free from fog but storm clouds were gathering above. A ferry to Nólsoy Island that loomed out to sea idled dockside; Skansin Fort, perched on top of a rocky outcropping above looked on. The low thrumming of the ship's engines drifted in as the café door opened behind a new customer.

For Hannis – a broad-shouldered man in his 50s, sporting a thick woollen jumper to combat the elements – Faroese football runs through his veins. Decades of voluntary service to his beloved club side, B36 Tórshavn – one half of the big Tórshavn derby match with HB – meant he appreciated that the performance the night before far outweighed the result.

'We are learning how to play attacking football, after nearly 30 years of a more defensive style,' he said, staring out at the traditional grass-roofed buildings of the Tinganes, the Faroe Islands' parliament comprising a warren of attractive red wooden buildings and houses crammed onto a rocky outcrop that bisected the harbour in two. The passengers en-route to Nólsoy would enjoy a birds-eye view of one of the world's oldest democracies in action, as well as a couple of lounging cats hunkered into sheltered spots among the weave of narrow alleyways.

'The Nations League means that we can go out to win. But that takes some getting used to. We have always had to play with a counter-attacking style against most teams. But we were very good technically. We could pass and press against Azerbaijan, we just couldn't score!

'It was a pity that our midfield wasn't as strong as they have been recently. Due to injuries there were a few players playing out of position. But that is how it goes when you have a small squad. Who knows what the score might have been otherwise.'

Outside, the odd car crept past and on into the narrow streets of the quiet town centre. Small, neat houses huddled along cul-de-sacs, while on the compact high street immaculate shops displaying Faroese woollen products attempted to lure in the few remaining tourists brave enough to linger on in the islands. A knit of small streets providing a collective sense of safety in what could be a wild environment.

'Hopes were high of winning our league, which was a first for us here on the Faroes! That is why the concept of the Nations League is such a good one for teams like ours,' Hannis went on. 'But Kosovo are just too strong this time round. We are hopeful moving forward though. Maybe the next Nations League we can achieve something special. This experience will help improve the team. They will be better equipped and more confident after a decent campaign here. It will help them against the bigger teams as well, having more belief in their ability.'

The last time I met Hannis was in August 2006, in the same café. Him and his friend Jakub had just returned from Suðuroy, the most southerly island of the Faroes, where they had been watching Hannis' B36 play. A successful season had seen them progress in Europe past Birkirkara of Malta, before bringing Fenerbahçe, a team full of international players who had finished third in the 2002 World Cup with Turkey, to Tórshavn.

A relatively benign summer by Faroese standards had made me question Hannis back then when he had said that teams rarely left the Islands with a heavy victory, no matter their ability. 'Players don't like coming all the way out here, facing terrible weather, and a Faroese team who always give 100 per cent. Some of them leave their ability in the warmth of the team bus!' Now, on the cusp of winter, the Faroes felt like a different, more menacing place to call home. A dark, fog-bound journey on twisting roads across a landscape of sheer cliff faces falling hundreds of metres into huge, crushing breakers confirmed that.

And when Hannis mentioned a 2-1 defeat to Italy in recent years, he reiterated the point. 'Our decent home form is down to a combination of nations underestimating us, and some star players not fancying the trip out here. They think it is a done deal before stepping off the plane. They don't anticipate our passion. At all.'

As Hannis spoke of his childhood, it became evident that even on these isolated islands, football is more a religion than a simple sport. 'When I was little, the only football we saw outside of our domestic game was when a VHS copy of a match from England that had been recorded in Denmark the week before, come over by boat and was aired on Faroese TV. We would sit glued to the screen, even though the game had long been decided. Sometimes the next game too! But, long before the internet or satellite television, we didn't know the score, so it was live to us. 'Ever since those days, I have dreamed of the Faroe Islands facing England, but we have never drawn them in qualifying. It would be a happy headache to have, as I always support them at World Cups. The only time I haven't supported them is the Iceland match in 2016. There was a big screen up in the centre of town, and so many came out to watch. All supporting Iceland.

'They are our neighbours,' he shrugged. 'Our cousins out here in the Atlantic.'

So strong was the passion for the game and, more importantly, the Faroese game on the islands, that not even the advent of satellite television had had any effect on attendances for domestic matches. 'Everyone comes out and supports their local team, because the football club is a big part of peoples' lives. They are a big part of communities here, some of which are very small (the second largest town on the islands, Klaksvík, is home to just 5,000). These symbols are very important and precious. Nearly every family in each town and village will have at least one person playing for their team, either at senior level, or in the boys and girls age groups below. It is a vital sporting outlet, but also a social one too.

'No matter where you go, you will see these clubs almost in constant use. Men's, women's, boys' and girls' teams training at different times. And if not them, then a few children with a ball, just having a kickabout in one of the goals.

'All the pitches here on the islands are artificial as grass pitches couldn't survive the climate. So often it is only the snow that halts play out here. Or a really bad storm.'

He nods outside when I mention the plan is to visit some of the more isolated football communities later in the day. 'That may not be such a good idea today. Or if you are going to do it, do it now, as a bad one is closing in. I am supposed to be flying out to Copenhagen tomorrow, but I am not so sure the plane will be able to get to us.

'The under-21 team are meant to be playing Lithuania this evening over at Svangaskarð stadium in Toftir. But it is so exposed that there is no chance, it just couldn't happen, so it has been switched here to Tórsvøllur. At least there is a little shelter here.'

'It's that bad?'

'That bad. If you make it out there you will see just how exposed it is. It looks out over the water, and any storm just blows straight through. Vicious winds. Dangerous.'

The weather, the isolation, just as it is breathtaking and terrifying in equal measure, so too it can be a hindrance to furthering the national team. 'Outside of qualifying games it is really hard to arrange friendlies, because it is so expensive to get out here. Why come all this way when most nations can arrange friendlies within mainland Europe? It holds the national team back. There can be long gaps between games, so the Nations League, with six games in three months is great for us. More games mean more experience, and more time working together as a national team. It is invaluable, even though the weather is wild this time of year!'

In the shadow of Tórsvøllur sits Gundadalur, the home to both HB and B36 Tórshavn. Perennial rivals for the league title, this rivalry is intense on the pitch, but typically Faroese off it. Hannis' best friend, Jakub, is a HB supporter, yet he goes with his friend to watch B36 play. Each club has a stand and clubhouse either side of the halfway line, decked out in the red and black of HB, and the black and white of B36, and on derby day both are packed. Behind one goal, wooden benches sit precariously over a steep grass bank, and opposite the clubhouses, a long wooden stand houses the neutral or the more reserved supporter.

The 90 minutes of the game is a full-blooded, passionate derby. But at the final whistle, both sets of fans mingle together and head back into town to celebrate or commiserate, depending on their persuasion. It is a by-product of living in such a small community, this passion with perspective. Surviving, thriving in such rugged isolation is tough enough. Why introduce such unnecessary animosity with half of your fellow townsfolk?

Despite this lack of hatred that seems to fuel so many derby rivalries the world over, there can be no denying the pride that Hannis feels for his club; that every fan across these islands feels for their team. It is as all-encompassing, all-consuming and unfathomably significant to his very being as any other supporter anywhere else in the world.

It is just that the Faroese can bring a little perspective to bear. Though that doesn't dull the sparkle in his eyes when he talks about his team. 'We have a few B36 players in the national team squad right now. And that will grow over the next few years. We are a young, homegrown team. A bit of a work in progress. We don't have so many foreign players. We are trying to focus on the youth, the future a bit more. And we have quite a few players in the under-21 squad.

'Even though we are a young team, we have done well this season,' he said as the door of the café rattled in its frame, the longer tufts of the grass roof of the old building opposite whipping in the ever-growing wind. 'We beat HB in the Cup Final. We had two players sent off and then equalised in the last few seconds. Then we held on and won on penalties. Now that was a good day! I was very happy!

'We also did well in Europe this season. We beat teams from Malta and Montenegro before losing 4-0 on aggregate to Beşiktaş. And we did it all playing neat, technical football like the national team play.

'Some sides here still like to play a more direct style, but it is better for the league, for the national team that more play with an emphasis on technique. Twelve of the 23 national team squad play abroad, mainly in Denmark, Norway, Germany and Iceland. They develop a technical style that our national team boss, Lars Olsen, wants to use for the national team.

'Now that B36 and some others are focusing on developing that, it is no longer a barrier to the national team to stay playing football on the islands. The league is beginning to keep up with the development players gain from moving abroad, though players will move still, as the league here isn't full-time. And becoming a full-time professional footballer is nearly every child's dream here on the islands.

'We are proud though of our playing style at B36, that we can help develop players for the national team. It is a good feeling.'

As he spoke, the door rattled once more, and the road began to stain with rain. Rows of fishing boats moored among a maze of pontoons dockside bobbing and rocking in the wind.

'Though I don't have a good feeling about that,' he said. 'Are you sure you want to head out exploring today?'

When a Faroe islander questions whether you should do something due to weather, it is best to listen to them – is a lesson learned within an hour of leaving the relative shelter of Tórshavn far behind.

As the crow flies, nowhere is that far away from anywhere else among the islands that are connected by undersea tunnels. Geography, however, can, and does, make reaching many parts of the country a spectacular white-knuckle ride of awe-inspiring views, and single lane roads winding and teetering close to sheer drops or hugging vast rock faces. Monstrous swells crash against headlands, growing faint among veils of sweeping rain whipping across exposed bays with ever-growing ferocity. Looming mountains menace among the black cloud that drains the day to a monochrome grey.

Among this ungodly storm raging across the vastness of an unforgiving Atlantic October, a small hire car has no choice but to go with the gusts of wind, pushing tyres onto gravel verges and potential catastrophe without the intervention of some serious tugging of the steering wheel. Thankfully, the approach to Saksun, the first and now last port of call on an abandoned itinerary, runs through a sheltered valley in the remote north-west of Streymoy island.

Saksun (population: 14) is during the summer months one of the Faroe Islands most popular stops on any tour. A classic example of the rugged, isolated life some Faroese choose, this hamlet comprising three habitable dwellings, a church, and some grass-roofed outhouses stands out as the poster child for the remotest spots on the islands, courtesy of the breathtaking natural amphitheatre it looks out on.

Mountains and vast headland wrap round Saksun bay, the waters still while all hell is breaking loose just out of view beyond the narrow tributary that heads out to sea. Waterfalls tumble from out of the mountain tops, their roar muted by the howling winds that race down the valley and into the bay. Even in such ungodly weather, where the driving rain hits you horizontally with a wind at its back so severe that you could readily believe the rain may never even touch land if whipping across a flatter landscape, this is a beautiful, timeless spot.

Sheltering in the lee of the thick, whitewashed walls of the small church, Saksun exists as a physical manifestation of the Faroese passion for these islands; that even the most remote and seemingly inhospitable spot has value and is home to someone. That a car park, toilet block and information board for visitors (who often temporarily swell Saksun's population ten-fold during the summer) exists and is immaculately maintained tells of the pride the people have for the land. That the only car in the car park, growing faint behind veils of driving rain and being buffeted by the wind to such an extent it looked capable of being flipped over told of the dire need to abandon sightseeing and respect the storm.

Despite the stands that protected two sides of Tórsvøllur stadium, it would be the weather that dictated the play between the under-21 teams of the Faroes and Lithuania that evening. Goal kicks from in front of the sports complex, where gymnasts and athletes limbering up in studios with large glass fronts looked out, caught the wind before looping back the way it had come. No doubt shaking their heads and celebrating their sporting choice, the gymnasts turned back to the warmth of their task at hand. Above them, and two men battled to bring down the flags of the two nations, and that of UEFA, from three poles on the sports complex roof that looked ready to snap in two. The rain, as in Saksun, rarely fell vertically. Wicked twisters of wind and rain danced across the pitch, swarmed about the floodlights, tore along the rows of seats in the stand. The hundred or so souls brave enough to take in the game winced and shrank ever further into the hoods of their coats.

Somehow, despite it all, an entertaining European Championship qualifier broke out. The hosts were more defensive than the senior team the night before, and they dealt with a Lithuania team who were very good on the ball but lacked a cutting edge. A last gasp penalty denied the Faroes a 2-1 win that would have seen them leapfrog Lithuania into second-last place in their qualifying group. Despite their lowly positions, both sets of players sank to their knees at the final whistle, exhausted, but also devastated that a rare opportunity for a win had been missed. Ultimately, the weather had robbed them both, and sent the supporters, substitutes and the senior team who had been watching on from above the empty Skansin Ultras block scurrying into the night for shelter and a warm drink.

October, among the fishermen of the Atlantic, brings with it a sense of dread. A sea, unruly enough at the best of times, begins to flex its ungodly muscles with a terrifying regularity. Storm swells rising up from the deep waters either side of the mid-Atlantic ridge help focus the mind of fishermen from Newfoundland and all the way down the eastern seaboard of the Unites States, across to skippers of boats based as far afield as Iceland and Portugal. A billboard by a wharf lined with brightly painted former traders' houses marked the wreckage of every Faroese fishing boat lost at sea, a reminder to the rows of boats moored alongside of the dangers beyond the harbour walls.

Fishing is still the largest industry on the islands, and every spot of bad weather can't put a halt to their work. Calculated risks with the lives of the fishermen and the crew are made every day as they pull out of port, past the dry docks with its vast cradles, into which ships in need of repair are winched. Sparks from welding tools spray down onto kelp-littered slipways from the hulls of boats that have not been so lucky. Silent prayers that they won't need the shipyards services, or worse, become a statistic on the billboard are uttered from skipper and deckhand alike as they draw out toward open water.

To the untrained eye, the worst of the storm is not over. Huge breakers crash violently against headlands. Waterspouts grow and fade, grow again as they skitter over churning whitecaps, twisting and lurching through the chaotic winds both out to sea, and on into the network of fjords around the islands. Waterfalls tumbling from the mountains whip back on themselves in the gale, writhing violently like a businessman's tie. And among it all, a fishing boat bobs and plots a course out to sea. The clear, blustery skies above and a favourable shipping forecast are all the omens they need to get back to work, no matter how impossible it seems.

Beyond the capital, the islands are an amalgam of impossibilities made possible. The isolated village of Tjørnuvik (population: 71) balances on a strip of land at sea level with a beach of black sand before it and a horseshoe of basalt rock towering over it from behind. Allotment-style plots, more sand than soil, line the beach, providing the most unlikely crop of potatoes year on year. The narrow road labouring up the steep cliffs that link the village to the rest of the islands easily made impassable in bad weather.

Eiði (population: 669), the most northerly village on the island of Eysturoy, shelters in the lee of a harbour wall, spreading out up the side of a modest (by Faroese standards) grass incline. The narrow strip of flat land that runs from the harbour across to a far shore of vast cliffs and open sea hosts one of football's most incredible pitches. Facing down the ocean, and reachable only by a narrow isthmus protected by a sea wall of boulders, stands the home of the now defunct Eiðis Bóltfelag. Its artificial playing surface pocked with small numbered squares marking out pitches for caravans, this one-time sports facility turned summer campsite feels the most unlikely of places for both endeavours.

A decrepit clubhouse, now home to the most basic of facilities for campers, looks every bit a building that has faced down some of the worst storms for who knows how many years of the club's eight-decade existence. As waves crash on the sea defence, sending sheets of spray across the pitch, it is a wonder that a club formed back in 1913 could play out its existence in the second and third divisions of Faroese football in such a fragile and exposed spot. However, at the time, this sliver of isolated land, which looks set to be submerged at any moment by any of the monstrous waves lurching toward shore, was the only flat and available land for a football team. A desire for football outweighed any potential calamity with the sea, and the club was built.

When Eiðis merged in 1993 with the team from Streymnes, a village of 199 souls 17 kilometres south, EB/Streymur played at a new 1,000-capacity stadium closer to the village. From there, progression up into the top-flight was swift and, in 2007, the club won its first ever major silverware with the Faroese Cup, that saw them drawn against Manchester City in the first round of the UEFA Cup.

This amalgamation of communities, totalling less than 900 people, lost 4-0 on aggregate to a side featuring Dietmar Hamann, who played in the 2002 World Cup Final, Brazilian internationals Robinho and Elano, and club stalwart Vincent Kompany. It is miracle enough that such a small community can compete against B36 and HB from the capital, let alone Manchester City. Place, belonging – it can clearly inspire way beyond your supposed potential.

The village of Funningur clings to the face of a treacherous basalt drop, looking out across crystal blue fjords at snow-topped mountains. Leirvík, another village whose football team merged to form a stronger proposition in Víkingur with nearby side Gøta, still lovingly tend their pitch that stands above the village and looks out across spectacular fjords and the islands of Kalsoy and Bordoy.

In Klaksvík, the Faroes' second city (population: 5,000), a coach barks out orders to the squad of KI Klaksvík. Running through drills, their shouts echo out across the steep valley in which the town sits and out toward the harbour. Meanwhile, a group of boys sit impatiently in the little stand dwarfed by the mountains surrounding it, waiting for the pitch to become free.

From Klaksvík, the last point on the islands reachable by car and tunnel is Viðareiði on the island of Viðoy. Home to 300 people, it sits sandwiched between two mountains that stretch the width of this, the most northerly of all the islands. A single lane, two-way tunnel stretching for more kilometres than a first-time user cares to drive links Bordoy and Viðoy. Narrow passing points forged out of the rock enable traffic to flow in this dark, oppressive underworld, if you can gauge the distance of the lights of the car coming toward you. Beyond this nerve-wracking tunnel, a second, burrowing beneath the mountain of Malìnsfjall that cuts off Viðareiði from the rest of the world. Houses huddle on vertigo-inducing clifftops. A church looks out on the wild sea, and a cautionary tale glimmers on the far banks of the fjord.

Even the fortitude of the Faroese can sometimes be undone by nature and isolation. Múli, a hamlet of three dwellings sits empty, abandoned by the tiny community that tried to call it home. Still habitable and used by shepherds for shelter in the winter, and by tourists in summer months as an extreme holiday let, Múli is one of many abandoned settlements on the islands, a reminder that humankind's reach still has its limits.

Svangaskarð stadium in Toftir, on the southernmost protrusion of Eysturoy Island, basked in the most unlikely of setting suns. A pale pastel light grew fainter as it began to sink behind the mountains on the far side of the fjord. Carved into the rock and looking out to sea, the exposed rows of roofless, weather-beaten seats that lined the pitch rattled in the wind as local side B68 Toftir ran through an array of set-pieces. With only two games to go, promotion back to the top-flight remained possible and, with it, the Faroes first ever international stadium would return to the big time. This was, after all the venue that bore witness to a national team humbling for Scotland in 2002, having to come back from 2-0 down to rescue a point in a European qualifier.

With the thought of winds and rain buffeting this stadium from all sides on a bad day, Hannis' notion of teams not fancying the battle seemed to cement themselves into lore. There would simply have been no way the under-21s' match could have started, let alone finished here 24 hours earlier.

In 2011, NSÍ Runavík, a town a kilometre or two up the road from Toftir, drew Fulham, UEFA Cup finalists the year before, in the first qualifying round of that season's competition. A 3-0 victory on a warm summer's evening on the banks of the River Thames saw Fulham take an unassailable lead to Svangaskarð for the second leg. Despite that, a near strength side of internationals from around the continent, who had fought with Atlético Madrid for the trophy 12 months earlier, scrabbled to a goalless draw. Even in the relative calm of a Faroese summer, sides come unprepared for the fight that awaits them. It is a fight epitomised by 28-year-old B36 Tórshavn centre back and captain, Ódmar Færø.

Hotel Føroyar is virtually invisible to those not in the know. A single storey, grass-roofed complex on a road seemingly leading to nowhere; stretching across a steep hill that looks down on the capital below. From Tórshavn, the location of its most exclusive hotel simply looks like more pastureland for grazing sheep, and large boulders for the Huldufólk, so successfully is it designed into its environment. At night, the only assurances that you are on the right path is a sign a few metres before a turn-off into its car park. It is an oasis of calm and safety built into the rock of the hillside, looking down at the twinkling lights of Tórshavn and the inky black sea beyond.

It is the perfect location to prepare for an international football match, as witnessed from the foyer as a carefully orchestrated timetable saw the Faroes team leave the restaurant only a few minutes before the delegation from Kosovo arrived for their evening meal. Whether there had been an even greater logistical nightmare a day or two earlier with Azerbaijan and Lithuania also in town, we will never know, though this would have no doubt been a tale for the hotel's concierge to spin at the pub in years to come.

No matter how smooth an operation, there was an awkward, respectful clash of opposing tracksuits in the foyer and bar as stragglers from the Faroes team lingered over coffee while the Kosovans passed through. Heads down looking at their phones or distracted glances out the window masked the desire for each side to check out their opponents for the following day. And as the Kosovans passed by and into the restaurant, Odmar Færø wandered across the bar and shook me warmly by the hand.

With fair hair, broad shoulders, and a thick beard, Odmar looked every bit the centre back as well as a proud descendent of the Vikings. Though when he began to speak, there was more than a bit of an Aberdeenshire Scots inflection.

'I was born here in the Faroes, in Tórshavn, but our family moved to Aberdeen when I was a boy. My father worked as a dentist, and he got a job there. We would be back in the Faroes whenever we could. And we supported the national team from afar. We the Faroese are very passionate about our team. And my family maybe a little more so,' he said, taking a sip of coffee.

'My father and grandfather also played for the national team. They are both called Odmar Færø too! When I first made it into the national team as well, UEFA kept posting lots of articles on how we were the first son, father and grandfather in world football to play for the same national team with the same name!

'It was always my dream to follow in their footsteps and play for the national team as well, though from Aberdeen it was quite hard to get spotted. In fact, I first got called up for the under-19 team after playing against them in a youth tournament in Aberdeen!

'I was invited to play in the next game for the Faroes. It was such a wonderful moment to pull that shirt on. I was so proud,' he said, the emotion evident in his voice.

Outside, the glow of the floodlights from Tórsvøllur stadium on the far side of town lit up the low-lying cloud that had descended. Hannis had explained that they are left on the day before a match to make sure they are working fine, because they are not used too often.

'The neighbours complain about it,' he had said, shrugging, 'but that's what they do. It's only one night.'

All football roads in the Faroe Islands lead to Tórsvøllur and, when Odmar and his family returned to Tórshavn in 2007, he got to play there for both the under-19s and under-21s while making a name for himself at the heart of the B36 defence in the Faroese top-flight. But it was while he was back in Scotland studying that he got his first call up into the senior team in 2012.

Playing for Forfar Athletic in the third tier of Scottish football, Odmar became the first ever Forfar player to be called up to a senior international side when he joined the national team to face Germany in the opening round of World Cup qualifiers.

'It was their first qualifying match for the 2014 World Cup. A World Cup they would go on to win, beating Brazil 7-1 at the Maracanã in the semi-final. They were the best team in the world, by far,' he said.

'They played their strongest team, with it being the first qualifier, they wanted to get off to a strong start. It was at the Olympic Stadium in Berlin, in front of 40,000. And I was in the starting line-up! I can name that starting eleven to this day: Neuer, Lahm, Mertesacker, Hummels, Badstuber, Khedira, Müller, Özil, Götze, Reus, Klose. They also brought Schürrle, Podolski, and Draxler off the bench!

'Özil scored twice and they won 3-0. But I loved every minute of it. I didn't feel overawed. In fact, I love the bigger games in the biggest stadiums. You have nothing to lose and can just give your very best. You're not expected to do anything. You get to play against the best players in the world in front of huge crowds and try for a good two nil loss or something like that. It is performance and pride over points and victories. I love it. So do our fans, who support endeavour. They know what we are up against. We all have a "maybe next time" philosophy when we play the big teams. But for a first taste, that game in Berlin was something else.

'I remember a few minutes before the final whistle, we were 3-0 down, I was marking Özil and the ball had gone out of play, so I asked him if he would swap shirts at the end of the game. He said sure. The game carried on, but at the final whistle we were nowhere near each other.

'There had been about 500 Faroese, mainly students, who had made the trip from Denmark to support us, and we all went over to applaud them and thank them for their efforts. I looked behind me and the German players had already applauded their crowd and had left the field. I was gutted!

'But as we left the pitch, standing by the tunnel among all the security guards, officials, technicians that were setting up interview zones was Özil. He had waited a good five-ten minutes for me, and we swapped shirts.

'I will always respect him for that. What a wonderful gesture. He didn't care that it was just some guy from the Faroes. It will stay with me forever, the respect he had. That is what it is all about. Some players have more ability than others, but football is football.'

Along with facing future world champions, Odmar had also played against European champions Portugal in another World Cup qualifier, this time for the 2018 edition. Cristiano Ronaldo had scored a hat-trick in a 5-0 defeat. But it was talking about Faroes victories and the reaction of his fellow islanders that animated Odmar the most.

'The supporters are great whatever the score. But when we win!' He shook his head and smiled. 'The atmosphere after the Malta game was amazing.' (The Faroes had opened their Nations League campaign with a 3-1 win – their first win on home soil for a year.) 'But beating Greece home and away during the last European qualifiers was crazy! We beat them 1-0 away, but then we won 2-1 at home. They had been European champions ten years earlier! The whole town partied long into the night. It was something else! We are a nation of 50,000 people!'

And thanks to the Nations League, Odmar is hopeful of more celebrations for the Faroese. 'The Nations League means everything to us. Six games in a short space of time is great for the development of the team. Next year we have just eight games scheduled. So, to have six games in three months is great for the players, for the fans, for everyone. Any opportunity to play wearing the national team shirt is priceless.

'It is really hard for us to arrange friendlies outside of the World and European qualifiers, so this competition gives the manager time to really work on the team. It is invaluable.'

Odmar's enthusiasm for the Nations League, for any opportunity to represent his country is palpable. As he talks, his legs fidget under the table, wishing away the 24 hours until he can get back out there beneath the Tórsvøllur lights.

'This new competition is a great opportunity for us to attack, to properly show what we can do, to play with more freedom. It is a new philosophy for us as we only get the odd game in qualifying where there is a realistic chance of us winning. Against Azerbaijan we nearly had it, we just couldn't get that goal. Now we focus on tomorrow and Kosovo.' He took a sip of coffee.

'We had hopes of winning our Nations League group, of reaching the play-offs, of daring to dream about qualifying for the European Championships. But Kosovo have proved to be too strong. They would be much higher up the rankings and in a higher group if it wasn't for them being a new football nation. They were very good when we played them away. It will be very tough tomorrow. If we win, then there is still a chance that we can do it. If not – no problem. It has been a great experience. We will move on. And hopefully there will be another Nations League where we can dream once more.

'For the national team it's all about tiny steps. The fans are proud of their team. They are realistic, however. We're not going to beat France. Despite this, they are as proud of the shirt, the spirit, the fight as the players are. It's all about a good performance, a goal, a draw. The odd win. We know we aren't going to qualify for the World Cup, but the team is moving up the world rankings.

'For the next World Cup qualifying campaign, we will be seeded in pot four, not pot six. All that hard work will give us better opportunities in the future. Tiny steps forward. Especially with our boss guiding us.' He shook his head. 'We couldn't believe it when he was announced as coach. He is a legend. We all have so much respect for him. He has really helped us all.'

Lars Olsen will forever be remembered as the captain of the Danish national team who, in 1992, were recalled from their summer holidays at short notice to replace war-torn Yugoslavia in the upcoming European Championships. With only ten days' notice, Olsen and his teammates went on the most unlikely of runs to the final, defeating then world champions Germany 2-0 to lift the country's only major silverware.

Winner of the Danish Superliga six times, as well as the Turkish Cup with Trabzonspor as a player, Olsen then set out on a managerial career that saw him lift unfancied Danish teams up into the top- flight. A perfect cv for a team like the Faroe Islands, who he has been coaching since 2012.

'The squad has improved so much,' Odmar continued. 'There are about ten of the squad now playing full time abroad, in Denmark, Norway, Sweden, Germany. It is great for us as the experience has improved them and the team. Five years ago there were maybe only five playing abroad.

'If you play in the Faroes, you are part time. As well as playing for B36, I am just finishing a degree in West Nordic Studies, covering Iceland, the Faroes and Norway, focusing on history, sustainability and conservation. The match fee you get for playing for the national team is very welcome to a student!

'Other players work in the fishing industry, for local government or in the private sector. We had one national player who was a bus driver. He would collect visiting national teams from the airport and drop them at their hotels, then the following day he would be out on the pitch marking them!

'The league is strong now. It doesn't hold you back if you want to get into the national team. The club sides hold their own in European competition. B36 got to the second qualifying round of the Europa League and played Beşiktaş this year. We held them to 2-0 over here before they overpowered us in Turkey.'

After more than 200 games for B36, and with his studies complete, Odmar is mulling over a few options to play abroad next year. 'I've had a few offers. My studies are done, as are my wife's, so there is nothing stopping us. And at 28 I get the feeling that it might be now or never if I want to play full time. We shall have to wait and see what the future holds.

'If it doesn't happen, I would be as proud as ever to wear the B36 shirt again. Pride, identity, development. That is what it is all about here. We are a small nation, taking small steps. But we are so proud to represent our country. It means everything to play in front of our people. And we can improve, as individuals and as a team. And we will keep trying, keep working. As always.'

Match day three and Tórshavn woke to bright sunshine and benign winds. Three kittens playfully scrapped and explored the myriad nooks and crannies of a deserted dry dock, precariously traversing the lip of a large skip full of old steel. Joggers took to the coastal roads without as many layers of protective gear as usual, while others idled dockside or sat on their boats, the crystal-clear waters shimmering

enough to make one squint. The pinks, blues and yellows of the former traders' houses and storerooms along the wharf lifted the mood
further as people sat outside cafés taking their coffee. Making the
most of such an unlikely treat this late in the year, young families
took walks in the park that wound from the centre up to Tórsvøllur
stadium. Toddlers waddled ahead along winding paths hemmed in by
swathes of trees and thick, lush ferns, climbing up to its highest point
and a statue to all those that had been lost at sea over the years.

In town, people lingered to chat outside a small convenience store
while cross-trainers and treadmills whirred silently in the windows
of the gym above. Gone were the skittering runs for shelter between
shops. No longer were the bells of shop doors opening and shutting
beacons of safe harbour to those caught in a storm, but simply the
chimes of a population temporarily coming out of a storm-battered
hibernation. The close-knit streets and pathways provided pockets of
pure sun. No wind – just the warmth on your face.

The pitches outside Tórsvøllur teemed with groups of children
also making the most of the sun. Taking up balls found behind the
goals, small-sided games chaotically broke out from all angles. Excited
shouts smothered as the speakers about the national stadium crackled into life, echoing to all points across the sports complex thanks
to Tórsvøllur's exposed, undeveloped side. Stewards in their bright
yellow jackets began to drain down the terraces, linger by the gates in
preparation for any early supporter that wanted to make the most of
their seat being drenched in sunlight.

Taking up the spot that the handful of Azerbaijan supporters had
just three days earlier, the first of the Kosovan fans slowly filed down.
A couple of men in their 20s asked the stewards if they could hang
their banners above the sports complex behind the goal. And with
remarkable generosity, they helped them up onto the roof, and showed
them the best spots above studios of unsuspecting gymnasts stretching
out and performing tumbles below.

As the banners were set and attached, a family gingerly made its
way down the steps, and found seats a few rows from the pitch. An
elderly couple, a son and a granddaughter settled into their spots,
before the girl, decked out in a Kosovo shirt and scarf, began running excitedly up and down her row of empty seats. She ignored her
father's pleas to put her coat on, too focused on running and jumping

in the air, as if practising her goal celebrations, or better yet, imagining her scoring a winning goal for her country. Being no more than eight years old, she had been born into a relatively peaceful, independent Kosovo and this trip to a magical far away land was a simple, if very exciting, act of supporting her beloved team.

For her father, who had taken his seat having given up on his daughter, and her grandparents, with Kosovo flags retrieved from their bag and draped over their shoulders, this devotional trip held a greater significance. It would be a significance she would eventually discover in her studies at school. For now, at least, her love for her team, like millions of other children around the world, was simply based on an innocent joy that it is *her* team playing the game she loved. For her dad, her grandparents, this fixture against the Faroe Islands meant an awful lot more and marked the end of only a second year being able to support their team in competitive international football. For them it was as much an overwhelming, unique experience as it was for the little girl that danced among the seats. Only age, embarrassment at such unrestrained public abandon and the burden of a bloody history prevented them from joining her. Being able to take these seats in a sun-drenched Tórsvøllur stadium had been hard-fought, hard-won, and the ghosts of those lost along the way could have filled the empty spots around them countless times over. And that would forever temper their emotions.

Kosovo's history is one of turmoil. In 1912, after 500 years under Turkish Ottoman rule, Serbia regained control of a Kosovo that had once been the heart of the Serbian empire in the 12th century. Under Ottoman rule, many ethnic Serbs had fled Kosovo, leaving a mainly ethnic Albanian population to fall under the rule of Belgrade. During World War II, Kosovo was absorbed into a Greater Albania controlled by Italy. In 1946, it was made a part of the Yugoslav Federation and given autonomous status in 1974. With the rise of Slobodan Milošević to power in the 1980s, there began the stripping of autonomy and a campaign of sacking ethnic Albanians from government and media positions after ethnic Albanian leaders declared independence from Serbia.

As Yugoslavia began to fall apart in the 1990s, Kosovo elected a president to this self-proclaimed Republic, escalating Milošević-fuelled ethnic tensions and unrest. In 1998, open conflict broke out between Serb forces and the Kosovo Liberation Army. After international talks to halt the war failed, and amid claims of a campaign of brutality, including ethnic cleansing being meted out on the Kosovan population, NATO intervened.

Seventy-eight days of air strikes finally forced a retreat by Serb forces, but not before an escalation in the horrors handed out to the Kosovan Albanian population. A NATO-led peace-keeping force maintained the status quo while a UN-sponsored administration took over. In the days and weeks that followed, stories of massacres and forced expulsions began to reveal the true horrors inflicted upon the Kosovan people. Thousands remained unaccounted for, feared victims of the ethnic cleansing. Tens of thousands more remained displaced, now refugees after their homes were destroyed.

As the 21st century began, this fragile peace was threatened with ethnic clashes in Mitrovica, north-west of the capital Prishtina. Nineteen people died in the ensuing violence throughout 2004. Later, in 2006, Serbia voted in a referendum to declare Kosovo an integral part of Serbia. While in 2008, after Kosovo is declared an independent state, Kosovan Serbs set up a rival administration in Mitrovica.

While 'normalisation talks' between the two states remain ongoing, the open wounds of the recent past continue to create tension between ethnic Serbs and Albanians within Europe's youngest country, as witnessed at the 2018 World Cup. Xherdan Shaqiri, a Kosovan refugee who fled the fighting as a young boy, scored a last-minute winner for his adopted Switzerland against Serbia in a group stage match in Kaliningrad, Russia. Celebrating his goal, he made a two-handed eagle gesture that represents the black eagle on the flag of Albania – a source of great pride for all Kosovan and ethnic Albanians, but a red rag to the furious Serb supporters in the stadium and beyond.

There is still much work to be done before the country that this little girl, still twirling and jumping about in the sun, calls home is truly at peace. Whether she will ever see a time where Kosovo can play Serbia in the game she loves, who knows. It seems unlikely.

For now, celebrating what they have, rather than what they have not, is the order of the day. And as the little girl and her father and grandparents are joined by another 30 or so Kosovan supporters in the rapidly filling stadium, the emotion of seeing their national team walk out beneath the fluttering flag of their people remained a raw, overwhelming experience. Two years of being able to see your team play competitive football matches is surely not enough time to enable that emotion to level out.

After everything that this father and his parents have seen, it may take a lifetime, possibly the length of his daughter's, for that to subside a little. The opportunity to celebrate such a hard-won identity, to sing the national anthem, to see your team – arms locked, eyes closed, singing with such an intensity – is so precious that a gruelling trip to one of Europe's most remote and distant outposts is deemed necessary.

As Odmar Færø's team grouped together for one last motivational roar near the centre-circle, arms around each other's shoulders, as the Skansin Ultras behind the goal started in on their never-ending repertoire, the meaning of this 'meaningless' match in the eyes of many beyond these two countries felt palpable. The air was choked with emotion on all sides. This was an occasion, one witnessed by 3,000 people shielding their eyes from the sun so as to fully take it all in An occasion soon to be marked with a great goal as Lazio's Valon Berisha teamed up well with Werder Bremen's Milot Rashica, who slammed the ball home in the ninth minute to give Kosovo the lead. The entire bench ran out to the ecstatic Rashica, everyone celebrating in front of their supporters – among them a little girl wildly twirling her scarf above her head.

New to the international scene Kosovo may be, but inexperienced they are not. Complimenting Berisha and Rashica were players plying their trade in Holland, Belgium, Norway, Turkey, Switzerland, Denmark, Ukraine and England with Sheffield Wednesday's Atdhe Nuhiu. They would not be at the foot of the world rankings for long.

Kosovo's passing, pressing game meant the Faroes had to revert to a more familiar, counter-attacking tactic. And as the game wore on, they grew into a bigger threat. Early in the second half, their dogged perseverance paid off as a wicked Gilli Rólantsson cross was swept home by René Joensen. It was a moment of pure joy which swept around the stadium, with it a touch of self-depreciating slapstick magic. Goalscorer Joensen, who plays for a Grindavik team that narrowly avoided relegation from Iceland's top-flight, ran to a point on the pitch and stopped. Eyes closed, he lifted his head to the skies and raised his arms out wide while his rushing teammates bent down and lifted him up, like someone ascending the rapture, or a human facsimile of Rio's imposing Christ the Redeemer statue.

Lowered back to earth, a laughing Joensen took in the moment – the berserk ultras and the near 3,000 crowd cheering and clapping. Somewhere just out of view, a young girl slumped forlornly in her chair. For Joensen, this is what it is all about, a lifetime's ambition fulfilled: representing and scoring for your community, your nation.

Across two teams, two sets of supporters, the passion and electricity of international football moved the 90 minutes along in what felt like a captivating flash. And at the final whistle, a draw was good enough for Kosovo to maintain their stranglehold on the group, and a strong display against a very good team more than enough to sustain the Faroes' belief that the future was bright. The Faroes team applauded the ultras' dedication while the Kosovans came together with their fans to celebrate another precious milestone in a fledgling international endeavour.

As the sun set and the crowds drained away, there were echoes of young children who had rushed back out onto the pitches beyond the national stadium, retrieving the balls they had left in the goals. Playing out what they had just seen, they no doubt dreamt that maybe, one day, it might be them out there.

For the little girl and her family, for the teams and supporters of every club and national team that make their way out to the Faroes, Vágar Airport is their first and last impression of these islands, an airport that today receives five flights and sees five depart – aviation Faroes style. Heathrow Airport handles 1,400 departures and arrivals every day. Looking out across the runway flanked by a rugged hillside dotted with sheep seemingly immune to the occasional roar of a jet engine, it is hard not to feel a pang of sadness. A sharp take-off over vast clifftops, and the inevitable choke of cloud waiting to swallow your flight, will signal the end of your time on the islands. Gone, as if they had never been there in the first place.

It is a land of marvels. That a people survive – and thrive – among such devastatingly brutal, but breathtaking geography, amid the hardships of an Atlantic winter being the most fundamental marvel of all.

The people, their love for football, the world in which they exist deserves the respect of UEFA and should never be consigned to some pre-qualifying tournament. The pride and meaning of represent-ing and supporting your nation alone demand a level playing field. Because who can rank passion, identity, belonging? Thankfully, UEFA understands this, and the Faroe Islands and their brethren nearer the foot of the football rankings will continue to take their rightful place alongside world-beaters in qualifying groups. After all, why would anyone want to deny themselves the opportunity to follow their team out to such a unique and unforgettable place?

CHAPTER THREE

Locos, Chuff Chuffs, and Can Cans – Inverurie Loco Works and Forres Mechanics

VIOLET ANN OMAND, or Granny as I knew her, was born on 31 August 1926 at 6 Hawthorn Terrace, Aberdeen to Samuel Alexander Omand, a water bailiff at Cruives of Don, Old Machar, and Jessie Omand, a domestic servant. Samuel and Jessie had married in Banchory, a small town 18 miles west of Aberdeen only 13 days before Violet's birth. Violet's brother, Charles, was born 14 months later in a gardener's cottage in the village of Druim Auldearn, between the small towns of Nairn and Forres on the Moray Firth coast to the east of Inverness.

We know nothing of Violet's childhood. She never spoke of it. All that can be gleaned from official records is a nomadic existence, following work along an agricultural belt that wraps around the foothills of the Cairngorm mountains between Aberdeen and Inverness. Across which Samuel had been registered as being a water bailiff, monitoring weirs and dams used for trapping salmon, a gardener, a chauffeur, a shepherd and a trapper. From Banchory to Nairn, Violet's lost childhood plays out somewhere among the countryside, villages and towns of the eastern Highlands of Scotland. Why Violet never spoke about her youth, we can only speculate. She never spoke of her father either. Both were closed books, that only began to open a little after her death in 2004, where ancestry records discovered that her father had spent time in Peterhead Prison. For what, it would take a little while longer to discover, and would go a long way to explaining a discarded childhood and parent. It transpired that, in 1939, when Violet was 12, her father secretly married an Edith Ross in Elgin. They proceeded to have four children between 1940 and 1944, until his secret was discovered and he was convicted of bigamy in 1945. Violet's mother had had some part in the conviction, bringing an end to her marriage of 19 years.

77

During the early part of World War II, Violet had worked in the dockyards of Aberdeen as a rivet catcher. Freshly 'cooked' rivets would be thrown from the furnace to a catcher, who caught them in an ash-lined basket before hurrying them to wherever they were needed to help fix or construct warships and merchant vessels – ones that Violet's brother had signed up to crew. Later, during the war, the opportunity to join the Auxiliary Territorial Service arose, which she took willingly. It would be a fresh start all the way down south in Brighton, where she would become a cook feeding new recruits as they were assessed and made ready for the frontline. It was her job to build up those soldiers that had come to training underweight and help those with a few too many pounds to diet.

As Nazi Germany faltered and fell, and her father's double life began to unravel, Violet met an officer of the Royal Artillery named J Bunbury. Shortly after her father was convicted, she fell pregnant and was promised marriage. But as the war effort slowed down and broke apart, J Bunbury disappeared. Military records suggest that he had already married in 1940. Whether the humiliation and hurt of her father's actions prevented her from returning to the Highlands, or whether her pregnancy or other factors did, we will never know. But David James Omand was born on 30 July 1946 in Worthing, just outside Brighton.

Violet married a David Keyes in Worthing in 1948, another man she never spoke about in later life. Evidence for why came in a letter she wrote to the Royal Caledonian School in Bushey, just outside London, formerly the Royal Caledonian Asylum, a school for the children of deceased Scottish soldiers, in February 1951. She wrote enquiring about a place for David at the school because her husband '[did] not take to him which [made] things quite uncomfortable at times'. She went on to say she thought the school would give him that chance in life which she wanted him to have and she was 'pure scotch'. David was admitted in September 1951, not long after his fifth birthday.

A month later she wrote to the school to say that her husband would not let her have the money from the housekeeping to visit David at the school and, as that was the only money coming in, she had left him and changed her name. David's younger brother Chris, born in 1949, was admitted into the school aged eight in 1957 and described life in the school as being very tough. By the time Chris arrived, David had spent seven of his 12 years at the school and explained that it was every boy for himself, that he couldn't fight his younger brother's battles for him. He had rose up to become a respected and tough 12-year-old boy, which was just as well, as life was as rough outside the school as it was within.

They would attend local schools during the week and the boys from the Royal Caledonian would be teased and picked on. It was well known that children from the Royal Caledonian were Scots, orphaned or destitute in some way, who wore kilts while at the RCS. They were different, an easy target. And while it was every boy for himself within the RCS, when out at their day schools, they fought to protect one another, resulting in the entire RCS population being expelled from one school after a particularly large skirmish.

Meanwhile, Violet settled in Salisbury, working for 30 years at Wellworthys, a large factory that made pistons and piston rings. She became involved in the works' football team, who had a pitch on-site and played in the Salisbury and District League. After working a half day on Saturdays, she would make sure the kit was ready and washed, as well as getting the half-time tea ready for the players, officials and supporters.

Fate and misfortune had brought her to this point – the actions of men having destroyed any future that she may have envisioned for herself. But she didn't give up and attempted to create a new landscape as best she could for her and her children from the wreckage of deceit at the hands of her father and J Bunbury, and the cruelty of David Keyes.

If not for the war effort and her father's betrayal, Violet Ann Omand may have never left the Highlands, protecting her from the predatory Bunbury and the suffocating Keyes. Instead of falling in with the football team at Wellworthys, she may have gravitated towards one of the local Highland sides that litter the agricultural belt that had once been home. From Nairn County and Forres Mechanics – which were close to the birth of her younger brother, Charles, to the north-west – to the towns of Elgin, Keith, Turriff and Huntly to the east, Lossiemouth, Deveronvale, Buckie and Fraserburgh along the Moray coast, and Cove to the south, any town could have enticed her in. She had embraced the community spirit at Wellworthys and willingly given her spare time to the works' football team. There is little to suggest that the same couldn't have happened had she remained in Scotland.

Looking at a map of the Highlands, one can only wonder at the towns and villages, and whether they played a part in Violet's nomadic early life. Some towns seem more likely than others, such as Inverurie. North of Banchory, and north-west of Aberdeen, Inverurie – or Inbhir Uraidh in Gaelic – is a small market town of some 11,000 people. Called Inverary until 1866, Inverurie's name was changed back to its ancient spelling when the town's post kept getting sent to another Inverary on the west coast of Argyll. Like so many towns and villages of the eastern Highlands, it is constructed from the same grey granite that gives Aberdeen its distinctive pallid look, and the nickname 'the Granite City'.

Currently one of the fastest growing towns in Britain due to its proximity to Aberdeen and the prosperous oil industry out at sea, Inverurie was the industrial heart of the Highlands for the best part of a century, and the source of work to those that needed it. The Great North of Scotland Railway based its locomotive construction and repair works on a 15-acre site in Inverurie in 1902. Closing some 70 years later, the town remains synonymous to this day with an industry mothballed half a century ago. Despite the business created from the North Sea Oil industry, and a number of decades in the late 20th century where the town's population found work at a paper mill, it is the locomotive works that remains at the heart of the community's identity.

Loco Works Road still exists, though it now leads into an industrial estate that is bordered with a Lidl supermarket. Road sign aside, the only tangible remnants of what had once been the dominating factor in Inverurie are a weave of tracks and sidings that still feed the town's train station. And a set of floodlights.

Inverurie Loco Works Football Club was formed in 1903 and played an important part in the social life of the works, just as Violet's Wellworthys team did at the other end of the British Isles. To some, half-day shifts on a Saturday would not be complete without a few beers after, then walking along Harlaw Road to catch the Locos playing junior football among the Aberdeenshire Leagues. For them, it would be an action as regular and pre-determined as clocking in and out. And when the works closed, the club continued, becoming an ever more important outlet for those clinging on to friends made over decades on the shop floor, and to happier, possibly more prosperous times.

The Locos stepped up into senior football in 2001, joining the Highland League. Since then Inverurie have won the Highland League Cup twice, in 2008 and 2009, but have yet to lift the title, despite some lofty finishes. Their most celebrated moment in recent history came in 2009, where victories over Deveronvale, Banks O' Dee and Vale of Leithen saw them face Scottish Premier League side Motherwell in the fourth round of the Scottish Cup. A capacity crowd of 2,500 crammed in to Harlaw Park to see the Locos lose 3-0. A more than respectable result against a professional team playing four leagues above them and well used to rubbing shoulders with the likes of Celtic and Rangers.

No matter the decade, history repeats itself around institutions like these, especially on match day, or match night in this case. The rituals of pre- and post-match are ingrained, unwritten laws rarely deviated from, handed down from generation to generation, knitting into a weave of intermingling traditions as the crowd gathers. This night was no different, as Locos supporters began to descend upon Harlaw Park

Optimism sprang eternal in a couple of middle-aged friends as they stepped out of Hopeville Social Club and crossed Harlaw Road, drawn toward the floodlights burning into the night. The ghosts of long-gone childhood match days spent weaving between the tables, scuffing an old ball about outside while their fathers laughed and drank at the bar, spilled out behind them, snuffed out again as the sliver of warm light from within recedes as the door yawned shut. The steady stream of bodies along the pavement and the clack of the turnstile ramped up the atmosphere – it was game night with the Locos.

Sounds echoed about the compact ground: the crack of balls being pinged between warming up players; the shrill whistle of a trainer; orders being barked, encouragement shouted. It all spilled out over the external wall and into the queue. Slivers of a shimmering emerald pitch could be seen beyond the turnstiles, taunting those outside with the little piece of footballing magic being cast within. Because night games feel that little bit more special.

The gleam of the pitch and the mesmerising glare of the flood-lights seemed to concentrate all that is intoxicating about football into a sharp focus. The world beyond lost in the dark, the pitch cocooned in a dome of brilliant illumination. It is a scene set for something magical, regardless if it actually manifests within the white lines. The anticipation leaps across years, decades, generations, to that first magical night game witnessed. A moment etched in every fan's memory. Maybe for some child holding their parents' hand in the queue, tonight was that first night, a life-long addiction or affliction potentially about to be born.

Inside, a young girl sat in a small booth selling half-time fifty-fifty tickets. Another poured tea from behind the counter of a burger van. In another life, in another time, this could have been a young Violet Ann Omand. A ticket from one and a cup from the other seemed the right thing to do.

Harlaw Park is a small, neat and well-loved little ground. A stretch of covered terracing running along one touchline mirrors a small, modern main stand of no more than 300 seats on the far side of the pitch. A flag fluttered the Locos colours of red and black, while friends drank and laughed in the Locos social club behind the Harlaw Road goal. Netting suspended from stanchions behind the posts pro-tected them from wayward practice shots that bulged, then dropped harmlessly to the ground. The odd unsuspecting punter stood outside in the smoking section flinching at what their instincts believed to be impending impact, spilling their pint a little to the mockery of their friends.

The pitch slopes down toward the far goal that sits in front of a cement works. Towers, conveyors and other units needed in the pro-cess faded into the darkness, their white façade a ghostly apparition of the real world beyond the floodlights. A world on pause, for a couple of hours at least. Two spectators wandered past and looked up at the industrial scene. One of them pointed.

'It's just as well this isn't a cup game, otherwise the result could be on aggregate.' He paused, expecting some recognition of the pun. His friend just shook his head, sighed.

'To hell with you, that was funny. Philistine!'

Harlaw Park was teeming with expectation, especially among a coachload of lads no more than 16 years old who, having draped their Deveronvale flag across the barriers of the covered terrace, couldn't wait for the game to begin before starting in on their repertoire of songs. Bouncing in unison, this 40-strong band of brothers cheered their visiting heroes as they finished their warm-ups. Outside, their coach driver sat in shell shock. Like a latter day, benign pied piper, having driven the male youth away from their home in Banff (albeit it a fully sanctioned and paid in full endeavour), the songs seemed to still ring in his ears, the 40-minute drive down from the Moray Firth Coast feeling twice as long with such a relentlessly energetic cargo.

Banff (population: 4,000) looks across the mouth of the Deveron River (where the town's football team derives its name) at the town of Macduff. Those not making the trip south to Inverurie were in for a peaceful Friday night, shorn of these excitable teenagers, who wouldn't get it all their own way when it came to singing, as their main competition began to assemble and set up behind the cement works goal.

Three men in their early 50s and a boy no more than 13 set about erecting a flag of their own, piecing together a collapsible flagpole before threading a large Inverurie Loco Works flag onto it. Dressed in red train drivers' hats, red Loco shirts beneath red and black checked fleeces with the arms cut off, there could be no confusing who the three men were there to support. The boy, who helped two of them hoist the straps of two large bass drums over their shoulders was dressed more conservatively. A Locos beanie hat pulled down onto the rims of a pair of thick lensed glasses, this apprentice had a little work to do before he could be fully affiliated into the Chuff Chuffs – the Locos' very own ultra-group. Like a prospect in a biker gang not yet ready to wear the full club colours, one could imagine a ceremonial presentation of a driver's hat and cut-off fleece somewhere along a long trip back from Wick or Fort William, having finally paid his dues. No doubt he would wear it with pride, just as he stood alongside his comrades as they began in on their own back catalogue of chants.

The barrage of abuse from the Deveronvale lads was inevitable. But when you have two bass drums and a third Chuff Chuff wielding a snare and a cowbell, this was easily drowned out. Their apprentice also stood firm alongside his comrades who were old enough to

83

be his grandfather, twirling his Locos scarf above his head proudly. And the Vale supporters had no answer when the Chuff Chuffs pulled a bespoke, self-penned theme tune out of the bag, regaling all with who they were, what they did (complete with a short solo on each instrument that they played to prove the point). It was a symphony of dedication, passion and true love. The back of the team sheet revealed that the Chuff Chuffs also sponsored talismanic striker and leading Highland League goalscorer, Neil Gauld, and when the teams ran out it was Gauld's appearance that sent them into a frenzy of beating drums.

On paper, the match looked a banker for a home win, with the Locos attempting to chase down the Rangers from Cove and Brora at the top of the table. For a community out on a limb along the coast, and numbering just 4,000, mid-table obscurity seemed a decent return from the season so far for Deveronvale. But every dog has its day, even such a small one, as witnessed by the Vale winning the Highland League first in 2003, then again in 2006. When the pieces fall in place, anything can and will happen. Every Highland League supporter drinks at the Hopeville Social Club, as do supporters the world over. This year could be our year. Though this year it is far more likely to be the Locos' than the Vale's.

The margins between decent and great can be very fine, and often come down to the rarest of commodities in football: a goalscorer. For the likes of Deveronvale coming from such a small community, finding that player to make a difference is that much harder, especially when you are within commutable proximity of Scottish Football league sides Peterhead and Elgin, as well as perennial Highland League front runners Fraserburgh and Inverurie. And so, it played out beneath the lights and a 600-strong crowd, as Inverurie threatened and the Vale counterattacked without any real cutting edge in front of goal.

Being able to cast their net out towards a city the size of Aberdeen, the Locos are a decent draw for players. They have the look of a professional set-up in a semi-pro league, with realistic aspirations of joining the pro leagues above them. As such, they were just that half a pace faster than their visitors, and it was no real surprise when they made that count with a sublime free kick by Jamie Michie halfway through the first half. Running away to the sound of frenetic drums, he attempted a cartwheel into a backflip. But the cartwheel went awry, his legs never extending, and he just about salvaged the flip without causing himself any damage.

Things got better just before the break, when Chuff Chuffs' sponsored striker Neil Gauld cut inside his man and curled a pinpoint shot into the far corner for his 38th goal of the season. Drums and cowbells exploded into chaotic life despite one of the Chuff Chuffs having made his way past the terracing on his way to the toilets. Frozen for a second, he toyed with the idea of running back to his post for a belated celebration, but the call of nature was obviously too great. Content with the sight of their little apprentice just about managing to wield the cowbell above his head without causing himself serious harm, he carried on.

A two-goal advantage to Inverurie is a worthy lead at half-time and had what is left of the Chuff Chuffs in good spirits as they began to dismantle their flag, take up bags and coats in preparation for the trek round to the social club goal where their beloved Locos would be aiming in the second half.

When asked if they take all the drums and paraphernalia to matches home and away, the chief Chuff Chuff smiled proudly and proclaimed 'Aye' in a heartbeat. A second passed before he repeated his affirmation, this time in a softer, self-depreciating tone – a tacit acknowledgement that this isn't how most people show their affection for their team, just him and his band of chuffing brothers.

'It can be a bit of a squeeze in the car on those long away trips, but aye, we manage to fit it all in, for every game.' He introduced his colleagues. Gordie nodded, unable to shake hands as he is was poised with a drumstick in each one in readiness to strike the large bass drum that was strapped to his chest.

'We'll be at Forres in two weeks, no doubt about that,' Gordie said, more as a simple proclamation than any kind of brag. It is, quite simply, what they do.

Brian, the pre-teen apprentice, looked up at me from beneath his beanie and thick spectacles with a little suspicion. Having never seen me at a Locos game before, he asked the obvious question: 'Do you support Deveronvale?' When the response came back in the negative, he relaxed, clearly wary of the large away support, and their unkind chants at the Chuff Chuffs at the start of the game. It wouldn't be enough to stop him walking proudly past the bank of visitors on their way to their vantage point for the second half, however, despite the feeling of intimidation a boy in a junior year at school would no doubt feel walking past a large group in their senior year. Pride in your team gives you courage in the face of provocation.

'My name is Cuikie,' said the lead Chuff Chuff, 'but you've missed the last in our group. He won on the dominoes earlier today, and in his excitement, he keeps needing to go away to the toilet! He'll be kicking himself that he missed the second goal!'

Brian, exemplary apprentice that he was, had already prepared the errant Chuff Chuff's snare and cowbell in readiness for the off up the slope to the far goal. And with a wave of the hand they were away, like a gaggle of one-man bands that had taken a tumble down some steps. They headed off in a tangle of flagpole and drumsticks, coats tucked under chins and bags hanging from arms that cradled drums. A double beat on his drum, a shout of ''Mon the Locos' and a last wave of the hand and Cuikie and his travelling band turned the corner, slipping out of sight behind the terracing.

Playing down the slope in the second half and Deveronvale continued to play the ball along the floor, preferring composure and neat passing over hoofing the ball into the danger area, no matter the two-goal deficit. Both teams could really play and did as the match opened up and the visitors pressed for a way back into the game. Close misses from both sides saw an entertaining contest level out a little and it became clear, as the clock wound down, that the Locos' two first-half goals were fast becoming insurmountable.

With the points slipping away, and despite their team's unwavering efforts to achieve the near impossible, the young coachload of visiting supporters found their own entertainment, as a couple of their group were frogmarched out of the ground by stewards, much to the delight of their remaining colleagues. Singing and bouncing escalated, then was replaced by cheers as the heads of the two ejected boys peaked up above the external wall.

In as good natured an ejection as had ever been witnessed, the boys happily left when told to do so, the victims of swearing at the stewards one time too many. Not wanting to miss out on the fun, and with the game ebbing away, another roar went up, more laughter, as another beaming kid found himself taking the long walk to the exits. In time, another head popped up over the wall.

At the final whistle, after 90 minutes of fast, incisive football, the crowd of 600 (minus three) applauded both teams from the field. An excellent advertisement for Highland League football, the endeavour and passion on both sides of the white lines served to underline the mission statement of the league:

> Having now survived over 100 years, and the many obstacles history has placed in its path, the Highland Football League has become a part of the northern spirit, displaying the strength of commitment to the game from the meeting rooms, the players and from the supporters who loyally support their chosen team. Although the Highland Football League is a small speck in the increasingly global world of football, it is a league with a special character, a sound commitment to the game, exceptional skill, strong pride and an integral part of the communities within which it is a part.

As the large Friday night crowd began to drain away into the night, the Chuff Chuffs took pictures with members of their beloved team as they trudged into the changing rooms, Brian's beanie hat barely visible above the hoardings. The three ejected teens met up with their mates, excitedly recounting their tale at the steps of the coach, rejoicing in their dubious newfound badge of honour. The coach driver, hopeful that defeat might have subdued his cargo, slumped onto the wheel as they noisily embarked.

Pavements streamed with happy Locos, a few children looked back at the floodlights burning into the sky, one last glimpse of the magic, while others, optimism restored, headed back for a nightcap or two in the Hopeville Social Club.

And for Inverurie Loco Works Football Club, in gaining another three points; entertaining the crowd; providing a place for friends, old and young, to meet up and enjoy each other's company at a game of football; bringing the past and present of this little market town together, it was a case of job done, lights out. Until next time.

Bagpipes startled the hotel guests at breakfast the following morning, drowning out the gaggle of voices talking over one another in the adjacent bar. Men and women decked out in waders, sporting fishing rods that had to be lowered as they passed through doorways, began to file out onto the forecourt. Forming a semi-circle around the piper, they adjusted jackets and flat caps, before setting off in procession along the pavement behind him, the sound carrying long after they had slipped from view.

'It's the first day of the new fishing season,' one of the hotel staff explained, shaking her head. 'They all get dressed up and march down as one to the River Don, every year. Behind that piper.' She raised her eyebrows and smiled a smile that said what she couldn't – that it was all a bit much just to go fishing, but bless them, they were doing no harm, except to those with a sore head from the night before.

* * *

Brian, Gordie, Cuikie and the toilet-bound third Chuff Chuff's next away trip to Forres in a fortnight's time would be my Saturday afternoon. Wending my way across a landscape that is part of my family heritage, though having no idea which bits exactly, the trip from Inverurie to Forres normally takes 90 minutes. Stopping off at Highland League points of interest along the way extended matters significantly as the A96 skirted the foothills of the Cairngorms to the west. Rolling hills stopped farmland in its tracks, larger summits beyond topped out in snow hinted at the wilds this sprawling national park contained. Villages and towns came and went, along with them the nagging wonder at whether any held a familial significance that warranted more than a passing glance. Some you hoped might, such as Forres' Highland League opponents Huntly.

A pretty little town of some 4,500 people, Huntly is a picture postcard of old terraced cottages, churches and monuments lovingly tended among neat and welcoming parks. Frozen in time, it is a place you would hope your ancestors could have found some happiness, for a time at least. Christie Park, home to the town's football team, blends into this weave of old-time charm seamlessly. The weathered walls of the football ground mirror the rustic grey of the terraced streets across the road; an idyllic hush falling across this meeting of residential and sporting worlds.

Images of children playing ball in the street, standing on one another's shoulders to get a glimpse of the pitch, the grandstand, came as easily as the reality of smiling dog walkers watching a grown man attempting the same thing, catching a leg-up from a foot-sized crack in the stone masonry. A quick glance at a tree-lined football amphitheatre, barriers surrounding the pitch painted a vibrant yellow and black; the seats in the stand, arranged in alternating rows of the same colours, basked in a warm sun. This is a place that could feel like home, if only it had played host to a young girl washing kit and knocking up urns of tea...

The park looked every bit its 91 years, as lived in and embedded in the community as anything else. But despite its age, this is an institution clearly loved by the people of Huntly. The narrow doors to the turnstiles are painted with a relatively fresh coat of yellow, the framework a shiny black suggested that a small army of volunteers dedicated their spare time to the upkeep of Christie Park, as had an army before them and who knows how many before them, right back to the club's formation in 1928. And every now and then, that faith and passion is rewarded with some success on the pitch.

Having won the Highland League title at only the second time of asking in 1930, it would be a long wait for more glory to reach this part of the Highlands. But when it came, it heralded a period of five league titles in five years between 1994 and 1998. A seventh success in 2005 remains their last piece of silverware.

The echoes of cheering supporters filing away back down into the nest of narrow streets came easy that lazy Saturday morning. The unseasonably warm sun hinted at end of season weather, or the opening throes of summer, rather than the reality of being far from either. It was easy to imagine a lazy summer in Huntly, a summer that would have tasted all the sweeter as champions during those glory years.

Back in the present, the club began to stir a little in preparation for the trip to Forres, bodies fetching out bags of kit and the like, dropping them by the entrance ready to be stowed on the minibus that would take the team west. Sitting mid-table, it would be a trip purely for the pride of it, the chance to win a game of football on any given Saturday. Incentive enough to get those bodies out of bed and down to the club, to do their bit.

On the road and the A96 leads indirectly to much of the Highland League. Just past Huntly and a right turn will take you to Turriff, and then on to Fraserburgh. A fork in the road at Turriff takes you to Banff, the home of Deveronvale. North of Huntly, you find Keith,

Highland League members since 1924. A left turn here and Rothes and Strathspey Thistle reveal themselves, along with the long drive to Fort William. North of Keith and the coastal towns of Buckie and Lossiemouth look out on the Moray Firth, while the A96 takes a turn west through former Highland Leaguers Elgin towards Forres, Nairn and Clachnacuddin in Inverness.

It is often a thankless, anonymous life for players and supporters of these Highland teams, only rarely intercut with a club making the headlines for a cup run and occasional giant killing. An unsurprising existence for these remote communities that make up the league, facing down North Sea storms, bitter winters and relative isolation from the rest of the country.

Findhorn, a village just north of Forres, bears witness to such struggle. On a road leading to nowhere but there, the third incarnation of this community looks out across the calm waters of Findhorn Bay. A first Findhorn was buried by sand dunes that create a natural buffer to the open sea, leaving just a small inlet into the bay. A second was submerged by flooding a century later. Edition 3.0 appears safe enough beneath benign skies that has day-trippers squinting against a low winter sun. On the far bank, the ribs of two wrecks jut out above the waters at low tide – two fishing boats moored by men who went off to fight in World War 1. When they didn't return, their boats were left alone, a solemn, decaying monument to young lives lost more than a century ago. Bothered only on occasion by basking seals that dot the sand bar looking out at the Moray Firth and the long coastline up to Wick and John o' Groats, it cuts a melancholy sight to those who know the tale played out in decaying timber.

Forres (population: 13,000) stands on more solid ground than the shifting Findhorn. A few miles inland, it rises out of the countryside forged from the large granite blocks that typify Highland living. Multiple-time winner of the Beautiful Scotland competition, a Neo-gothic church looks out across an attractive town of characterful period buildings that mark the spot of a community mentioned in the writings of Claudius Ptolemy, a 2nd century mathematician, astronomer, geographer and astrologer from Alexandria in the Roman province of Egypt. No doubt he had been fascinated by Sueno's Stone, a monument thought to have been carved by the Picts, who lived in northern Scotland during the late Iron Age and early medieval period. Standing some 21 feet tall and intricately carved, it is a commemoration of a battle against Norse invaders.

Forres also lays claim to have inspired literary greats, as well as ancient scholars. In Shakespeare's *Macbeth*, Duncan's castle is located at Forres, and the three witches meet in Act Three on a heath just outside the town.

Not only at the vanguard of history, literature and floral displays in the Highlands, Forres is also home to the oldest still active football club in the north of Scotland. Formed in 1884 by a group of players frustrated at the lack of opportunities at the St Lawrence club, the main team in Forres at the time, Forres Mechanics, was born. They settled on 'Mechanics' as it was a common factor between the disgruntled players – mechanics at the time meaning 'people who are employed in manual occupation and as craftsmen'.

The Can Cans joined the inaugural Highland League season in 1893 alongside Thistle, Caley, Union, Citadel, Camerons and the only other ever-present Highland League side, Clachnacuddin (formed a year after Forres). It would take 54 years for Forres to win their first silverware, lifting the League Cup in 1947.

At the end of World War II, the Can Cans arranged a series of matches against teams of servicemen from around Europe who had been stationed in the town. To the consternation of the local press, who gave up on trying to spell these foreign players in their reports, the games were a huge success. A number of the Polish players became regulars in the Forres post-war team, with the likes of Mrowonski, Drynda, and Lesz helping them to that first League Cup trophy. For a time, the team was affectionately known as 'Foreign Mechanics'.

It would take a further 39 years for Forres to finally be crowned champions of the league they had helped create some 92 years earlier. That first title in 1986 was followed by another League Cup success in 2011, and a second championship in 2012 – four trophies the sum total of more than 126 years of membership, though by no means the sole defining moments in the Can Cans history.

In February 1957, more than 7,000 spectators crammed in to their Mosset Park home to witness a Scottish Cup fifth-round tie against Celtic. A 5-0 defeat was no mean feat against one of the giants of Glasgow. In more recent times, Forres would, in 2016, take

Stenhousemuir of League One to a third-round replay after a 2-2 draw at home.

However, titles and cup-runs do not make a football club. The passion, endeavour and dedication between them are the cement that binds a club together, anonymous match days down the years populated by those for whom Forres Mechanics is the only team that matters. Match days like the one I'd come to watch.

A speaker system crackled into life, music echoing up into a blustery sky like a call to arms, the wrapped up faithful beginning down steep pathways from the centre of town toward Mosset Park. A man dressed up in a suit and club tie stood expectantly by a trestle table adorned with club scarves, beanie hats and polo shirts. Situated just past the turnstiles, he doubled up as fifty-fifty ticket seller and team-sheet distributor. Eyeing the darkening skies above, he stood poised to scoop the lot back into a cardboard box beneath the table and retreat to a lesser, more sheltered spot.

Beyond, there are a handful of steps that lead up to the Can Cans' field of dreams, a natural amphitheatre surrounded on three sides by grass banks that rise up to act as terracing. As lovingly tended as the pitch itself, the terracing had been freshly cut and felt heavy underfoot. Like the pitch itself, the immaculate billiard finish of pre-season had succumbed to the rigours of winter, patches of wear appearing that not even the enthusiasm of those that tended them could prevent. As much at threat of waterlogging as the playing surface, it would be quite the spectacle to witness supporters slipping and sliding as they attempted to extricate themselves from the steeper spots on a particularly wet day.

A smattering of regulars, already gathering at their favourite grassy knoll, chatted over cups of tea, turning their collars to the onshore winds. For those unwilling to risk the slopes behind the goals, a large grandstand beckoned, complete with a wooden plaque at its entrance commemorating those who helped contribute towards it. The plaque, as polished and pristine as the day it had been erected more than 30 years earlier, bore testament to the love and care poured into the club. A similarly polished handrail led up to banks of freshly swept yellow and black seats, emptied bins, and cleaned Perspex windbreakers at either end that attempted to protect those huddled between from the wilds of the countless highland storms that blown through on match days. All the love afforded the stand belied the fact it was well into its fourth decade, having been built once Mosset Park had been shunted some 50 metres further into the lee of the town to accommodate the new A96 route from Elgin to Inverness.

At the top of the grandstand steps, a young lad attempted to take the pound entrance fee from those willing to part with it. Some do so happily, others look at him as if he has been forced to sit there as a punishment for committing a heinous crime, passing by without engaging with him. He didn't protest. Possibly the worst of the volunteer positions at Mosset Park, he no doubt dreams of a life behind the tea bar, or as a turnstile operator. But for now, this was how he could help his club, even if it garnered disdain and suspicion. He got neither from me as I hand over my pound and settled among the odd old-timer still wheezing from the exertion of the steps.

As the locals gathered, both teams continued their pre-match warm-ups, the starting eleven on both sides finishing up with a game of close-quartered two touch football while the substitutes descended into a chaotic taking of pot shots at the goal. Like some kind of tacit protest at being benched, this is the preserve of substitutes the game over, lashing the ball at a sometimes empty net, possibly venting the frustrations of another weekend without a start – maybe picturing a cowering manager between the sticks as they slam yet another ball towards them.

An outfield Forres sub gleefully took up the goalkeeper position, a manic grin on his face as he dived here and there after the balls raining down on him, his shoulders slumped a little when forced to retreat to the bench as the teams came out just before kick-off.

He would cut a forlorn figure at half-time as well, when the goal was descended upon by 20 or so children all playing out their own goalscoring heroics. Balls pinballing about the goalmouth in a whirl-wind of youthful exuberance as multiple chaotic games play out, the sub stood near the halfway line passing the ball around his fellow subs, looking on enviously at the muddy chaos.

Like Inverurie, Forres were aiming to keep within touching distance of Cove and Brora at the top of the table. And after the announcer, sat with the microphone with his mates in the main stand, had read out the line-ups, the hosts – a team of seasoned Highland Leaguers, some with experience of the professional leagues above – played out a dominating game against a Huntly side just aiming to hang on in there.

As Fort William's gate-man Sam Lees had offered, it was a semi-professional league, but some were more so than others. And with Huntly's league dominance in the mid-'90s, anyone could find themselves top of the pile given that all too elusive winning formula: clean sheets and a goalscoring touch. And this season, the stars, along with an extraordinary amount of selfless volunteer work, have aligned for the Can Cans, who threatened with every possession.

A Huntly supporter, chatting to the stranger in the seat next to him, shook his head and said, 'The wheels have come off a bit in the last few weeks. We look beat already.'

But it hadn't put him off from driving the hour to see those wheels fall off. For many, it was an act of belonging far more significant than any score-line.

Just as well, as after some determined defending, the inevitable happened, much to the delight of the few hundred assembled Can Cans and the announcer, who fumbled about his feet for the microphone before booming the name of the Forres scorer up into the rafters. It would be a relatively busy day for him, the Can Cans finishing as 4-0 winners, along with numerous substitutions to call that had him scrabbling about for his team-sheet to get the visiting names right.

Despite the drubbing, no one could accuse Huntly of not giving it their all, despite the anguished rollockings doled out by exhausted defenders who, having thwarted yet another attack, saw their strikers fumble their touch, the ball falling back into the hands, or feet, of Forres to launch another attack.

No matter the foregone conclusion, protecting the pride of the team, the club and its 90 plus-year history was worth going right to the very last. This was the unsaid minimum requirement of every player and every supporter – the fan in the stand choosing not to dip out early, but to sit and suffer with his team, applaud them for a job well done in getting away with just the four conceded. Any less application and it could have been much, much worse.

It was Forres who were then far more likely to break the monopoly at the top of the league. But as Huntly and Deveronvale proved, being off the pace for a time and coming from a smaller community doesn't mean you can never have your time at the top. The summit is not insurmountable, which is hope enough to shake hands with your opponents at the end of a defeat, console teammates while trudging off, weaving between scores of children descending on the nets to play out the goalscoring heroics just witnessed.

The stand and grass banks drained away to empty as players leaned against the perimeter barrier to chat to friends and family. Supporters slipped back up into town or pulled out of the car park and into the A96 traffic. The speakers crackled, then died as Mosset Park began to hush. The excited echoes of the last few kids playing on the pitch were the only accompaniment to the handful of volunteers beginning to sweep the stands in readiness for next time. As the floodlights snapped off, the last few die hard children took the hint, scuffing their ball away and along the pavements and back up into town. Another match day complete, like the countless games that have gone before and those yet to happen. A ritual of no importance to the wider world, save only in an understanding that, like those frequenting the Camp Nou of Barcelona, Old Trafford or Celtic Park, if it means the world to you, then it means the world.

Six Hawthorn Terrace, Aberdeen was hidden by an early morning dusk and the five preceding cottages that obscured it from the road. Accessible only by a narrow alleyway barely a shoulders' width across, it looked uncannily like the alleyway that led to the house Violet Ann Omand finally called home in Salisbury. Born in one, died in the other, much of what happened between the two places is seemingly forever lost to time. She was a young girl prepared to do her bit during the war, from rivet catcher to cook – her heritage betrayed by her father, her future derailed by a deceitful army officer. How Violet's life may have played out in the absence of these two events is now the preserve of an alternative universe, one in which the familial role that Wellworthys football team played in her life could have been replaced with Inverurie Loco Works, Huntly or Forres Mechanics. The sense of togetherness, pride and belonging that she found in the former, and that is on display any given match day in the latter, would no doubt have attracted her and her young son David.

Free from the brutality of the Royal Caledonian Asylum, would the childhood of her son, David – or dad, as I knew him – be populated with chaotic half-time Highland League kickabouts while his mum served out the tea to recuperating teams? What loyalties might he have handed down to his children as a result? Given the passion, humour and strong sense of community experienced, along with a cracking standard of football that could capture the imagination of any youngster peering over the barriers for the very first time, it would have been, in a parallel universe, more than enough I am sure to have captured my heart.

And that is my loss.

CHAPTER FOUR

No League of Their Own – Liechtenstein

UEFA STATUTES DECREE that a senior national football league must comprise no less than eight teams. Among the confederation's smallest members, 51,000 Faroe Islanders have ten teams in their Betri Deildin. There are also ten sides for 33,000 Gibraltarians to support in their Premier Division. UEFA's smallest nation, San Marino, have 15 sides spread across two groups in the Campionato Sammarinese di Calcio to occupy a population just a shade smaller than Gibraltar. The Primera Divisió in Andorra operates with just the eight teams. If ever one of Encamp, Engordany, Santa Coloma, Inter Club d'Escaldes, Lusitanos, Ordino, Sant Julià, or UE Santa Coloma disbanded suddenly, the league could be bolstered by one of the six teams playing in the second division.

What happens, however, if you just don't have eight teams?

Liechtenstein, a micro-state that is 24 kilometres long and 12 kilometres wide, sandwiched between Switzerland and Austria in the Rhine Valley deep within the Alps, is UEFA's anomaly. Only seven teams play the beautiful game beneath a spectacular alpine backdrop, servicing a population of just 37,000. With just the seven clubs, there is no national league. The opportunity of qualifying for the early stages of the Champions League is forever denied them. The only national football competition within Liechtenstein comes in the shape of the Liechtensteiner Cup, where reserve and youth teams bolster the seven senior sides to create an annual knock-out tournament. For many teams in Liechtenstein, national competition every year can be fleeting at best.

There is no simple answer to Liechtenstein's missing football league conundrum. The seven teams that do exist play within the Swiss football pyramid. Their positions within it suggest that the notion of a reserve team simply reforming to create an eighth senior team in Liechtenstein could cause more harm than good.

The footballing giants of this minnow nation are FC Vaduz from the capital, who play in the Swiss Challenge League, Switzerland's second division. Relegated from the top-flight in 2017 after three seasons competing against the best of Swiss football, Vaduz dominate the game in Liechtenstein. Winners of the Liechtensteiner Cup on 20 of the last 21 occasions, FC Vaduz are the country's almost exclusive representatives in European competition, reaching the third qualifying round of the Europa League three times.

Beyond Vaduz, USV Eschen/Mauren play in the fourth tier of Swiss football in the regional I liga. The only other side to taste Liechtensteiner Cup victory in the past two decades (defeating Vaduz in the final in 2012), they took on FH from Iceland in European competition, losing 2-1 at home and 1-0 away in the first qualifying round. FC Balzers play in the fifth tier and last won the cup in 1997, resulting in a 5-1 aggregate defeat in the now defunct UEFA Cup Winners Cup to BVSC Budapest in the qualifying round. After Balzers, the remaining four clubs in Liechtenstein operate as amateur teams in the lowest reaches of Swiss football: FC Ruggell in the sixth tier, FC Triesenberg in the seventh and FCs Schaan and Triesen in the eighth.

However, when you are just one of seven, every dog can have its day, as witnessed by FC Schaan's Liechtensteiner Cup win in 1994 which resulted in their only foray into European football. Representing their nation, Schaan went down 4-0 on aggregate to Bulgaria's Pirin Blagoevgrad in the qualifying round of the Cup Winners Cup.

If ever an eighth team were formed, a national league with such a mismatch of abilities could very well do more harm than good. While a national division could be a source of pride for the country (a national championship was only ever run five times during the 1930s, ironically won three times by one of Liechtenstein's lowest ranked side, FC Triesen[1]), the league would be so one-sided

---

[1] During the early part of the 20th century, teams from Liechtenstein were not only affiliated with the Swiss Football Association, but also the regional association of St Gallen in the north-east of the country. The St Gallen FA placed all teams from Liechtenstein in the same regional division, declaring

that it would be rendered pointless. More than 70 years of teams finding their level in a much larger system would see to that. The only immediate outcome would be an inevitable talent-drain from FC Vaduz to teams in Switzerland playing at their current standard. Having a team in the higher reaches of the Swiss league is a great aspirational carrot for young players from the principality. Losing that would slam shut a major opportunity for young Liechtensteiners to develop.

As unique and quirky as it is, the current system of playing in another country's league works well for all seven of Liechtenstein's teams. Playing at a level in which they can be competitive and can have a chance of improving naturally is a perfect fit. It also elevates the near processional annual cup competition, despite it being heavily weighted in Vaduz's favour.

Such a rare opportunity to play in a national event, that for some may last only 90 minutes every year but represents the footballing passion and sporting heritage of this tiny mountainous principality, can raise the amateur up to unexpected heights. In 2015, FC Triesenberg made it all the way to the final for the first time in their history. A 5-0 defeat against a then Super League team Vaduz is still proudly commemorated on club house walls with photographs and paper clippings. The paucity of opportunity to play for national pride can do that, once the moment has finally been forged from hard work and desire. A seven-division gulf in standard not producing the cricket score that should have been inevitable. It is how a national team from one of Europe's smallest countries consistently punches well above its weight, against national teams whose stadiums could seat the population of Liechtenstein two or three times over, and with seats still to spare.

Narrow defeats shouldn't happen in situations like that. But they can and do, fuelled by the desire and passion caused by a rare opportunity to represent the nation of your parents and grandparents, and however many generations that have called Liechtenstein

---

the winners to be national champions. The Liechtenstein football championship of the 1930s struggled, however, resulting in only one participant in 1937, the final year of the championship. By default, FC Triesen won that final league, and therefore remain unofficial champions of Liechtenstein to this day.

home. England's golden generation of the early 21st century played Liechtenstein home and away in qualifying for the 2004 European Championships. Goals from Michael Owen and David Beckham gave England a 2-0 victory in front of 3,500 spectators at the Rheinpark Stadion, Vaduz in March 2003. The re-match in September saw Owen and Wayne Rooney score a goal each in another 2-0 win, this time with 65,000 watching on at Manchester United's Old Trafford. Results like this shouldn't happen, and often don't: defeats by seven or eight goals against the strongest nations in Europe are the inevitable consequence of such a sporting mismatch.

However, heroics against the newly crowned World and soon to be European champions Spain saw a 4-0 defeat at home in September 2010 (Torres x2, Villa, Silva) and a 6-0 loss the following year (Negredo x2, Xavi, Ramos, Villa x2). Respectable defeats (given the gulf in resources) against a team that tore the world's very best to shreds proves that victory sometimes doesn't just come from a positive goals tally. As Odmar Færø and his Faroes team displayed, nations at the foot of the UEFA and world rankings cherish endeavour as much as tangible wins. Small steps in an extremely aggressive environment.

It is an alien mindset to those whose national teams have grand aspirations of World Cup qualification, or European Championship silverware. But it is no less significant or worthy a target for one of the world's minnow footballing nations, garnering as much pride and celebration as any trophy could. And as my plane touched down among the rain of a grey November morning in Zurich, the hope of witnessing a little bit of that tangible minnow magic, albeit at a far more obscure fixture than that night at Old Trafford more than 15 years before, fortified me in the face of the least Swiss-looking scene you could imagine.

The flat lands around the airport, littered with industrial estates and municipal buildings, appeared even more drab and depressing beneath oppressive clouds of near freezing drizzle. Car exhausts smoked and choked pedestrians hidden beneath umbrellas and deep hoods. Picture postcard it was not. But as the road wound eastwards, the Switzerland that first springs to your mind's eye began to materialise, the landscape slowly rising up on an ever-grander scale.

Long tunnels beneath the mountains, like a finely engineered wardrobe door into a real-life Narnia, finally revealed a more picture-postcard alpine scene at the far end. Blinking back out into the light, the small towns of Quarten and Murg appeared, pinned between a vast, chill lake and looming snow-topped mountains. Seemingly unfathomable peaks slipped from view among a thick freezing fog. Steep snow-dusted forests of pine ebbing and flowing behind the cloud cover adding to a scene that was hard to take your eyes off in order to concentrate on a road lined with drifts of freshly ploughed snow.

The contrast from one end of the tunnel to the other was startling. As if to prove the point, fresh flurries of snow began to fall, shrouding the valley in another picturesque layer of alpine beauty. It was easy to imagine the dull tolling of distant cowbells, echoing across pastures among the mountains on which cattle grazed – an eternal soundtrack to rural alpine life. Imagination would suffice, as the bone-chilling air tempered any romantic notion of winding down the window.

Into the Rhine Valley and the main thoroughfare linking Switzerland, Austria and Germany snaked between ever-more startling scenery. Beauty-hardened locals, lorry drivers and commuters powered on, the impending winter and ski season just another facet of life up in the mountains, not worthy enough to linger in the slow lane to take it all in. There were jobs to reach, deliveries to complete, chores to do.

Even at such a slow pace, trying to take everything in, I missed Liechtenstein. Or at least, a significant chunk of it. Not quite a case of blink and you miss it but not taking the junction to Balzers, Liechtenstein's most southerly town, does result in missing roughly a third of this constitutional hereditary monarchy. Four more junctions missed in the time it takes to listen to 'Bohemian Rhapsody' and the entire country has been left behind for a crossroads toward the alpine pass into Austria and the southern tip of Germany and Lake Constance. It is easily done, hidden as Liechtenstein is behind a ten-foot-high berm that lines the great River Rhine, protecting the flatlands of the valley floor from flooding. Punt across this grand landmark of Western Europe to its mid-way point and you find Liechtenstein's constitutional border with the outside world, wending its way along the contours and currents of the river for the principalities entire western front. As the road hugs the flow of the river, those not in the know would have no clue as to the country they were passing by. Its closeted geography enables one of Europe's oldest counties to survive through the centuries, while borders were being drawn and re-drawn around them.

Dating back to 1342, the county of Vaduz had previously been a state of the holy Roman Empire, before centuries of benign alpine isolation. In 1699, Prince Johann Adam Andreas bought the Lordship of Schellenberg and then, in 1712, the county of Vaduz. Seven years later, the two regions were to become the Imperial Principality of Liechtenstein. Location and close diplomatic ties with its neighbours enabled the country to survive through Europe's great periods of political instability. The rewriting of geographical borders never threatening Liechtenstein's 300 years of sovereignty, though its close relationship with the larger states around them have left a somewhat chameleon-like façade. Standard German is the official language (though the spoken language is an Alemannic dialect specific to the Rhine Valley region that is close enough to standard German for tourists with limited vocabulary to notice no difference), while the Swiss Franc is the official currency. In another twist, Liechtenstein also uses the same melody as 'God Save the Queen' for its national anthem, causing even greater consternation to outsiders, although in reality the melody only became known as 'God Save the Queen' in 1745 and had been used in France, Sweden, Russia, Switzerland and Norway for royal or national anthems over the centuries. While Switzerland dispensed with the melody in 1940, Liechtenstein remain the only other country in modern times to use it as a national anthem, the common assumption being that it is just another of Liechtenstein's appropriations.

With the second turning into the principality successfully negotiated, only time would tell if Liechtenstein's identity truly was one of adaptation and assimilation – either by design or born out of some necessity of survival – or if a micro-state of some 37,000 souls could forge their own cultural footprint while being surrounded by political and historical powerhouses Austria, Switzerland and Germany.

While the nation of Liechtenstein celebrates its 300th birthday in 2019, the principality's largest sporting endeavour – the national football team – is a relative baby. Despite club football thriving in the Swiss leagues since the early 20th century, a national team was only formed and admitted into UEFA and FIFA in 1974. However, it wouldn't be until 1981 that a Liechtenstein national football team would take to the field, and in the most unlikely of places.

In June 1981, at a small tournament called the President's Cup in Daejeon, South Korea, it would be Ludwig Sklarski who made history by scoring the principality's first ever international goal in their first ever international match, a 1-1 draw with Malta. A 2-0 defeat to Thailand and a 3-2 victory against Indonesia in Jeonju followed, but it would be another four months before the team would play their first ever international on home soil. It would be Sklarski again who scored that all important first goal in a 1-0 friendly win in October 1981 over Malaysia, watched by 700 spectators in Balzers.

For Sklarski (who had turned out for the junior teams of Bayern Munich before playing in Belgium for KV Kortrijk and FC Zurich in Switzerland) that would be as good as it got as an international footballer, with the national team playing only two more friendly matches during the rest of the 1980s. Indeed, before the principality took part in its first ever competitive fixtures – qualifying for the Euro 96 tournament that began in 1994 – it played only three matches between 1990 and 1993. Despite that, it was far from a baptism of fire, losing 4-1 to Northern Ireland in the opening round of fixtures before narrow defeats to Switzerland and Latvia. Heavier defeats home and away to Portugal (7-0 and 8-0 respectively) were followed up by a 7-0 defeat in Austria and then a goalless draw at home to the Republic of Ireland. Pretty remarkable results for a tiny nation with such limited experience, though an 11-1 drubbing at home by the former Yugoslav Republic of Macedonia in their 1998 World Cup qualifying campaign added a perspective that international football would always come hard to them.

It would take four years of endeavour before a first ever competitive win, a 2-1 victory over Azerbaijan at Rheinpark Stadion during the qualifying for Euro 2000. And in the following 20 years leading up to the Nations League of 2018, Liechtenstein managed a further six competitive wins over Luxembourg (twice), Latvia, Iceland, Lithuania and Moldova. However, arguably more impressive than any of those results were their two close-run matches against England in 2003 and a 2-2 draw at home to Portugal in their World Cup 2006 qualifying fixtures.

The last qualifying campaign for the 2018 World Cup, Liechtenstein played ten and lost ten in a group including both Spain and Italy. Any positives, such as close-run games against Albania and Israel, or periods of play against some of the world's best are achievements to be celebrated when you are a micro-state, just as they are in the Faroe Islands. Performances over score-lines and pride over points are the only tangible football currency for a nation ranked 183 in the world, beneath the likes of Chad, St Vincent and the Grenadines and Guyana.

And with a paucity of players to choose from, qualification for the World Cup Finals is a fanciful notion. That doesn't stop players and supporters from the lowest ranked nations from trying, from dreaming. One moment of magic that can be savoured, added to those seven wins, and tales of heroic displays handed down from elder to junior. Which is why the inaugural UEFA Nations League was so eagerly anticipated down in the Rhine Valley. Just as it was in Tórshavn, Valletta, Chişinău and every other region in Europe deprived a regular opportunity to win football matches.

Paired with Armenia, Macedonia and Gibraltar in League four, group D, six games in three months against teams not so far out of sight on the FIFA rankings was an opportunity never afforded them before. As with all the minnow nations in UEFA, money and viable opposition largely prevents fixtures outside of the normal qualifying campaigns. Just like the Faroes, who have daunting isolation to contend with as well, nations like Liechtenstein, San Marino and Andorra can sometimes have only a handful of fixtures any given year. Six Nations League games in twelve weeks offered them a priceless opportunity to develop the national team, its tactics, confidence and belief.

A narrow 2-1 defeat in Armenia was followed with a 2-0 home win against Gibraltar in September. October's fixtures saw a much improved 4-1 loss in Macedonia compared to their horror show defeat in 1996, before a 2-1 defeat in Gibraltar. All four matches were competitive, enabling all teams the freedom to attack and explore their talents fully. A final Group D home double header against Macedonia and Armenia, played over four days in mid-November, provided one final Nations League shot in the arm for the players and supporters of Liechtenstein. And while Sandro Wieser's sending off early in the second half in the first game against Macedonia dampened the mood a little, a spirited rear-guard action limited the visitors and leaders of

Group D to a 2-0 win. A win, five goals scored and only ten against across five matches already constituted a decent campaign. But with one game to go, hope still sprung eternal.

Triesenberg (population: 2,000) was lost. The only major village in Liechtenstein, situated up in the mountains that stretch across more than two thirds of the country, it remained missing among heavy cloud that threatened more snow. With the car idling on the banks of the Rhine, the valley and indeed the entire country cowered beneath dark, looming waves of cresting rock, materialising and fading behind swathes of dense fog. Signposts for Triesenberg pointed up into the gloom but the town was nowhere to be seen.

A narrow road of twisting switchbacks ascended into a magical world of snow flurries and frosted pine trees. The twinkling lights of the valley below slipped away quickly the higher into the cloud the car laboured. Chalets began to line the road, seemingly impassable alleyways branching off, providing access to more dwellings beyond, fading in and out of view. On it went until the road levelled out a touch, and a church materialised looking out on a deserted village square, its bulbous spire a unique feature of churches in Liechtenstein. Engine off and the village fell silent, hidden in a fog that limited the view to a hundred feet or so. The road from the valley, heading on and up to the small ski resort of Malbun beyond tapered off, dissolving to nothing. Pathways deserted. Smoking chimneys the only signs of life until the drone of another car labouring up from the valley floor, the chime of a bell as an old man wrapped up warm stepped out from a little convenience store. This did not look like the home of a football team that as recently as 2015 had made it to the final of a national cup competition. But this was Liechtenstein.

Steep, treacherous pathways, a road easily cut off during the worst of the winter storms, houses clinging to the sheer rock face. Picturesque it may be, but there is a reason why Triesenberg is the only significantly habited mountain region in Liechtenstein: life is that much harder. On the valley floor there is fertile land, flat land, easily maintainable services even during the worst of an alpine winter. Life naturally gravitates to it. And so too do its football teams.

For the football loving folk of Triesenberg, nothing comes easy, as is witnessed at its home ground, Sportanlage Leitwies. A quick walk through the deserted streets of the village reveals one thing – no flat land. An odd patch of ground in someone's garden, a relatively benign stretch in the village centre that resembled those classic old non-league slopes that used to topple high-flying teams in the FA Cup. Beyond that, nothing where even a kickabout between schoolchildren could break out. Stood only a few feet away from Sportanlage Leitwies, it remains hidden to those not in the know. A narrow road off the main tract of switchbacks out of town reveal what looks like a municipal building of some kind. Undercroft parking spots on the ground floor line up behind large pillars of concrete. Beyond, stairways lead up into what looks like the belly of some strange, windowless building. The only thing that looks a little off are sets of floodlights rooted next to the road, which rise up and look in over what seems to be a fenced off roof. Its appearance is so unlike a football ground that you can't help but carry on, only turning back after the entrance to a small school and a little warren of houses, where the road quickly tapers away into barely a farm track plummeting into some treacherous looking pastures.

Steep icy steps up one side of this curious building are clearly rarely trodden on non-match days. A pristine pitch and clubhouse, complete with a few rows of seats to catch a match in stretch out across the rooftop. A wall of fog beyond the fenced in perimeter denies one of the most spectacular views in European football: the Swiss Alps and the Rhine Valley. Instead, silence. Absolute silence. The outside world lost. Only this wonder of design and architecture remains, a football pitch, floating among the cloud.

So desperate for a team (formed in 1972), Triesenberg created a pitch where there was no flat land to be had, no doubt at a great deal of expense. And all to play in the seventh tier of Swiss football. What a testament to the lengths people will go to for the love of the game. The village may never produce a team to rival Vaduz, or even USV Eschen/Mauren, but it is clear by the way the complex is spotlessly maintained that it is very important to them. That being an albeit modest part of Liechtenstein football is a source of tremendous pride.

On such a cold, lifeless day, it seemed hard to imagine a crowd of any size congregating here, the bulk of the 2,000 souls that inhabit the mountains remaining conspicuous by their absence as night fell. The hotel restaurant remained mostly quiet as dinner was served; mid-November being just a little too early for the ski season trade. What would have been panoramic views of the valley from a row of floor to ceiling windows remained lost behind the cloud; the only thing on show was your own dulled reflection that studied you as hard as you tried to discern anything out of the gloom. The one opportunity to do anything other than sit awkwardly in a room with two other people dotted about an otherwise deserted hotel had been denied. The eagerness with which individuals ate, then left for pastures less uncomfortable felt palpable in the silence.

Heading back down the switchbacks into the valley, the cloud finally broke. The lights of cars streamed in both directions along the motorway beyond the river, forming a twinkling border between Liechtenstein and the outside world. More vehicles poured over the bridges across the Rhine to join the throng, as the 20,000 workers who cross into the principality every day to work in its financial sector began to drain away.

Vaduz (population: 5,000) is the third smallest capital in Europe behind the Vatican City and San Marino. It's not even the largest town in Liechtenstein, Schaan having more inhabitants. But what it loses in size it more than makes up for in old world charm. Vaduz Castle perches on a rocky outcropping above the town. Home to the Princely family, one of the oldest noble families in Europe, the castle dates to the 12th century. Floodlights at its base illuminate the castle at night, a symbol of pride and identity in Liechtenstein, it seems to float above the capital in the dark.

That evening, it had competition for most visible landmark in this near invisible country. The burning floodlights of Rheinpark Stadion, home of FC Vaduz and the national team, made it virtually impossible for any football supporter to lose their way en-route to a night match.

With a capacity of 6,000, the national stadium sits right on the riverbanks of the Rhine. The berm runs behind a modest main stand, and along its spine there is a footpath from where those not wanting to pay for a ticket can catch snatches of Challenge League matches or national team fixtures. It may very well be one of the few national stadiums in the world where a hoofed clearance could carry into another country, and then possibly float away into a third. It is certainly in one of the most stunning locations for a national stadium in the world. And regardless of its modest capacity, it feels smaller again, cowering as it does beneath one of the most breathtaking mountain ranges in the world.

Despite being clear of the freezing fog that clung to the lower slopes of the alps, the temperature in the valley had plummeted to below zero. Exhausts and spectators' breath alike smoked up into the night sky as they began to congregate around the stadium for Liechtenstein's last Nations League fixture. An ultimately meaningless match in the outcome of League D, Group Four, with Macedonia taking a three-point lead into their final game at home to Gibraltar (a match they were unlikely to lose) meant that for tonight's visitors, Armenia, it was a case of so near and yet so far. But despite the reality that Nations League progress was unlikely, Armenian supporters began to materialize out of the darkness, drawn towards a very old-looking coach in one corner of the car park.

There was no way of knowing for sure just how far it had transported its passengers, its license plates having long since been obscured beneath layers of dirt and grime. But with its shabby, torn curtains in the windows and external panelling hinting at a lifespan dating back to the '80s and possible service during the Soviet-era, it looked every bit as downtrodden as a bus might after a 50-plus-hour, 4,500-kilometre journey from Yerevan all the way across Georgia, Russia, Ukraine, Moldova, Romania, Hungary and Austria to find itself here in Vaduz.

Crossing from Russia into Ukraine may have proven tense given the ongoing conflict between the two, but at least that route would have been open to them. The quicker journey across Turkey remains impossible due to the closed border between Armenia and its neighbour to the west – a result of the Nagorno-Karabakh war fought in the '90s between Armenia and Turkey's political ally, Azerbaijan, as the Soviet Union they had both belonged to disintegrated around them. A small circle of men huddled at the rear of the coach and listened as a lone voice sang a mournful lament of a song. Its meaning lost to most that heard it, the only thing that did translate was its importance, as more Armenian supporters drifted across the car park to join the circle, listening in with a hushed respect. In its lilting inflections it certainly carried the emotional weight of a song honouring those lost in a war that, barely 25 years old, would no doubt remain an open wound in the consciousness of those that endured and immediately followed it. Eyes raised to the bitterly cold skies or fixed on some point or memory way beyond the reach of any physical horizon, they looked just as the Azerbaijani players had as they sang their national anthem on the pitch in Tórshavn.

Bitter enemies to this day, where both nations are kept apart in qualifying groups for everyone's safety, they remain brothers in anguish over those who were lost in over six years of conflict. Song complete, a round of applause broke the silence, followed by the opening bars of a football chant that quickly had everyone joining in, twirling scarves and flags above their heads. The football lovers of Liechtenstein may not have the passion of identity that surviving a collapsing super-state or war can solidify, but in their reserved and understated way this lack of overt identity, of fervent sporting nationalism *is* the identity of this tiny principality.

In a country of 160 square miles (the majority of which is sparsely populated mountains), where the currency is Swiss, the language is German and the national anthem is regularly confused for that of the United Kingdom, traditional markers of identity don't necessarily work. The principality survived 300 years of political and geographical upheaval through diplomacy and understatement. Indeed, to the untrained ear, the language sounds purely German. The subtle differences that constitute Liechtenstein-German lost. The porous borders with Switzerland and Austria mean that you could find yourself in, and then back out of Liechtenstein without even realising it. The architecture is traditionally alpine, save for the odd bulbous spire on the odd church. In this near unique environment, traditional markers of identity make way for a far more subtle, internal certainty of who you are and where you are from. A football match, however, affords a more direct display.

Children proudly decked out in national team shirts that are normally much too big for them but fit a little better over thick coats and scarves looked up at the pennants and keyrings, flags and shirts of the small merchandise stall. Hands held tightly, their look of awe is familiar the world over when confronted with the badge of your national team, rows of shirts your heroes will be pulling on. Newly bought hand-held flags were unfurled until they hang from a little wooden pole, then waved enthusiastically above their new owners' heads.

The rich spices of glühwein, a drink synonymous with Christmas markets but traditionally served throughout the winter months in

Scandinavia and the Alps, elevated the atmosphere around food stalls, where friends decked out in scarves and flags met up to take a drink before heading into the ground. It felt like a typical lower league bustle back in England, but with the anticipation of an international football match.

While they may not be the typical drum-banging set of supporters, it would be a mistake to see the Liechtensteiners' reserved nature as apathy. They are both proud of and passionate for their team. A crowd of 1,200 may not back that up initially. But with a population of just 37,000, the numbers in the crowd mean that more than 4 per cent of the population have come to see a match that is ultimately meaningless. If a similar percentage of England wanted to see their national team play, Wembley Stadium would need somewhere in the region of 2.7 million seats.

Inside, boys stood by the gates handing out programmes. Eager to do their jobs well, they weaved between bodies so as not to miss any potential customers. With arms full of them, one boy attempted to hand one out, but missed. It fell to the floor. In his desire to retrieve it, he forgot about the laws of gravity, bent over, only for his armful of programmes to cascade and spill. Mortified, he quickly scrabbled to pick them back up, dropping as many as he retrieved with ever panicking and flailing hands. His friends, in typical young boy fashion, laughed hysterically at his misfortune, coming to his aid the last thing on their minds. As a few passers-by helped him gain equilibrium, the tannoy system spluttered into life, distracting others from his blushes and drowning out his cackling buddies. Back to square one, he began to hand them out once more, this time more gingerly.

With a squad comprising six players from FC Balzers in the fifth tier of Swiss football, and another three from fourth-tier USV Eschen/ Mauren, it is a miracle that Liechtenstein can compete even in the modest surroundings of League D Group four of the Nations League. It shouldn't be possible for Liechtenstein, Andorra, Gibraltar, San Marino or the Faroe Islands to do anything other than get beat out of sight every match, even against the likes of Armenia 81 places above them in the FIFA rankings. But with four other players turning out for FC Vaduz in the Swiss Challenge League – and a smattering of others playing lower league football in Austria, Switzerland and Germany – pride, passion and a siege mentality that is forged when the world perpetually writes you off can create a decent base from which to work. Add to that mix a few players who have managed to reach the rarefied air of senior football leagues, and a small team can quickly grow greater than the sum of their parts.

Martin Büchel and Dennis Salanović represent FC Zurich and FC Thun in the Swiss Super League respectively. Nicolas Hasler made the switch to America to play in the MLS with Chicago Fire. But it is Marcel Büchel who is the current talisman for the national team. Having been signed by Italian giants Juventus in 2010, he made his professional debut for 'The Old Lady' in a Europa League match against Red Bull Salzburg in November of that year. Loan spells at Serie B sides Gubbio, Cremonese, Virtus Lanciano and Bologna yielded more than 100 appearances in Italy's second tier before a move to Empoli and a taste of top-flight football. In an 18-month spell, he played more than 40 Serie A matches, scoring twice, before being loaned out to Hellas Verona back in Serie B.

As he jogged out to begin his warm-up in preparation for a 14th appearance for his national team, he was still waiting to play a first club match of the season. Empoli did not include him in their league squad, but also did not arrange a loan elsewhere. This freezing November evening was a rare opportunity to get out there on the pitch.

Just as he was the shining light for Liechtenstein, Armenia had one of their own, whose emergence onto the pitch with his teammates sent the travel-weary inhabitants of that Soviet-era bus, now dug in behind one of the goals, into song – banners fluttering across empty seats around them. Henrikh Mkhitaryan, captain of his country, has won the Armenian League four times with Pyunik, the Ukrainian double three times with Shakhtar Donetsk, the German Super Cup with Borussia Dortmund and the Europa League with Manchester United (scoring the winner). A move to Arsenal kept Mkhitaryan at the top of the game.

A young boy during the fall of the Soviet Union and the Nagorno-Karabakh war – Mkhitaryan's 78 national team appearances for a side that rarely threatens qualification to the big competitions suggests that he is rarely absent when called upon. Representing his nation is as priceless for him as it is for those who have made the arduous journey from a country bordering Iran to shiver in the arctic conditions in Vaduz. Identities that have been hard-fought, have seen fellow countrymen lose their lives in achieving it no doubt fuelling a desire to turn out in even the most hopeless of sporting causes.

It may well be a match with little riding on it, but it is far from lacking in significance to those who have braved the weather to be here, Mkhitaryan included. Whether those identities are being sung from the rafters in the Armenian end, or quietly considered among the reserved Liechtensteiners – making use of the free programmes to insulate the seats – this is a precious occasion to be savoured, to be honoured. It is a celebration of national and sporting identity, the standard being entirely irrelevant.

National anthems sung, including Liechtenstein's familiar 'Oben am jungen Rhein', the match began with the side 80 places better off in the world rankings dominating. There was no surprise when a neat move resulted in Sargis Adamyan, a striker from ssv Jahn Regensburg in Germany, scoring his first ever international goal on his 12th attempt. As he and his teammates celebrated, the players from Liechtenstein retrieved the ball, placing it on the centre circle. Used as they were to going behind, they lined back up, ready to go. Applause from the Liechtensteiners in the stands attempted to spur them on. With only eight minutes gone, there was plenty of time to truly express themselves. And as the game restarted, they did just that.

An existence carved out of occasional counterattacks saw the hosts grow into the game, making the most of Armenia losing possession. Martin Rechsteiner of fifth-tier FC Balzers battled with Europa League winner Mkhitaryan, snuffing out defence-splitting passes with desperate tackles and interceptions. And as the game ebbed and flowed towards half-time, it would be a moment of magic from Liechtenstein's poster boy Marcel Büchel that would have the home fans chatting excitedly over their interval Glühwein. Controlling the ball, he instinctively leathered it from far enough outside the Armenian penalty area that it should have been easy pickings for the keeper. Instead, it flew into the top right-hand corner, giving Henri Avagyan no chance. Liechtenstein's reservation disappeared in a roar of ecstasy from the stands, seats flipping up violently as supporters jumped to their feet, insulating programmes tumbling down the steps like paper slinkies. Witnessing a Liechtenstein goal is never a given. Indeed, they only scored once during the 2018 World Cup

Qualifying campaign – and that came in an away defeat to Israel. Seeing a goal, let alone one of such quality could do nothing but set the heart racing.

The boys who had been handing out programmes, now unburdened by their load, huddled by the hoardings at half-time, recreating Büchel's moment of magic. Sending air kicks toward the goal, showing a feint of the shoulders as he had done to create enough space to get the shot away, that one goal had done enough to inspire at least one small gaggle of Liechtenstein's footballing future. They could always say that they were there the night Büchel scored his first ever international goal, potentially the nation's best goal ever.

Things got better early in the second half when Varazdat Haroyan's limp back-pass was intercepted by Chicago Fire's Nicolas Hasler, who coolly curled it round the Armenian keeper to make it 2-1. Sinking to his knees, the defender from FC Ural in the mountains of western Russia no doubt feared being sent east to Siberia by his teammates for such a soft goal. Instead, his defensive colleagues patted him on the back of the head before they began an onslaught on the Liechtenstein goal. Mkhitaryan, instead of easing off in preparation for Arsenal's weekend Premier League fixture, drove forward, spraying passes left and right in search of that killer ball.

No matter that the game had no intrinsic value – Macedonia were comfortably beating Gibraltar in the other Group Four match – national pride was at stake. Having the honour of pulling on that national team shirt had been hard-won. It would not be dishonoured by giving anything less than their very all.

Liechtenstein held out until the 85th minute, when yet another wave of attacks afforded substitute Aleksandr Karapetyan a sight of goal that he didn't pass up. Scoring his first international goal in only his third appearance, Karapetyan, who played for Progrès Niederkorn in Luxembourg, was swamped by his teammates, the entire Armenian bench and an over-excited kit-man. The supporters behind the goal lost their minds and didn't stop singing until long after the final whistle. Heading out of the ground once they had received the applause from the appreciative playing squad on the pitch, not even the sight of that dilapidated old bus tempered their mood; their songs smoking and trailing up into the frigid night, echoing across the valley.

Driving a few hundred metres away from the stadium followed by a sharp right turn would see that ramshackle old bus bridge the River Rhine, crossing the border back into Switzerland before the heaters had even had time to warm up. From the motorway, the Armenian supporters could catch one last look at the floodlights shining above the berm, marking the spot of that glorious late equaliser, before the road wound north and away toward Austria, and a potentially brutal journey back home. No matter their route home, such dedication and passion proved that for many nations, there is no such thing as a meaningless match. Just another opportunity to celebrate an identity, to come together as a people, no matter how far from home.

As 4 per cent of Liechtenstein drifted away, wandering home in small groups while others began to scrape the frozen windscreens of their cars in the car park, it had been another momentous day in the life of the national team. Two goals – one world class – a draw and a battling performance had roused even the most reserved supporter as the team had held on to the death. Now that Rheinpark Stadion had fallen silent, save for some warm-down routines out on the pitch, Liechtenstein seemed to shrink away back into the dark, into the shadow of the mountains. Only the Princely home – glowing, hovering above the capital – remained. A quiet, understated existence returned. At least until next time.

The following morning in the restaurant of Hotel Kulm, those same few guests from the night before congregated for breakfast. This time lost in wonder at the view, the cloud having dissolved at some point during the early hours, there was no hint of even registering their fellow lone travellers, let alone noticing or fuelling an awkward silence like the one that had plagued dinner the night before. Beneath a crystal blue alpine sky, the mountains of the Rhine Valley rose up. Snow-capped peaks, sheer faces dotted with pockets of fir trees, glowed in the sun and loomed over the valley floor and Liechtenstein. Traffic on the motorway glinted as it snaked along silently, following the contours of the mountains on into Switzerland, eventually growing faint in a freezing haze.

A few switchbacks below, the home of FC Triesenberg stretched on its concrete stilts out into this view like some grassy infinity pool. As spectacular a setting for a football ground as there ever could be, you would have expected it to be an insurmountable weapon in distracting and defeating visiting teams. Sadly, for Triesenberg, these views

Claggan Park, Fort William. The Highland League's
very own Narnia.

Fort William fans supporting their team through thin and thin.

The fogbound Tórsvøllur Stadium, the Faroe Islands.

The Faroe Islands versus Azerbaijan.

Football in the Faroe Islands finds a way in Eidi.

F.B/Streymur once faced Manchester City in European competition!

Kosovo sing their hard-fought national anthem in Torshavn.

Odmar and his Faroe team before taking on Kosovo.

Harlaw Park, Inverurie.
Home of the Locos.

The Chuff Chuffs in
full song.

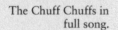

Infiltrating the Chuff Chuffs!
(photo: The Chuff Chuffs).

The colourful welcome at
Christie Park, home
of Huntly FC.

Kynoch Park, Keith.
Home of Keith FC and the
legendary Cammy Keith.

Steps leading up to Mosset
Park and the Can Cans of
Forres Mechanics.

Chaos in the goal mouth
at Forres.

Liechtenstein line up
against Armenia in Vaduz.

Attack versus defence.
Armenia versus Liechtenstein
at the Rheinpark Stadion.

The spectacular home of Triesenberg FC, Liechtenstein.

Washing day in Brora.

Twins at their regular spot in Harmsworth Park, Wick.

Wick Academy defend a Keith corner in galeforce winds.

The small but spectacular Estadi Nacional, Andorra La Vella, Andorra.

The Andorran Primera Divisió in full swing. UE Engordany versus Lusitanos.

Match of the day Andorran style. Saint Julià versus Inter Club d'Escaldes.

Young Cove fans at Berwick Rangers.

A heatwave stifling San Marino Stadium, Serravalle.

The heart of the community, floodlights lead the way. Serravalle, San Marino.

Volunteers tend the Mackessack Park pitch, home of Rothes FC.

Sunshine on Lossiemouth and Grant Park.

God is in their corner at Bellslea Park, home of Fraserburgh FC.

Finally, from Barcelona to Buckie Thistle
and Victoria Park.

Buckie supporters enjoying some early season sun.

were no doubt everyday for the local Swiss sides that made up their league in the seventh tier. But for the slack-jawed first-time visitor, it was hard to turn away from such an unbelievable snapshot of stunning natural beauty.

Competing with cooling toast and the breathtaking vista lay the final tables and results of this debut Nations League campaign. Spread out among cups of tea and glasses of orange juice, the campaigns of all 55 UEFA members revealed themselves. Back in England, supporters and journalists who had been critical of this new format softened after a successful campaign for the Three Lions. A first win in Spain since 1987, inflicting a first competitive defeat on their hosts on home soil for 15 years (England's 3-2 win also being the first time Spain had ever conceded three goals in a competitive match at home), was followed up by a cathartic last-minute victory over Croatia, the team that had knocked them out of the World Cup semi-finals that summer. Topping their League-A group meant qualification for the semi-finals and a shot at Nations League silverware.

North of the border and three wins out of four against Israel and Albania in League C saw Scotland reach the play-offs and a chance at qualifying for the next European Championships. For both it had been a gratifying experience, and far more valuable than a series of friendlies that would have taken their place in the international calendar.

Lower down the rankings, it had been a Nations League to remember for most. Of the five smallest UEFA nations, Gibraltar would make history with their first ever competitive international win. A Joseph Chipolina penalty was enough to secure three points away to Henrikh Mkhitaryan's Armenia in Yerevan. A first ever win would be turned into a first ever set of back-to-back internationals successes four days later, when they beat Liechtenstein on home soil. For Liechtenstein, a win over Gibraltar, their draw with Armenia and four close-fought defeats gave the team something to build on for the future.

The same could be said for Odmar Færø's the Faroe Islands who finished their campaign on five points – a home win over Malta and their draw with Kosovo was complimented with a draw away in Valletta in their final Nations League fixture. While Andorra didn't win any of their six games, four draws against Latvia (twice), Kazakhstan and Georgia provided this tiny principality in the Pyrenees with their most positive string of results in their history.

On the face of it, only San Marino had a Nations League campaign to forget. However, for the smallest country in Europe, everything is relative. In a strong group with Belarus, a quickly improving Luxembourg and Moldova, six defeats out of six wasn't altogether unexpected. Aside from a 5-0 defeat during the opening round of fixtures in Minsk, defeats by one, two or three goals suggested that they were, at least, competitive. Drawing a blank in front of goal throughout the competition suggested that finding a goalscorer among their 33,000-population remained high on the agenda.

No matter the scores, six games in three months afforded all five minnow nations a unique experience. With international friendlies hard to come by between qualifying campaigns, six matches against teams of relatively similar ability in a short space of time could only ever be a fantastic opportunity. Time to build team tactics, time to train and bond a squad that can sometimes have eight games a year to look forward to. Opportunities to play with more attacking intent on a consistent basis. To win, draw, or even lose in a close-fought battle can do wonders for morale and inner belief, of both individuals and an entire nation – steeling themselves and better preparing them for harder fixtures in future qualifying campaigns.

Six games in three months also enabled something far more basic: a true celebration of identity, of community, through sport. From the restrained Liechtensteiners to the raucous Skansin Ultras, via the embattled recent histories of Kosovo, Azerbaijan and Armenia – all displayed a passion for their past, present and future. No matter the numbers in the stands, this simple opportunity to celebrate a national identity, to sing a national anthem, is priceless. And for that reason alone, the debut Nations League can only be viewed as an unreserved success. While some will no doubt moan about meaningless, lopsided fixtures during World Cup and European qualifying, who can, in truth, deny those from Europe's minnow nations the right to celebrate their footballing and national identity among the top guns? That is something that can never be rated or quantified.

Leaving Triesenberg for the last time, navigating switchbacks with the extra distraction of an alpine view, it is hard not to want to turn off for one last look at Sportanlage Leitwies, the home of mountain football in Liechtenstein. The need for reassurance, that its awe-inspiring position hadn't been some trick of the mind, to savour it one last time tugged hard on the heartstrings. But there was a plane to catch. Down into the valley and a left turn led to a bridge and the motorway. And with that, Liechtenstein was gone – the trip from Narnia back into the real world a dispiriting one as the mountains began to recede.

Like its football minnow cousins at the foot of the rankings, Liechtenstein – a nation without a national league – offers so much more than a lowly position in a list of football's greats. You can't dismiss identity, history and community. They are, after all, elements that knit our very being together, our sense of place and purpose. We would not want to be excluded from sporting endeavour, to showcase the pride we have for our country, simply because of ability. Because international sport is rooted in so much more than ability alone. It is a celebration of nationhood, of community, of life. To exclude Liechtenstein and their fellow basement dwellers from competing against the best European football has to offer would be a crying shame for them, but also for those visiting to support their team.

Because sometimes it can be that they that have far more to offer you than you have to offer them, such as a different take on how passion and national pride can manifest. In the case of this unique Alpine principality, that is most definitely true.

CHAPTER FIVE

It's Grim Up North? – Wick Academy

A TRIP TO the football can sometimes come with a sense of trepidation. If your team are on a terrible run, the sheer inevitability that all your efforts in getting to the game, no matter how near or far, will result in deflation and a forlorn trudge home can sometimes – only briefly – make you question why you are putting yourself through it all.

Early morning starts for an exhausting round-trip across a choked motorway system. Bleary eyed stops at services, watching similarly fatigued supporters criss-crossing the country, shuffling from the toilets to a queue for coffee. Those same faces either animated on the return journey through victory or sitting, shoulders hunched; the disappointment of the day weighing heavily, aching limbs from too long spent hunched up in coach or car.

Along with distance needed to travel, time spent or wasted and the form of your team, trepidation can sometimes manifest as fear, either perceived or real. The reputation of opposing fans makes you wonder just how clever an idea it is to visit their patch. But rarely has a trip been prefaced with warnings of just how grim the place you are intending to visit is than the one I took to Wick.

Five and a half hours distant from Glasgow by car, significantly more by coach and numerous changes and connections by train making it an equally daunting prospect, the town of Wick looks out at the North Sea from the ragged coastline of eastern Caithness. Just a short distance from John o' Groats and the very tip of mainland Britain, a trip to Wick comes with all the standard foreboding for those hardy supporters making their way to Wick Academy – the most northerly senior football club in the most northerly senior football league in Britain. But with warnings about hours of long twisting roads that dwindle in size, wicked winds and a bitter cold that accompany the isolation in this part of the world also came a potential knock-out blow: that Wick is just bleak.

Forgotten, left behind by the rest of the country, run-down, boarded up, in terminal decay ever since the fishing industry the town relied on began its sharp contraction during the 20th century. It was a far cry from the picturesque market towns that populate a fair portion of the Highland League; towns that look out upon Scotland's astonishing country parks and towering Munros. Wick, it was said, was a place you simply passed by to visit the tourist spots about John o' Groats.

At a match earlier in the season, as one Highland League supporter chatted with a visiting fan who had mentioned Wick as being their next away trip, he exclaimed, 'It's a long, long way to go, only to find yourself in Wick.' Another, on hearing my intent to travel north just shook his head – 'Good luck with that. Enjoy.'

It would seem that Wick has been singled out as a forsaken place for the best part of two centuries, even during the economic boom of the 19th century, where fishing for herring had more than 1,000 boats in the harbour and 800 gallons of whisky sold every week in the town's 47 pubs. Robert Louis Stevenson, author of *Treasure Island* and *The Strange Case of Dr Jekyll and Mr Hyde* stayed in Wick in 1868 with his Uncle, Alan, who was a lighthouse engineer and was working on the building of the Noss Head Lighthouse. In a letter home to his mother he said that:

> Certainly Wick in itself possesses no beauty: bare, grey shores, grim grey houses, grim grey sea; not even the gleam of red tiles; not even the greenness of a tree. The southerly heights, when I came here, were black with people, fishers waiting on wind and night. Now all the SYS (Stornoway boats) have beaten out of the bay, and the Wick men stay indoors or wrangle on the quays with dissatisfied fish-curers, knee-high in brine, mud, and herring refuse. The day when the boats put out to go home to the Hebrides, the girl here told me there was 'a black wind'; and on going out, I found the epithet as justifiable as it was picturesque. A cold, BLACK southerly wind, with occasional rising showers of rain; it was a fine sight to see the boats beat out a-teeth of it.

In Wick I have never heard anyone greet his neighbour with the usual 'Fine day' or 'Good morning'. Both come shaking their heads, and both say, 'Breezy, breezy!' And such is the atrocious quality of the climate, that the remark is almost invariably justified by the fact. The streets are full of the Highland fishers, lubberly, stupid, inconceivably lazy and heavy to move. You bruise against them, tumble over them, elbow them against the wall – all to no purpose: they will not budge; and you are forced to leave the pavement every step.[2]

As the car came to a standstill, overlooking the same harbour as Robert Louis Stevenson described 151 years earlier, the wind buffeting the door with such a force that it was hard to open, there came the dread of his letter, his words an 'I told you so' through time as the bitter easterly gale cut through me with an icy blast.

The harbour was all but deserted. There were no 'lubberly, stupid, and inconceivably lazy fishers' to bruise against and elbow, or share a muttered 'Breezy, breezy' with. It did not bode well. But first looks can be deceiving and, no matter how respected a writer Stevenson is, you can't just give up on a place so easily.

It is true that the long journey from Glasgow sets a pretty high standard when it comes to beautiful scenery. And a five-and-a-half-hour drive isn't the best precursor to a positive outlook on anything. But Wick, despite it all, is anything other than the forsaken place that had been advertised. The only stereotype that remains true to its word is that this small fishing town is so, so far away from anywhere else.

Beyond Stirling and Perth, as Scotland's central belt recedes in the rear-view mirror, the Cairngorm mountain range and national park rises up. Steep mountainsides of browned heather, not dead but dormant in readiness for spring, skirt large patches of scree that rubble and skitter toward the roadside. Distant peaks, shorn of any vegetation, loom among the cloud. A shadowy world pocked with snowdrifts that tower over the winding road and the vast lochs that assemble at their feet. Fathomless black waters, eerily still, reflections of the great mountains above captured within, they appear mystical enough to home the odd sea-beast purported to linger about these parts.

---

2 From *The Letters of Robert Louis Stevenson*, University of Adelaide, 2014

Past Inverness, the Highland capital, and the mountains recede. A bridge spanning the Moray Firth leaves the last major town in Scotland behind. Ahead and roads that get narrower and narrower now skirt between windswept farmland, small villages and a coastline of ragged slate cliffs. Blackened by the sea spray, gulls nest among more sheltered alcoves where tufts of grass have found purchase. They twirl and sweep on the roaring easterlies above a churning North Sea. Whitecaps rise and fall, swamp one another among the chaotic swells that finally explode against the coastline with an ominous boom.

Beyond the picturesque towns of Tain and Golspie and life becomes more workmanlike, functional. Farming villages hunker on clifftops surrounded by vast swathes of fields, while fishing communities cower behind harbour walls, boats bobbing and rocking in the wind. Among these scattered villages, the odd farmhouse facing down the crosswinds, and a cemetery to those who fell during World War 1; their headstones neatly hemmed in by a dry-stone wall made up of reclaimed rocks from the foot of the cliffs it overlooked.

Somewhere between the small town of Brora, Wick Academy's nearest Highland League rivals, and Helmsdale, the radio signal began to falter. Voices and conversations that had been a faithful companion since Glasgow began to distort and echo, before failing altogether, small bursts of reception intercutting the silence. And there was still a good hour or so driving still to go, to reach Wick.

There can be no denying that Wick is a forgotten town, at least to those who don't call it home. Deriving from the Norse word *Vik*, meaning bay, the town still revolves around the harbour and river mouth first used by Vikings to shelter their longships. Despite the collapse in fishing for herring, when standing dockside meant you wouldn't be able to see the far side for the throng of boats and sails, the harbour still gives Wick its identity. A reduced herring fleet turned to white fish, and when that stopped being as profitable as it had, many of the small cluster of boats that survived turned to lobster fishing. Stacks of lobster pots litter the dockside, seemingly far too many for the handful of commercial boats moored alongside. Today it is all too easy to see the far side of the harbour, and Pulteneytown beyond.

The John o' Groats ferry idled close to the harbour wall; a good few months away from its relatively short summer season transporting tourists along to Land's End's northerly counterpoint. Complimenting the ferry and the fishing community were a cluster of support vessels for the oil rigs and wind farms just visible on the horizon. Taking up more room now than the lobster fleet, it is a case of adapt or die for the harbour and the town. And this relatively new offshore industry is most welcome indeed.

As the day began to grind into life, the odd fisherman decked out in thick jumpers and woollen hats made their way down to the harbour. One used a hose to wash down the deck of his boat, while another sat down to mend a few lobster pots, using twine to bind any unwanted holes shut. Most of the fleet remained dormant. There was little sign of any being readied to be put out to sea. Possibly a wise move given the squall.

Those souls that did wander down to populate the harbour seemed to do so more out of instinct than any pressing need. An attempt to feel busy, maybe to drown out for a while the fears of a livelihood in decline. Beyond a row of small warehouses, the harbour road forked left and right: up into the town and across a bridge into Pulteneytown. Runs of terraced houses and shops were dotted with sections of boarded up homes and businesses. At first glance an unappealing sight; the staple of a town in a terminal decay.

But Wick does not feel like a community that has lost the battle. Anything but. These boarded up buildings were free from graffiti, vandalism and serious degradation. They may be out of action, but they aren't down and out. Rather than derelict, they look more like homes and shops that are on pause, waiting for someone to take them back on, give them a purpose. The boards are a protection from the elements, to keep their integrity until someone comes along for them. How long that may take, no one can know. And until that time, streets stand unused, in a hushed stasis just beyond the sporadic thrum of buses and cars making for the high street and the unfurling Saturday beyond.

Charity shops, a convenience store, a bank and a bookies dot about the dulled windows of unused units along the main strip. A casualty of the newer retail park at the edge of town, the centre still served its purpose, however, as a hub for the community. Morag's Café was doing a roaring business in late morning breakfasts and early lunches. Every new admission takes the time to stop and chat with the tables of familiar faces about them, young and old. Across the way, others head into the Wetherspoons in anticipation of the televised lunch-time match from the Scottish Premier League.

Outside, families defy the vicious gales to make the most of the sunshine. Parents paused in a rare sheltered spot to feel the sun on their face while their children explored the riverbank at low tide, crabbing in tide pools in direct competition with skittering gulls looking for an easy meal. Others paused on the bridge looking out toward the harbour at the river running red beneath them. Stained by the iron-rich peat draining into it from the northern highlands inland, it finally diluted away to an icy blue as the river mouth met the deep waters and currents of the harbour and beyond. Those braver still faced down the winds to take the coastal path out to Old Wick Castle, along slate cliffs taking a pounding from the storm surge. Man-made sea-baths forged among the rocks are lost from time to time in the angry swell. That it ever became warm enough for them to be used will remain a mystery for those hardier than I to discover.

The ruins of Old Wick Castle, perched on top a treacherous sliver of rock high above the churning sea, stood as a metaphor for the town around it. For more than 800 years, it had put up a stoic resistance against the elements and the changing world around it, facing both down to preserve the history and identity of this isolated community. It may not be the most impressive historical ruin in Britain but to those about it, it is *their* ruin. And they are as proud of it as they are the town they come from.

Two identical twins in their late 70s, with collars pulled up about their faces, nodded in unison as they passed. The lasts wisps of hair on their identical balding heads whip violently in the wind like inflatable tube men writhing about on car showroom forecourts. Clearly a part of their daily or weekly routine, they took in the scene along the coast in quiet contemplation, looking out at oilrigs and windfarms that to most were some abstract concept way out to sea. But when you are from Wick, away out in the back of beyond, they are just over there. They, like the others braving the weather, showed that Wick was anything but finished. Down, maybe a little, the town teemed with life nonetheless, both young and old, utilising play parks, cafés, and coastal paths. Most would be present, the twins included, a few hours later when another old community institution ground into action: Wick Academy FC.

Nicknamed the Scorries, which is derived from old Norse, and is local dialect for the herring gulls that swirl and coast on the currents above Harmsworth Park, where the club has played out its entire history, Wick Academy were formed in 1893. Three seasons of friendly matches were followed by entry to the newly formed Wick League, where they gained full membership of the Scottish Football Association, enabling them to play in the Qualifying Cup. Then in 1926, they moved into the Caithness County League, where they would remain until 1960. When the Caithness League decided to switch to summer football, Wick withdrew so they could remain full members of the SFA, playing only cup-ties and friendlies for the next 12 years, until joining what is now known as the North Caledonian League in 1972. After numerous applications, they were finally received into the Highland League ranks in 1994, when Caledonian and Inverness Thistle amalgamated and left to join the Scottish Football League.

The Scorries' time in the Wick, Caithness and North Caledonian leagues were populated with titles and cup wins but, since stepping up into the Highland League, Wick have managed just the one success, winning the North of Scotland Cup in 2016. But impressive top four finishes in the league, and the odd near miss in the Highland League Cup appear progress enough for the Harmsworth Park faithful, who began to file in, bent double against the wind funnelling through the entry gate. Some paused to pick up a team sheet that they struggled to contain with both hands as the gale threatened to rip it in two before they could get to grips with it, battling the elements while they folded it up and pocketed it for safety. Team sheet under control, some congregated around the tea-bar, while others made for their usual place in the shelter of the small main stand, or the covered terracing opposite.

The twins preferred a spot in the sun. Their backs to the wind, they leant against the perimeter barrier and watched the players of Wick and Keith completed their warm-ups. Identical shadows stretched across the touchline before them, as if years of dedication to the same spot had become indelibly scorched into the turf. Away to their left the Academy keeper practised his kicking. He shook his head as he leathered the ball upfield, watched it travel 100 yards before it slowed, then turned back on itself, the wind propelling it the way it came a good 30 of them. He carried the look of a man who knew it was going to be a long day ahead.

He is proved right within ten minutes of kick-off. The visitors, Keith, kicked off with the wind and slope that built from the far corner flag behind their right-back raced into a two-goal lead, the first goal a shot volleyed into the roof of the net from a yard out, as a corner evaded all but Keith winger Michael Selfridge. A minute or so later and a Craig Macaskill free kick outside the box slammed into the bottom corner, seemingly picking up speed as it went, so Wick keeper Sean McCarthy could only stand and watch.

Alan Hendry, Wick supporter and local journalist looked on, beanie hat pulled down as far as it would go, coat buttoned up as high as it could nods at the pitch.

'Even for here this is pretty extreme wind. Though we have had the odd game called off before, just because it was too windy,' he said. 'It's a pity, as Academy like to play good, passing football, along the ground. They are not a physical team. It's going to be tough for them in these conditions. You don't usually even notice the slope, because of how they play. You can notice it today. The ball is flying!'

Like most of Wick, Harmsworth Park is exposed. Sitting on a large tract of open land, not even the housing estate between it and the cliffs provides any shelter. Rather, it seemed to channel the winds over it, sending bitter easterlies cascading down across the pitch.

A few years ago, at a Berwick Rangers match in the professional leagues, I overheard one friend scold another after complaining about how cold it was.

'Ah, you don't even know what cold is, not until you've stood on the terraces at Arbroath in the middle of winter. Their ground is no more than 30 feet from the sea. And when those winds come in, they damn near cut you clean in two.'

Having only ever visited Gayfield, home of the Red Lichties, on a benign September afternoon, I felt a sense that I had not passed the Scottish football initiation test: of facing down scything cold at a suitably windswept field of dreams somewhere far from home. Until now.

As the second Keith goal flew in, Alan sighed, shrugging his shoulders in a typically philosophical way that can be found around so many grounds starved of trophies and titles.

'Well, at least maybe that presenter of *Sky Sports Soccer Saturday* might be having a bit of fun with this. Sometimes, when they include Highland League teams on their vidiprinter – for cup games and the like, he always cracks the same joke about Keith, and how well he is doing up against 11 men. He never tires of it. Especially if they score and it's their number nine. His surname? Keith! Oh, he loves that: "Keith has just scored for Keith!" Little does he know that when Keith score, it is often Cammy Keith who does it. He is a club legend, played for them for years. Hundreds of games under his belt. In many ways, Keith is Keith FC.'

Why Keith, a small town of some 4,000 people on the road between Inverurie and Elgin, is called Keith is not definitively understood. It is thought that it is an amalgamation of the ancient Celtic word for wood, *coed*; the Pictish name for the area, *Ce*; and the Gaelic word *Gaoth*, meaning wind. Whatever the origins, it keeps Jeff Stelling amused.

As Academy struggled to grow into the game, Alan nodded at the bench. 'Wick are a good team, but they are thin on the ground right now. They struggled to get more than the bare 11 for last week's away trip to Huntly. They had a few kids and triallists to make up the numbers. We have a good few suspensions and injuries, I think six, which is a lot for a club our size.

'We are a semi-professional team. The players have a contract. It might not be a vast amount of money. But it is a contract, nonetheless. Even so, the manager has to deal with players being unavailable, for work, or personal reasons. Our top striker, Marc MacGregor, was missing last week as he was off watching the darts in Belfast! The manager wasn't happy about it, he's put him on the bench this week. But he can't be too angry with them. There are a limited number of players good enough to play in the Highland League up here. So, he needs to be diplomatic.

'After all, they do give up an awful lot to play for Wick. Ten-hour round trips on match days are the norm. They have to get time off work for mid-week matches. They give up a lot of time with their families to do what they do. Even Brora, the big local rivals, are a good hour's drive away. The manager understands that.'

So, too, the supporters, who encouraged rather than chastised the Wick players as they toiled against the gale. They knew that they would give their all. Game after game, it is a given in a community so small, where they all need to stick together. Their beloved football club deserves no less. It is a club so ingrained in the town it inspires a passion and dedication in people, on and off the pitch, that goes about its unsung business and keeps the Wick Academy ship set fair. Alan pointed out examples all around us.

'You see the two photographers, one sat by each goal? They are a husband and wife team. They go to every game, home and away, to take pictures of the team. They sell the odd one to local papers, but it's not even enough to pay for their petrol. It's just what they do. They never miss a game. They have built up this amazing photographic history of the club

'The man stood away by the players changing rooms?' He pointed across the pitch to the outline of an old man in a suit, watching the game from his position as changing room security. 'He is on the committee, and he has been here forever. No one knows how long. Not even him I suspect. I dread to think how many games he has seen. He is a walking encyclopaedia of all things Wick Academy. He gives me cracking statistics for the paper all the time. Including about that man there.' Alan pointed at the Wick number 10 and my wind-battered team sheet, when finally brought under control, revealed him to be Richard MacAdie.

'It's Richard's testimonial dinner tonight. He has pretty much played his entire career here with us. Though he had no idea that today's game would be his 525th appearance. He had our man over there to thank for that information. There is nothing that he doesn't know!

'There are so many characters with the Academy in their blood. And I've not even mentioned Barmy Army yet! Wick's most vocal supporter! He always starts in on his barmy army chant mid-way through the second half. Just him. No one else. No idea why he waits till then. That's just when he starts! His claim to fame came a few years back during the Ashes cricket series out in Australia, when the TV cameras picked him out among the stands, bellowing out his one-man barmy army chant! We couldn't believe it. Barmy Army from Wick all the way out there in Australia, and on TV!'

A man in his late 20s, who was stood a few paces further along the perimeter barrier, couldn't help but turn in when he overheard talk of Barmy Army. 'You want to know why he always starts singing halfway through the second half?' he said. 'You know that bag he always carries around with him? He has two small bottles of wine in there for every match. Once he's drunk both he's got the courage to sing. It always takes him till mid-way through the second half to down them both!' When I mention that I have already experienced the Chuff Chuffs down in Inverurie, they both smile.

'Aye, they come up here with all their drums to support the Locos,' Alan said. 'It can be quite the din when Barmy Army starts up as well!'

Despite its size and isolated location, Wick's passion for football, stretching back to the 19th century, helps to bolster squads far and wide across the northern Highlands. Unlike their brothers in isolation, Fort William, who come in a distant second to shinty in their community's sporting affections, football is ingrained in Wick life. It has been as far back as when the harbour was black with people, and a vast herring fleet obscured Pulteneytown on the far riverbank with a throng of masts and sails.

'There are a good number of lads from the town who have headed down to the academies of Inverness Caledonian Thistle and Ross County,' Alan said. 'But as they have risen up into the Premier League, they have started looking further afield, and lots of these youth players are released. I think about nine of the Wick squad came back from Ross County's youth team.'

Blair Duncan, the young man with the inside track on Barmy Army is a footballer himself, having just won the North Caledonian League with Golspie Sutherland – a club a good hour and a half south of Wick.

'It is a cracking standard of football, the Highland League,' he added. 'Every season, a good few teams cause upsets in the Scottish Cup. And a number of them could hold their own in the professional leagues.'

The North Caledonian League is a step below the Highland League. With teams stretching from around Inverness up to a representative side from Orkney, there is no less need for dedication among the players. However, there is no promotion or relegation between the two. When asked why, Blair shakes his head.

'The set-up at Highland League level is much better. Only my team Golspie really compare. We are the only side affiliated to the Scottish Football Association in the North Caley, so we get to play in the qualifying rounds of the Scottish Cup. Though we usually draw one of the bigger teams like Cove and get battered! Most of the North Caley don't have stands, floodlights, all the stuff you'd need for the Highland League. And the standard of football is that bit better too.

'I am lucky at Golspie. It is a decent set-up. They look after us. There are about seven or eight players from Wick who play down there, and the club have a minibus that they use to bring us down for games.'

When asked if he had ever thought about trying his luck in the Highland League, he nodded.

'Aye, I started out here at Wick for a few seasons, and have played off and on in the Highland League since.' He smiled. 'I remember once turning out for Brora Rangers against Wick here at Harmsworth Park on a Wednesday night, then ended up playing for Wick here on the Saturday!'

When asked if he fancied it today, in this gale, he shook his head and shrunk a little into the collars of his coat. 'No, you're alright! Plus, I'm injured. I tweaked a ligament in the last game of the season up in Orkney. We won the league that day, so I didn't care. Nor the ferry trip home!' His smile dimmed a little at the thought of how long it might take to heal as, even though the North Caley season had come to an end, there was plenty more football to be played.

It was something that Alan had mentioned earlier, the summer leagues of the Highlands, and a competition called the Highland Amateur Cup. And as the half-time whistle blew to end a deflating 45 minutes for the Scorries, a whole new football world was mapped out for me by Alan and Blair. As it turns out, the Highland League may be the most northerly senior league in Britain, but the most northerly league of all? It wouldn't even make the top five! Spanning from April to August, most Highland counties and islands host a summer football league. From Aberdeenshire to the Outer Hebrides, Skye to the Shetlands, teams from tiny hamlets, villages and towns play out leagues sometimes only populated by four sides. Home and away fixtures that are reached by trawler in some of the more remote areas are supplemented by county cup competitions and friendlies. An undertaking that simply couldn't be contemplated during winter, every corner of the Highlands breaks out in football fever during the summer months. This passion to the beautiful game culminates in the Highland Amateur Cup, which, Alan describes, takes amateur sporting dedication to new heights.

'Eighty-four teams take part, from all over the islands and mainland. It is a straight draw out of a hat, so a team from Aberdeenshire could be drawn away to a side from the Outer Hebrides. Any team that progresses to the semi-finals or beyond has usually racked up some serious miles by that point, via bus, boat and plane,' he said, shaking his head in admiration. 'Lerwick Spurs from the Shetlands reached the final last year. I remember they posted online just how many ferry journeys they had taken, and how many hours of travel they had undertaken to get to the final. It was the equivalent of a professional team playing in European competition, the time and distance travelled. And every single player is amateur! They do it for the prestige of the event, and the pride of their community. For their little club to be Highland champions, it is a big deal up here. It is a hidden football gem.'

Blair nodded in agreement with Alan. 'They lost the final by the way. Lerwick. After all that, they got beat by a late goal in extra time,' he shrugged his shoulders in the way footballers do when confronted with extreme sporting cruelty, it being the bedfellow of anyone who had tied their boot laces in anger and crossed that white line.

'I've played summer league all my life. It's all about playing with your mates, those you grew up with. And the games are usually played mid-week, so you get the weekends to yourself. That is nice.' A real treat to someone like Blair, whose North Caley exploits will often result in an entire Saturday given up to travelling to and coming back from the game.

'When I was younger, I would play wherever and whenever I could,' he went on. 'You could sign for up to three different summer teams at a time, as long as they were in different county leagues. At one point, I was playing for Wick Groats in the Caithness League, Golspie Stafford in the Sutherland and Eastern Rose in the Ross-shire League! I couldn't do that now,' he said, instinctively touching his injured leg. 'It would probably kill me! That kind of behaviour is a young man's game.'

As we spoke, the kind of fathomless youthful energy he had once relied upon to turn out for so many teams manifested itself in the guise of a young girl, no more than seven or eight, Wick Academy beanie hat pulled down over her ears, coat zipped up tightly as she ran and weaved between us. As she dodged about us, she would bellow 'HELLO!' to all and no one at the same time, before running to the foot of the floodlight a few yards away, then on to a small wall by the path to the covered terrace, tagging it and retracing her frantic steps to swerve between us again.

'Hello,' Blair responded every time, smiling and looking at Alan and me. 'Is she yours?' he asked. We shook our heads.

'I thought she was yours!' Alan said, and we watched as a microcosm of lower league life spent its energy about us. Clubs like these, ingrained in their communities, are a safe space where identity, friendship and play are free to manifest as they see fit. There are no airs and graces. If you'd rather run about like a loon, then do it. If you want to play in the goals at half-time, no one is going to stop you. It is an institution for all. And how you choose to utilise it is up to you.

Excitable children; parents looking on and chatting with friends; old-timers craning to see the pitch from their benches at the back of the terrace; more anguished, hand-wringing supporters putting the footballing world to rights at the perimeter barrier below after a dismal first 45 – it is all a part of the fibre that makes game-day, no matter where, such a vital experience. It is an intricate weave of meaning and belonging, companionship and identity among the 300 or so present. You take as much or as little as you need. From Barmy Army to the elderly twins, the pals roaring with laughter behind the goal to the old man quietly studying his team sheet, and ll the eccentricities and the familiarities in between, you need it all. And as the players ran out for the second half, focus began to turn back pitch-side, to a Wick team trying to make amends. But it just wasn't happening.

Kicking down the slope with the wind at their backs, these supposed advantages seemed to be only making matters worse. In trying too hard, passes kept going astray or running away from their intended recipient, the wind pushing them on and out of reach. A desperation to put things right soon turned into frustration and a wild tackle brought about a 20-man melee. As arms flailed and the referee's whistle sounded a shrill and wholly ineffective deterrent, things finally calmed down enough for the meting out of punishment. A conversation with one linesman, followed by a second with the lineswoman on the far side suggested that the referee had no clue as to who should be brought to task.

A woman behind the goal seemed to have a clear idea of what should be done and let the referee know. 'They didn't see what happened, but I did, ref. Come speak to me. It was that dirty bastard, the Keith number two. NUMBER TWO! NUMBER TWO!' she kept on, the referee stopping himself from looking over at her.

But knowing that someone needed to be disciplined, and he was running out of opinions to help him, he showed a red card to a player from either side. The Keith number five put his head in his hands when the card came his way. His protestations were bolstered by the gesticulating woman behind the goal.

'No, you idiot. NUMBER TWO. That dirty bastard over there.' Keith's right-back flashed a cheeky grin at the woman, which only served to make her more-irate, pointing wildly here, there and everywhere. 'Dirty bastard,' she shouted.

Meanwhile, Wick number 11 David Allen trudged off the pitch after the Keith player and disappeared past the walking encyclopaedia of a committee man holding the door to the changing rooms open for him.

'Ah Jesus, not David again,' Alan said. 'He's only just come back from a suspension!'

Blair shook his head. 'The funny thing is, he is such a lovely bloke off the pitch. Quiet as a mouse. But on the pitch, he always seems to find himself in the middle of all the trouble. You see it so many times with players. Shy, polite off the pitch, but as soon as they cross that white line, they turn crazy! Now I am a bit older I try and talk to players like that, but they are going to do what they do, no matter what you say.'

'How is your disciplinary record, Blair?' Alan asked.

'Well, it's pretty good really. I'm not one for dissent or anything like that. But when I tackle, I like the player to stay tackled,' he flashed a wicked grin. 'I can sometimes get in a spot of bother over that.'

With both sides down a player, the game seemed to begin to peter out. And if anyone looked like scoring, it was Keith, who broke with intent. Club legend Cammy Keith unlucky on a few occasions not to kill the game off.

As the second half reached its mid-way point, regular as clock-work, an unassuming man wrapped up in his coat wanders past.

Blair and Alan smile. 'There he goes, Barmy Army.'

On reaching his favoured spot just beyond the covered terracing, the man places his bag, shorn of the two mini wines, at his feet, and begins in on his song.

'Barmy army. Barmy army. Barmy army.'

'I swear to God,' Blair said 'you could set your watch to Barmy Army. No trouble.'

Despite Barmy Army's new support, Wick just couldn't get their passing game together. Always misjudging the weather conditions, passes kept going astray. These weather conditions, to be fair, had everyone on the back foot; with the bitterly cold wind and the clear blue skies above, it was hard to know if you were under greater threat from frostbite or sunburn. Squinting against the sun upfield to keep up with play, both seemed a fair bet.

As the clock began to wind down, the Wick manager made one last throw of the dice. Darts fan Marc MacGregor, having patiently sat out his punishment exiled on the bench, got stripped off in readiness to join the action.

'Let's hope he hits the bullseye,' Alan said and chuckled as MacGregor took up his position in the Wick frontline.

'In reality, I know it doesn't matter if we win or lose. The top six in the league are too far away to catch. But the manager has said that he wants to win the battle to be the best of the rest. There are a few sides with budgets that Academy can't compete with. Brora down the road being one of them. Right now, seventh spot is as good as it can get. So that is what he wants.'

Within minutes, MacGregor sprung the offside trap that had, until that point, had the Keith goal comfortably fortified. Taking a touch, he slid the ball past the Keith keeper and into the net. 2-1. Game-on.

Though it would take until the last minute of time added on for MacGregor to complete his darts-related redemption. Bringing a bouncing ball under control well outside the Keith penalty area, he took a touch, then on the half-volley leathered it into the top corner that sparked pandemonium in the 300 supporters that had followed it on its way. Keith players sank to their knees, while Barmy Army, the twins and everyone else celebrated the last second equaliser in a match that, ultimately, would have no major impact on the league table.

Impact or not, for everyone present, it was the only match that mattered that blustery Saturday. A full-blooded encounter that ended with Wick and Keith players sharing hugs and handshakes, children rushing to emulate MacGregor's heroics in the vacated goals and friends excitedly chattering about what they had seen as they made their way home and into the warmth.

Blair, Golspie's right-back, waved his goodbyes and slipped into the crowd making for the main road and home, while Alan slipped off to take some pictures for the paper before heading down to the site of Richard MacAdie's testimonial dinner. And with that, this remote football institution began to wind down. Terraces falling silent, the ever-present and unsung volunteers shutting up tea-bars, sweeping out changing rooms, before heading for home. Ready to go again next time.

It would take the best part of two and a half hours to drive back down the coast to Inverness, another three through failing light and the stunning, towering Cairngorm mountains to reach Scotland's central belt and Glasgow, Wick returning to a dim and distant point at the furthest extremes of the map.

Distant, yes, but forgotten, most certainly not. Because Wick, this oft-forsaken town, had revealed itself to be so much more than the moth-balled houses and businesses that first greet you. It is a town of great heart and pride, unprepared to slip into the stereotype of a grim and broken community in terminal decay. It may never win any tourism awards or Britain in Bloom, but it is a place that has nurtured a people who can see what Wick is, not what it isn't. The harbour and its industries fight on, adapting to the times as best they can, while places like Morag's Café and the football club provide spaces to meet, to natter with friends and make new ones. It is a town with beautiful coastal paths out to Old Wick Castle, and trails deep into the Highlands' interior. It is a town that, despite a steady decline in population from census to census, is home to a stoic community. And for those who stay on, it is a town worth fighting for, worth persevering with. Look beyond the boarded up streets, and a gem in the Highland League community begins to shine through.

Just don't ask Robert Louis Stevenson!

CHAPTER SIX

The Primera Divisió – Andorra

EXPLORING THE ROADS less travelled near the foot of the UEFA rankings can take you, constitutionally speaking, to the strangest of places. From the more traditional Republics of Moldova and Malta, UEFA's lesser lights can often comprise a more complicated proposition, evolved across centuries of political change. The Faroes are a 'devolved government within a parliamentary constitutional monarchy'. Liechtenstein is a principality ruled by a constitutional monarchy, as is Luxembourg, which remains the last of Europe's grand duchies. San Marino is a unitary parliamentary diarchic directorial Republic – 'diarchy' meaning that two people rule at the same time. The two Captains Regents of San Marino, elected every six months and coming from each of the two political parties of San Marino, rule in unison. But it is one of the most overlooked footballing nations in Europe that arguably has the strangest constitutional make-up.

Andorra, a tiny principality of some 468 square miles hidden among the Pyrenees between France and Spain, is also a diarchy. Ruled for more than 700 years by both the leader of France and the Bishop of Urgell in Northern Spain, they remain in the roles, albeit now in an honorary capacity. Two heads of state, neither of whom come from the country they represent.

Indeed, it wasn't until 1993 that these roles became honorary, when Andorra became a constitutionally independent nation, establishing a parliamentary government and joining the United Nations. Before then, the people of Andorra, living at the foot of a series of steep sun-blanched valleys among seemingly impassable mountain ranges, simply got on with life, unfazed by the dramas of the outside world. Life that dates back more than 12,000 years.

The small town of Sant Julià de Lòria (population: 7,000) is the first significant staging post on the road north from the Spanish border. Like all towns in Andorra, the steep, claustrophobic valley that closes in around it means that Sant Julià stretches up rather than out. A paucity of flat land has necessitated multiple storey buildings to accommodate the population. Buildings, old and new, nestle closely together to create a bustling community weaving among one another along snaking pavements. Sharp mountain air with an edge in the shade, it is a scene that could just as easily be in Nepal or Bhutan as in Europe.

First settled, at least on a seasonal basis, in 9500 BC, Sant Julià was a passing place across the mountains for Mesolithic hunters. The lush forests and rivers that still tumble across the mountain slopes facing away from the worst of the day's sun are a constant source of fish and meat. Permanent settlements began to appear during the Neolithic Age, with Escaldes-Engordany to the north dating back to 6400 BC and Ordino to 4900 BC.

The Roman Empire came and went between the 2nd century BC and the 5th century AD, to be replaced by the Visigoths for 200 years. When they fell to the Muslim Empire sweeping across Iberia, Andorra remained relatively hidden and protected by Emperor Charlemagne of the Franks to the north. And there it stayed. Looked out for by both Spain and France, Andorra lived out a relatively anonymous life save for the odd constitutional crisis such as that of 1933, when a Russian adventurer attempted to crown himself King Boris I of Andorra. The dispatching of a few French Gendarmes to intervene soon sent him off on another adventure.

Andorra also gave sanctuary to Spaniards fleeing the fascist Franco during the Spanish Civil War between 1936 and 1939, many of whom chose to remain. Indeed, of the 77,000 population of modern-day Andorra, less than half are Andorran. The majority hail from France, Spain, and Portugal.

Having, on paper, a population superior to the other UEFA minnow nations of the Faroes, Liechtenstein, San Marino, and Gibraltar, they are, in reality, no better off. And despite bordering both France and Spain, Andorra is also one of the more inaccessible minnow nations. With no airport or rail system servicing these Pyrenean valleys, the only way in and out is via narrow, winding roads from the north and south, all leading to Europe's highest capital city: Andorra la Vella (population: 22,000), 3,356 feet above sea level.

For such geographical and sporting isolation, it is no small irony that a trip to one of Europe's most obscure footballing institutions must start in the shadow of one of the world's greatest. Camp Nou, Barcelona, has the majesty to take your breath away even a few thousand feet above its towering façade. As the plane banks right in its approach to El Prat airport, its occupants stare out at the sprawling city below. Some linger on Gaudi's astonishing and still unfinished cathedral, La Sagrada Familia. Multiple spires cast shadows across matchbox tour buses and sun-drenched residential blocks.

Others search for the equally dominating colosseum across town, home of the world's greatest team, Barcelona. They can spot of green and vast banks of seats rising up around it in a nosebleed inducing sheer slant into the sky. A cathedral to football, seating 100,000 on match days, and attracting as many slack-jawed visitors as its orthodox cousin, even when there is no match to be played, it induces wonder no matter at what altitude.

These sporting tourists to the city rarely stray much further than the vast gift shop, or the long queues for the Camp Nou stadium tour that weaves in the shadow of those towering walls rising up into the sky, housing the greatest show on earth. They almost never bypass it altogether for one of Europe's lowliest footballing sons, Andorra.

As passengers disembark the plane, there is an extra sense of excitement about the city, because today is El Clásico: Real Madrid versus Barcelona. The Spanish capital versus the fiercely independent Catalan region, still smarting from a supressed independence vote, resulting in an exiled leader and Spanish troops on the streets of Las Ramblas. That night would be an opportunity to bloody the nose of the old enemy in Madrid and deal them a catastrophic blow in their forlorn chase after Barcelona at the summit of La Liga.

As the latest wave of arrivals dissolve into the tangle of buses and taxis for the city, some making a beeline to one of the countless bars that would be screening the match, my hire car swims against the tide, heading north and deeper into Catalonia, a picture postcard image of old Spain. Timeless churches adorned with weathered bell-towers look down at small, sun-bleached, dusty communities housing its flock. Villas, remnants of Templar castles among the arid and undulating hillsides, some perched on scrubbed mesas, intermingle with sleepy towns – all of which are forged from the pale limestone that gives the region its wild, distinctive look. So familiar is the join between land and building that it seems as if these towns and villages simply evolved out of the seam of rock beneath them. The skeletal remains of castle ruins return from where they came, it appears a geological and architectural evolution in progress. The only thing missing among this arid, sun-baked vista that prevented one from thinking they had somehow driven on to the set of a 1950s spaghetti western was the absence of large plains of cacti trailing into the sunset or cowboys lazily herding cattle on horseback.

By car, Andorra is a good three-hour drive from Barcelona. For visiting national teams and their supporters, taking coaches and buses that would labour and creep up steep, twisting inclines as dusty hills gave way to the towering Pyrenees, it could take much longer. Across mountain roads traversing spindly viaducts that straddle stomach churning ravines and gorges, the journey could take up to five hours – depending on the state of the transport. An act of bewildering, travel sickness-inducing dedication to the uninitiated or unprepared; twisting and turning beneath breathtaking, sheer slopes of fathomless rock and scrub.

Unlike the Alps, whose temperate latitudes create a rich vein of pasture and forest that nestles on and among mountains stretching from France to Slovenia, the Pyrenees are an altogether more alien scene. Like grainy images of Mars or the high peaks of the Himalayas, the Pyrenees appear an inhospitable place. Running east-west along the French-Spanish border, they are an arid, parched environment. Even on the lower slopes, threadbare pockets of shrub, the odd spindly tree cling to desolate walls of rock and scree, sun-baked the year round, life is hard-fought in these conditions. Shallow roots forage for an unlikely source of water.

When the Tour de France ventures up into the Pyrenees' most challenging of climbs, it is as if the cyclists, lungs heaving, have ridden up into some otherworldly state. The summit of the Col du Tourmalet is a barren, lifeless scene 7,000 feet above sea level, seemingly as incompatible to human life as Everest – just a narrow road winding around a rocky, sun-blanched moonscape. It is a relentless world where there is no respite from that dizzying sun during the day or the bitter cold at night, its rarefied air making breathing that bit more taxing.

Like the Faroes before it, Andorra is a place where the journey to it, and the scenery about it, can magically manifest niggling hamstring injuries, a calf strain in those players less prepared to experience footballing life away from the plush big leagues and tournaments. But for the license plates, and the nagging certainty that you haven't travelled *that* far, the scenery could easily convince you that you are in the Hindu-Kush of Pakistan or on the Tibetan Plateau.

Despite that, the Pyrenees have a somewhat schizophrenic appearance. As with Sant Julià and a history dating back 12,000 years, life in the Pyrenees found a way. Crammed into sheltered fissures and mountainsides shaded for part or most of the day, thick forests prosper. Trees cluster together, branches intertwine, tangled as if clawing at their neighbour, attempting to prevent them from spilling out into the withering scrubland beyond. A little respite from sun and anything is possible, as is witnessed when the road occasionally plateaus out into pockets of unlikely, verdant pastures, grazing cattle, water gurgling over shallow, rocky riverbeds.

It is among one of these oases that the town of La Seu d'Urgell, home to one of Andorra's honorary rulers, appears. The last stop before the principality, La Seu d'Urgell, a sleepy town of some 12,000 souls, appears deserted on a late Saturday afternoon. The heat of Barcelona left far behind, the sharp mountain air cuts deep in the shade, while the sun does enough to make sitting in it pleasant, and a few do in the town square lined with spindly plane trees not yet in bloom – branches, like thick, gnarled fingers clawing up toward the sky.

It could be any old picturesque small town anywhere, were it not for the snow-topped peaks shimmering in the far distance reminding all of the precarious winding journey needed to get here. Echoes of dogs barking, the distant honking of a car horn, a bus rumbling in low gear. The streets are deserted, the main drag empty, until firecrackers begin to explode in the road and a wall of sound from a festival procession begins to grow, turning off a side street and bearing down on the sleepy town centre. Floats, dance troupes grooving to ABBA, waving flanks of people dressed as dinosaurs, cartoon characters and pirates roll down the road. Pavements lined with parents and children, also dressed in countless different outfits, follow the display, waving back.

It is an assault on the senses after the quiet of the mountains and the town. Too much for some of d'Urgell's youth, who retreat to the water park that was built for the Barcelona Olympics in 1992. Gates once traversed by canoe and kayak in the pursuit of gold medals still hang suspended above the white water cascading down a twisting course. Benches that were once the best seats in the house are now a refuge to teens too cool for festival.

With the chaos of carnival over, the town slips back into hush, as its population make for home, bars and restaurants in readiness for the big match.

Barcelona represents far more than the city of its origin. It is a symbol, a beacon of Catalan identity across the entire region, a region that displays its flag from every available spot. Everyone supports Barcelona, even if they follow a local team primarily. And when they play Real Madrid, even those with little interest in football become Barca fans for the evening.

The club is a religion to its fans, its players deities. But if these living gods abuse their flock, that adoration can turn to hatred, as witnessed in November 2003. Luís Figo, Portuguese superstar and Barcelona legend, did the unthinkable – moved from Barca to the enemy, Real Madrid. This betrayal led to one of the most infamous moments in any El Clásico. As he went to take a corner for his new team on his return to Camp Nou, a severed pig's head was thrown at him from the crowd, narrowly missing him, gawking up at him from the turf with dead eyes.

Despite this act of vengeance at a perceived betrayal, there doesn't appear to be any real hatred toward the institution of Real Madrid in my hotel bar. The only exception being Real captain Sergio Ramos. They hate Ramos. While other Madrid players can play for free kicks, or commit fouls, remonstrate with the referee without causing ire among the packed bar, as soon as Ramos gets involved, the howls of derision rain down on the large screen above the breakfast buffet table. His antics over the years have afforded him special treatment.

Madrid shots narrowly missing the target draw sharp intakes of breath around the room. Misplaced crosses the same. There is no need for jeers, even though it is Real. In the end, it is a routine away win for the Catalans, taking them ten points ahead of Real at the top of La

Liga. That it was achieved at the Bernabéu in Madrid makes it all the sweeter, one last beer before home tasting that bit better.

From La Seu d'Urgell, the drive to the border with Andorra is a short one, the checkpoint at border control denotes not only the beginnings of a country barely 25 years old, but also a ramping up of the Pyrenees' majesty. Like the trash compactor scene in *Star Wars*, vast mountain walls squash the valley into an ever-narrowing taper. At Sant Julià, the road creeps between a town in shadow beneath the precarious cresting wall-face behind it and a sparkling shallow river that doubles as a guide the deeper you push into the principality. With every twist of the road, it is hard to imagine who would feel the most discomfort – someone that suffered with claustrophobia as the mountains closed in, or an agoraphobic having to deal with the unfathomable blue skies above. Suffering from neither, both situations brought a shiver to the spine and a tightness to the chest, maybe because of the thinner mountain air, more likely that the awesome sight makes you forget to breathe.

The Primera Divisió, or the Lliga Multisegur Assegurances as its sponsors would prefer it to be known, is the top-flight in Andorran football. Eight teams compete to be champions of the principality. Sant Julià are the southernmost team, with Encamp and Ordino representing communities of 13,000 and 3,000 respectively from the north of the country. In between, five teams play from the three towns that merge together around the capital, Andorra la Vela – Engordany and Inter Club d'Escaldes at the northern edges of the capital, FC Santa Coloma and UE Santa Coloma a kilometre or so further south. Somewhere in between, representing not an area but the Portuguese community that have made Andorra home, are FC Lusitanos.

Beneath the top-flight, a further ten teams compete for promotion from the Segona Divisió. La Massana and UE Extremenya come from the north-west, while Penya Encarnada, Carroi and Rangers are based in the capital. Atlètic Club d'Escaldes and Sporting Club d'Escaldes bring the senior sides in their small town to four, rubbing shoulders with Inter Club d'Escaldes' B team in the second tier. With the B teams from d'Escaldes, Encamp and UE Santa Coloma (who complete the division) ineligible for promotion, seven sides battle for a spot at the top table – a typical endeavour the football world over. Promotion and relegation aside, however, football in Andorra is anything but typical.

The Andorran Premier League wasn't formed until 1995, a year after Andorra became an independent country and joined the United Nations. Though new to the international scene (the fledgling Andorran Football Federation being accepted into UEFA and FIFA in 1994 and the new Andorran national team competing in international qualifiers for the first time two years later), football wasn't a new concept within the principality. It had existed in the shape of informal leagues and challenge matches, arranged on an AD hoc basis between local teams ever since the game had been introduced into the mountains in the early decades of the 20th century. The only national identity or 'organised' football among the valleys came in the guise of FC Andorra, formed in 1942, who have exclusively competed within the Spanish football leagues, and are now owned by Barcelona defender Gerard Piqué.

With the principality's best players drawn to the only source of 'official' football in the region, FC Andorra, a de-facto national team for more than 50 years reached the Segunda División B (the third tier) in 1981, having moved up through the Catalan regional leagues. Just missing out on promotion to the second division in 1989 and 1990, their greatest achievement came in 1994 when FC Andorra won the Copa Catalunya. Knocking out Barcelona in the semi-finals 2-1 on aggregate before beating Espanyol on penalties in the final, this was no mean feat despite the region's bigger teams fielding a mix of first team, reserves and youth players in the competition. It was the inspiration for taking the leap into international football when independence had been confirmed.

World beaters they may never be, as witnessed by FC Andorra dropping down in recent years into the fifth-tier Primera Catalana. But the love for football among their supporters and players, along with those competing in informal mountain leagues across their little slice of the Pyrenees, was enough to sustain belief that joining the likes of Spain, France and Germany in international qualifying tournaments was the right thing to do.

A new presence on the international scene would be solidified by a national identity through football and a new Andorran football league. Encamp, the oldest football club in the Andorran system, having been formed in 1950, was joined by sides such as FC Santa Coloma, UE Engordany and UE Santa Coloma – all formed in the

1980s to create the very first UEFA-sanctioned and fully ratified Liga Nacional de Fútbol Profesional.

A new league, offering greater opportunity for competition and participation in UEFA qualifiers for the league and cup winners, could only boost the talent pool available to Andorra's first ever national team boss, Isidre Codina. But despite this new league and national team – Codina's first taste of international management ending in a 6-1 defeat at home to Estonia – football has never had its own way in the principality, as witnessed on a seemingly sleepy Sunday morning, basking in a glorious late winter sun.

Despite the snow glinting on the mountain tops beyond and families decked out in winter wear – goggles perched on their heads, loading up skis and snowboards on top of rental cars outside high end hotels – it was t-shirt and sunglasses weather in the valley floor. The sun, having long since crested the mountain tops, beat down on Andorra la Vella with only a hint of a winter chill lingering in the shadows. Straining eyes tried to adapt to the fierce glare of the crystal-clear gurgling river bisecting the capital as they watched cyclists setting off for a day of labouring up mountain switchbacks, which would take them up across slopes more protected from the sun, forests offering respite along the way, ticking off the few small hamlets clinging to the gradient.

Whirring bikes passed joggers following the river's contours further on into the sleepy capital that, like Sant Julià, rose up to compensate for a lack of space on the valley floor. This valley is so narrow that it could surely be cleared by a golfer with a decent driver and downswing. Athletes made use of the track around the Estadi Comunal, a small stadium next to the river that could seat no more than 1,000. More seasoned joggers gave way to athletes pounding down the home straight, others stretching out in preparation for their session, while elderly couples took in the fresh mountain air and the vitamin D-rich sun along a tow path at the river's edge. It comes as no great surprise that Andorra has the highest life expectancy in the world.

For those who preferred to watch rather than take part, the national stadium is abuzz with activity as basketball fans queue, talking excitedly in the mother tongue, Catalan, waiting for the gates to open into the large indoor arena adjacent. Andorra's basketball team are taking on Real Madrid in a league fixture, and hope is building of another Catalan victory to compliment the one from the night before.

TV crews unload ribbons of cabling, feeding it into the arena while security guards man the players' entrance. Beyond, the national stadium sits quietly. Dwarfed by tall apartment blocks that rise up the mountain behind it, overlooking a pristine artificial surface lined by rows of seats no more than six or seven deep, the inhabitants have box seats for when the world's best come to take on the Andorran football team.

Vast alien-looking floodlights tower like martian death-rays from *War of the Worlds* at each corner, casting shadows across rugby posts affixed at either end of the stadium, the national football team sharing the stadium and complex with both Andorra's rugby and basketball teams, teams whose history and popularity can sometimes knock football into third place in Andorra's affections. Beyond the rise of apartments, the arid, scrubbed mountainside suggests that the floodlight death-rays have already scorched the earth at least once in recent times.

Despite its modest size, the national stadium is of a grand scale amid such awe-inspiring Pyrenean landscape and claustrophobic apartment blocks reminiscent of those grand façades that line the Monaco Grand Prix. The whitewashed walls of the stadium pop in the sun, adding to the illusion of that you could just as easily be on the Côte d'Azur as in the high mountains.

From the old town, high above the valley floor, Andorra la Vella and the valley shimmer in a heat haze. The chiming of a bell from the medieval church tower echoes through the nest of narrow streets huddled against the mountainside. Sheltering your eyes from the sparkling river, you can just make out a modest sports complex in the distance. Isolated in a no-mans-land of industrial units and garages that link the capital and nearby Santa Coloma, it is here that around 17 of Andorra's Primera Divisió football fixtures will be held. Not the poor relation – it is a modern, lovingly tended facility – but late to the sporting party, there simply wasn't any room for the Centre d'Entrenament de la Federació Andorrana de Futbol (Centre de la FAF) any closer to the town centre.

A couple of policemen yawn and lean against the wire mesh fencing at its entrance, taking no particular notice of those coming and going. Pacing themselves for an eight-hour, four-game football marathon that will see them act as security, ball-boys, player tunnel erectors and dismantlers and crowd control for crowds that remain largely absent, they simply nod and sip at their Sunday morning coffee as bodies file past them. It is free to watch the Primero Divisió, so unless you are causing a fracas, or messing with the players' tunnel, you are of little significance as you pass in and out.

The Centre de la FAF is a symbol of how unique football is in this tiny principality. With an organised football league being merely 25 years old, its position out of town fits the uphill battle it faces against the better established rugby and basketball fraternity, as well as FC Andorra and its 75-year history in the Spanish football system. Clubs younger than some of the players that play for them have had comparatively little time to bed into the communities they represent. Tradition and history is a work in progress given the century of informal football, AD hoc competitions and transient clubs that went before it. Players' friends and families bolster the small pockets of supporters that follow their team. So limited are space and facilities about the mountains that traditional clubs with their own grounds are an impossibility for all but a couple of teams.

It is the Football Federation who built the Centre in order to home the fledgling clubs of the Primero Divisió, and it is they who allocate venues for league games. On occasion, the municipal stadium is called into use, as well as pitches in Ordino and Encamp. However, the domestic football calendar is mostly played out at the Centre de la FAF, with home and away fixtures only distinguishable by which kit the players wear.

Two pitches stand adjacent, separated and serviced by two small back to back stands of vibrant blue, yellow and red seats – the colours of the Andorran flag. Four sets of changing rooms beyond the retractable players' tunnel enable one match to be played on the main pitch, while the next fixture's players can change and then warm up on the second. The entire Primero Divisió rolls in and out of the centre over an eight-hour period, from midday to 8.00pm.

A lazy Sunday morning. Players decked out in club tracksuits wandered in in dribs and drabs. A quiet, mostly empty municipal pitch. A few children played in a spare goal. Dog walkers and joggers wandered past. It was a scene from Sunday League matches the length and breadth of Britain. However, this is no Sunday League.

Yes, it is played exclusively on a Sunday, and some clubs in the Andorran Primero Divisió are operated on an amateur basis. But that is the only resemblance to the British institution of substitutes running the line balancing a cigarette and a can of lager with the linesman's flag, hungover players from the night before attempting to commit occasional outbreaks of football on mud pitches, those still drunk attempting unlikely skills, often to the derision of their teammates.

The Andorran Primero Divisió, though shorn of many of the institutions that define the football experience the world over, is a thrilling and unique experience because of it. With no entrance fee to watch Primera Divisió fixtures, the eight teams rely heavily on sponsorship for those lucky enough to find it, funding from the Football Federation and prize money earned from competing in Europe in order to survive.

Qualification for the preliminary rounds of the Europa and Champions League can earn €220,000 and €240,000 respectively. Progression to the next round, something the current members of the Lliga Multisegur Assegurances have achieved on four occasions in their short history, can double the prize pot. It is the difference between remaining an amateur outfit and turning professional, something that those without European experience do well to hide against their more successful opponents.

While the basketball stadium in the centre of town fills up for the visit of Real Madrid, a crowd of some 150 assemble to watch the midday football. Most linger by the touchline barriers to enjoy the sun, meet friends or watch their children having a kick about on the spare pitch. Others who have already decamped into the shade of the stands put jumpers and coats back on, the air cold and sharp out of the sun's reach.

UE Engordany and FC Lusitanos walk out from the police-monitored players' tunnel and applaud those assembled, before breaking away for one last warm-up sprint, a round of high fives with teammates and a few leg-stretches until the referee blows his whistle. The referee, his assistants and the fourth official will become familiar faces over the course of the day. As with the paucity of pitches in the principality, there also appears to be a finite number of qualified officials. In fact, there seems to be just the two sets, who each officiate two games, the ref in one becoming a linesman in the second, the lineswoman switching to fourth official, and so on.

UE Engordany, formed in 1980, didn't affiliate with the Andorran Football Federation until 2001, and spent their first decade of senior football in the Segona Divisió. Promotion in 2013 was followed by coming runners up in the Copa Constitució in 2017, and then runners up in the Primera Divisió a year later brought a first ever European campaign for the Guerrers (Warriors).

In their first attempt, they did something so few Andorran club sides have achieved: victory in Europe. A 3-2 Europa League preliminary round victory over Folgore of San Marino saw them face FC Kairat of Kazakhstan in the first qualifying round. A 3-0 home defeat was followed up by a 7-1 loss in Almaty – a city at the furthest reaches of UEFA, some 6,000 miles away from Andorra and further east than Islamabad and Kabul. Though they took one hell of a trek, and a 10-1 aggregate defeat at the end of it, Engordany's first taste of European football gave them the money to seriously compete at the top end of the Andorran league and a desire to repeat the European experience.

Which is why in this match they went at Lusitanos from the very off. With only one substitute available to them on the bench, it is clear Lusitanos were having a tough time. Psychologically they looked beaten from the off, the match an exercise in damage limitation. They remained as compact as they could be, finding an outlet in Mark Withers – an American playing for a Portuguese ex-pat team in Andorra. With the ball at his feet, he attempted attack after attack, hoping desperately that support would come before he was finally closed down, which he inevitably was, the support often failing to materialise. It is sad to see one of Andorra's more successful sides of recent seasons suffer in this way.

Having been formed as recently as 1999, Lusitanos provides a sporting focus for the Portuguese community living in Andorra. They won the league twice, and came runners up twice between 2012 and 2016, and have played in European competition six times, taking on the likes of Valletta from Malta, EB/Streymur from the Faroes, Rabotnički of Macedonia, Domžale from Slovenia and Varaždin of Croatia. But their biggest European night came in 2015 when 35,000 packed into the Boleyn Ground, then home of West Ham United from the English Premier League, to see Lusitanos hold the Hammers to a 3-0 win.

A 1-0 defeat in the home leg, barely three and a half years ago, seems a lifetime away from the Lusitanos now struggling before a huddle of despondent supporters slumped in their seats. Engordany striker Joël Thomas threatened with every possession, his skill and trickery unlocking passes into dangerous positions, wicked shots thrashing balls narrowly wide of the goal. It came as a great surprise that, when the goals start flying in, it wasn't Thomas – a player whose long career has taken in spells at Bordeaux, Kaiserslautern in Germany and Dinamo Bucureşti, along with spells in Britain with Hamilton Academicals, Raith Rovers and Colchester United – ending up on the scoresheet.

As the game wore on, 5-0 seemed like a let off for Lusitanos, who visibly withered in the second half, especially after former Andorra national team player, Victor Moreira, came off the bench and promptly scored twice without seemingly breaking sweat.

It is a fine line in the Andorran Premier League, where those flush with European success can afford better players to hopefully maintain a life at the top, and those without must rely on passion and hard work in order to bridge that gap. Lusitanos, it would seem, have lost their way, only early season form keeping them hovering above the foot of the table.

At the final whistle, the mechanics of an entire league being played out on one pitch ground into life. At half-time of the Engordany-Lusitanos match, most of those sat in the shaded stand had slipped round to its smaller sister behind it. Looking out across the second pitch and on into the staggering valley and mountains beyond, it basked in a warm sunshine that had those wrapped up in coats shedding them for 15 minutes of bliss. As they warmed themselves, the players of FC Santa Coloma and FC Encamp trotted out from the second sets of changing rooms and began their stretches in preparation for the second match of the day.

While the Engordany match played out its inevitable conclusion, the noise of barked instructions, balls being pinged about, whistles denoting new exercises to be undertaken rose from the second pitch with increasing intensity in readiness for kick-off. And no sooner had the Engordany and Lusitanos contingent left the pitch, disappearing down the tunnel only to reappear at its conclusion back out into the sunshine in front of the row of changing rooms, the players from FC

Santa Coloma and FC Encamp were assembled and marched out for the second game.

And so it went on, game after game, from high noon until long after darkness had descended across the valley. FC Santa Coloma versus FC Encamp, top versus bottom, champions versus a team who narrowly avoided relegation last time around line up on the pitch and applaud a virtually empty stand. A cameraman filming events and a couple of children taking a breather from their kickabout on the sister pitch were the only witnesses.

It seems bizarre that Andorra's champions and most decorated team would start a match in front of so few. But the four-game, one-pitch Primera Divisió works to such a tight timescale that supporters don't have time to wander out to the garages on the main road for a coffee and a sandwich in between fixtures. At least not without missing some of the action. And as Engordany and Lusitanos players, friends, family and supporters slip away, freeing up car parking space on the main road, the next wave of Santa Coloma and Encamp support begin to take their place and file in.

FC Santa Coloma are the dominant force in Andorran football. Winners of the title 12 times and the Copa Constitució on ten occasions, El Don (The Lord) have only failed to finish in the top three once in the league's history. They have played in European competition in 15 seasons since 2001, when clubs from the principality first entered the qualifying rounds. That first experience in the UEFA Cup was a true baptism of fire, facing Partizan Belgrade in their intimidating 32,000-seater Partizan Stadium, where they lost 7-1.

They did, however, become the first ever team from Andorra to win a match in Europe, when Juli Fernández wrote himself into the history books by scoring the only goal in a home win over Maccabi Tel Aviv in 2007. Santa Coloma lost the away leg 3-0, but they did become only the second Andorran team to win a European tie seven years later. A 1-0 home victory over Banants of Armenia in 2014 was followed up by a 3-2 defeat away – a remarkable goal in the fourth minute of stoppage time by goalkeeper Eloy Casals earning them a spot in the second qualifying round of the Champions League on the away goals rule. A familiar foe in Maccabi Tel Aviv stopped them progressing any further with a 3-0 aggregate defeat.

Their opening adventure in Europe would be the only time that El Don found themselves losing heavily. Spirited displays against teams from Iceland to Bosnia, via Denmark, Switzerland and Kosovo have seen them become a respected team in the European qualifying rounds, and a feared side in the Primera Divisió. The reasons why were becoming quickly apparent on that glorious Andorran Sunday afternoon.

FC Santa Coloma started the game in complete control, barely needing to break out of third gear. Their goalscoring hero of that 2014 European Campaign, keeper Eloy Casals cut an isolated figure, with enough time to smile and wave back at his little son and wife gesticulating frantically at him from the touchline, having just arrived. Captain and centre back Marc Rebés passed the ball around and set up attacks like the experienced international he was. And like his keeper, he too had been the goalscoring hero before, this time for his country, where his goal against Hungary in a World Cup qualifier in 2017 was enough to secure Andorra a first competitive win since 2004. And against a side far above them in the FIFA world rankings.

Rebés is one of five Santa Coloma players who regularly feature for the national team, linking up with the ten or so who play for FC Andorra in the Spanish leagues. Though not being a part of these two teams doesn't exclude you from the chance of international football. Five other Primera Divisió clubs boast players in around the national team squad on a regular basis. But not FC Encamp, who, despite that, play without fear against El Don – playing fast, passing football, attempting to break down their stubborn and experienced opponents through neat and incisive moves, mostly spearheaded by Tomás Lanzini.

If he was Andorran, there would be no doubt that Lanzini would be an international footballer. However, he, like a significant number of the players playing in Primera Divisió, are not. Whether from a family now settled in Andorra from another country – a community in the principality totalling more than 50 per cent of its population – or on a footballing odyssey in search of that break into Europe's big leagues, players from as far afield as South America and Africa have found themselves in Lliga Multisegur Assegurances.

Lanzini is Argentinian and came up through the River Plate youth system in Buenos Aires before a season in the first team of second tier side Club Atlético Platense. Ninety appearances in the second division in Chile with Union San Felipe and Ñublense followed before he tried his luck in Europe. However, he eventually found his way to FC Encamp, he gives his all for his team, and helps to keep the Santa Coloma defenders honest, though not over-worked.

Since a period of success in the early years of the Primera Divisió, where they won the league in 1996 and 2002, and were runners up a year later, the lot of FC Encamp has been one of survival in the top-flight. When that failed, Segona Divisió titles in 2006, 2009 and 2012 helped the oldest team in the league find their feet again.

It must feel a lifetime ago since Encamp played in Europe, where a 13 0 aggregate defeat to Zenit St Petersburg in 2002 was followed up a year later by an Intertoto Cup loss to Lierse, 7-1 over two legs. But those who made the winding journey through the valleys from the north to follow them seemed happy with what they were seeing, though didn't appear surprised when Santa Coloma scored what would turn out to be the only goal of the game. At the bottom of the league, it would be another battle to remain in the top-flight for one more season. But it was a battle the players were fully committed to, playing their fast, passing game no matter who they were facing.

For Santa Coloma, a professional display by this professional team was the bare minimum of requirements. But even though they were in control against their largely amateur opponents – moments of breath-taking skill such as centre forward Diego Quintero crashing an overhead kick against the bar threatening to add to the score – they still demanded more of themselves, and the referee if they thought he had gotten a decision wrong. Sick of the constant niggling, the referee simply stopped listening to the imploring David Sebastian Cortez as he attempted to argue yet another point in favour of Santa Coloma, a ploy that would lead to comedy gold as the referee booked one of his teammates, took down his name, then inadvertently dropped his pencil onto the pitch. Sebastian Cortez picked it up and shouted to the ref, jogging after him with his pencil. The referee, certain he was about to be nagged at again simply ran off following the play. When Sebastian Cortez caught up with him, the referee turned away once more. Sebastian Cortez held his pencil forlornly, jogging about the pitch after him for a full minute until he finally realised that ref wasn't going to stop blanking him. Unsure what to do, he stopped, looked about him, shrugged, then dropped the pencil back onto the pitch and wandered back into position.

At full-time, as the Primera Divisió machine rolled seamlessly on, FC Santa Coloma headed past their village rivals UE Santa Coloma in the tunnel. Supporters of one vacated their seats in the stand, being replaced by followers of the other. The two policemen stood at the player tunnel unfazed by this sporting migration, knowing full well that any rivalry there may be among these small pockets of supporters was of a benign kind. Men, women and their children swamped in adult-sized shirts of the team they were here to follow mingled together with an assured knowledge that support never spilled over into any-thing more malicious. Maybe a by-product of a fledgling league pop-ulated by fledgling clubs – I am more than ten years older than all but FC Encamp – combined with the fact that the Lliga Multisegur Assegurances can often be fourth choice in Andorra's sporting interests behind basketball, rugby and FC Andorra, has meant the evolution of bitter rivalries between teams seems not even at an embryonic stage.

In such a small community, as with the other mini UEFA nations in this book, the concept of a violent hatred of another, simply because of the football team they support, is a seemingly abstract one. When the Andorran Football Federation and its league come to celebrate its 125th anniversary in a century's time, you can feel confident that not much will have changed among the atmosphere of those populat-ing the Centre d'Entrenament – just as it hasn't in the Faroe Islands, whose league is closing in on its 70th birthday, while its biggest rivalry between HB and B36 is entering its 84th year as peacefully and sport-ingly as the previous 83.

It would be wrong to see a lack of flare wielding, Poznań-bouncing ultras complete with a 90-minute song book of chants in the Andorran league as a negative. The genteel observation among the few hun-dred assembled across an eight-hour marathon is a lack of passion, of legitimacy, of purpose. Football, thankfully, comes in all shapes and sizes and at the remotest edges of the footballing map, among small populations whose very existence is predicated on everyone pulling together to overcome the wild isolation of the Faroes, the mountain-ous extremes of Liechtenstein and Andorra, a hatred built on noth-ing more than sporting preference appears counter-productive at best, dangerous at worst. Pointless, plain and simple. As in Liechtenstein, by not displaying your support through pyrotechnics and song, you are simply weaving a different, more reserved thread into the intricate fabric of the footballing universe.

However, while the rest of the league, its spectators and the country at large exists in this beautiful mountain scape vacuum of sun-drenched calm, there is one exception. Víctor Bernat Cuadros, centre-forward for UE Santa Coloma, is a one-man army for any pent-up rage, frustration and injustice that may exist among the valleys of Andorra. As match three kicked off, surely the angriest man in the principality, Cuadros complained to the referee when he isn't given a free kick, even though the ref allowing play to continue resulted in a UE Santa Coloma goal. When waved back by his manager to form part of a wall to defend a free kick, he did so with gesticulating arms in every direction, muttering loudly enough so no one can be in any doubt as to his objections. When he was booked for a flagrant shirt-tug on an opponent, he laughed with a genuine disbelief at his misfortune. Being flagged, correctly, offside the first time provoked more gesticulation. After the fifth, all correct, his death stares suggested he was doing everything in his power not to stab the linesman to death with a corner flag.

The rest of team just get on with things, clearly used to playing with a Tasmanian Devil every Sunday. He must be a player worth persevering with, though there was little evidence of that against an Ordino side who, like FC Encamp, are fighting for their top-flight lives.

Despite their lowly position, and again like Encamp, they play a technical game, always playing out from the goalkeeper, threading passes about defence and midfield until an attacking opportunity presents itself. Formed as recently as 2010, Ordino (population: 2,700) have had to travel the furthest for today's games, coming from a valley in the north-west of the country. Their nine seasons have either been spent at the top of the Segona Divisió, or near the foot of the top-flight. One of only two Primera Divisió teams never to have represented their country in Europe, their style of play suggests that it won't be too long until they rectify that. It was hard not to root for them, willing them on along with their small cluster of supporters to find an equaliser. If only to see what Bernat might do.

As the shadow of the floodlights swept an excruciatingly slow path across the brilliant sun-soaked pitch, like the slowest set of windscreen wipers or a pair of sporting sundials, UE Santa Coloma saw out the victory. Regulars in Europe over the past ten years courtesy of a couple of runners-up spots in the league and three Copa Constitució victories, it would be the knock-out tournament that would be their best bet in reaching the Europa League once more, cut adrift as they were from the top four – two of which had been warming up on the second pitch while Cuadros stormed around for 90 minutes.

As Cuadros' fury propelled him down the players' tunnel, the match of the day began to come together as third place Inter Club d'Escaldes and league leaders – still unbeaten after 18 rounds of fixtures – Sant Julià walked out onto the pitch. Televised live on the Federation's YouTube channel via a single camera perched on a tripod, the commentators' excited chatter bounced around the little press box and out the open door. Animated gestures had the cameraman keep one hand on the camera, just in case, as his pre-match thoughts tumbled down across the seats where some of the players and supporters from the previous matches had come to watch. All aware of its significance in the race for end of season glory, they felt compelled to stay and watch, working over the potential ramifications any result might have for their own clubs.

Inter Club d'Escaldes, like Ordino, have never tasted European football. Formed in 1991, they came close in 2002, losing the Copa Constitució final to Lusitanos. Aside from a Segona Divisió title in 2017, their lot has been one of also-rans. Not so this year, which goes some way to explaining the animated anguish of their media secretary Coke González as the game began. Intercut with moments of calm to take action shots with his camera, uploading them to Twitter along with match updates to the club's 400 followers, he doubled over every time a Sant Julià shot stung the palms of Inter keeper Joan Bayona, wincing as if he has taken the shot to the groin. The odd misplaced pass or a Sant Julià shot fizzing just wide of Bayona's post had him jolting and contorting as if he has been electrocuted – his nerves not helped by the excited clamour from the press box.

'We are so close to the top of the league,' he explained in between official duties and supporter anguish. 'We have never been this close to the title, or Europe. After all, we are still an amateur club in a league of professional sides. But everything has come together this season. Our new boss has come in and implemented a professional outlook.'

He pointed at the figure of the Inter manager, Adolfo Baines, standing motionless in his technical area on the far side of the pitch, absorbed in the tactical manoeuvres of his team.

'He has improved the mentality of the players, made them professional in all but name. He uses sport science to improve their preparation. They are now professional athletes in an amateur team. And it shows,' he said, as Inter broke forward at pace against a Sant Julià side long since accustomed to high placed finishes in the league and cup.

The pace and intensity in the day's final match seemed a step above what had gone before it. There was an edge in the air above and beyond the growing chill as the sun began to sink into the mountains.

'There is a little spice between some of the players,' Coke nodded. 'A few left us for Sant Julià at the beginning of the season, and a few came the other way, leaving their contracts and European football behind because they believed in the project Adolfo is building.' He shook his head. 'That is no small thing.'

League and cup wins, runners-up spots in both on a regular basis since 2001 has seen Sant Julià, one of the league's elder statesmen having been founded in 1982, become regulars in the Europa League and, before it, the UEFA and Intertoto Cups. Fifteen campaigns playing teams as far afield as Northern Ireland, Russia and Israel culminated in Sant Julià becoming the first ever Andorran team to win a two-legged European tie, and in the Champions League no less. A 1-1 draw home and away against Tre Fiori, the champions of San Marino, saw Sant Julià come out victorious in the penalty shoot-out 5-4. Facing Levski Sofia of Bulgaria in the second qualifying round, they came unstuck, losing 9-0 on aggregate. However, given their resources compared to those from the many larger leagues around the continent, Sant Julià's results in European competition – like those of their compatriots – is nothing short of miraculous. Narrow defeats to sides from Denmark, Bosnia and Croatia really shouldn't happen, but they do, testament to the skill and passion that exists within Andorran football. This skill is what finally unlocked Inter's backline – Jose Antonio Aguilar finishing off a sweeping Sant Julià move to give them the lead.

The commentary box erupts as the commentator screamed, 'Goooooooooaaaaaaaaaaaaaaalll' for what seemed like minutes into his microphone. Taking a breath, he then repeated the feat in case his YouTube followers had been left in any doubt. 'Goooooooooaaaaaaaaaaaaaaalll Sant Julià Goooooooooooaaaaaaaaall,' before a ferocious retelling of the move that brought it about. Coke inhaled sharply and turned his back on the pitch for a moment.

'Aguilar was one of those who left us in the summer,' he said, shaking his head, the pained expression on his face etched that little bit deeper as Jose Antonio celebrated in front of the stand. 'Ildefons won't be happy,' he continued, pointing behind the goal that framed the despondent Inter keeper Joan Bayona, yet to stir from his prone position on the floor.

Ildefons Lima is an institution in Andorran football. Capped a record 119 times by his country, centre back Lima is also the nation's record international goalscorer with 11 goals to his name. His club career saw him start at FC Andorra before spells at Sant Andreu, Las Palmas and Rayo Vallecano in Spain, Ionikos in Greece, Pachuca in Mexico, Triestina in Italy and Bellinzona in Switzerland, before return-ing home with FC Andorra and FC Santa Coloma. Now, at the age of 39, he has signed up to the Inter vision, though injury has side-lined him for this round of matches.

'Whenever he is injured, he comes down to the matches and watches with his friend Koldo Álvarez. Koldo is the national team manager. Where else but Andorra could you find the national team boss and the national team captain, holder of the most appear-ances and goals for his country, just stood behind the goal? I will introduce you.'

Although nearly 40, Lima looks every bit the athlete. A tall wiry frame is topped off with a warm smile, creating crow's feet around his eyes from a lifetime of training among the elements. He is all wrapped up in a coat that was by now a necessity as shadow crept in a pincer movement across both sides of the valley. The last of the sun's warmth quickly lost, the snow-topped peaks in the distance the last to fall into shadow.

'I should be out there,' Ildefons explained, nodding at the pitch, 'but I picked up an injury.' He instinctively felt his hamstring with his hand. 'It's getting better. I should be fit for the two international matches in a few weeks,' he said, referring to the opening two fixtures of the Euro 2020 qualifying campaign against Iceland and Albania, both to be played at the national stadium in the space of four days. 'It is such an honour, to play for my country. I will do everything I can to be fit for them, and then see after that. I am getting on. I think my time as an international may be coming to an end. I don't know. We will see.'

For a player who has been a staple of the Andorran national team, making his debut some 22 years earlier, barely a year after the national side was first formed and accepted into UEFA and FIFA – a national team without Ildefons will be a strange experience for player and nation. It is remarkable, a player reaching 119 caps, in any national team. But for a team that never qualifies for the World Cup and the European Championships – and with it the opportunity to play a host of matches in a short space of time – for a team that rarely gets the chance to bolster qualifying matches with friendly fixtures, 119 caps is a real feat. It is a testament to the dedication and love for his sport and country.

Among those appearances, Lima has faced the world's best, marking Ronaldo, Bale, Henry, Totti, the untouchable Spanish front line of Xavi, Torres and Iniesta. He has played in iconic stadiums, facing down a 60,000 crowd at Wembley, and even played the Brazil of Ronaldo, Rivaldo, Cafu and Roberto Carlos in a 1998 World Cup warm-up match. He has an extensive shirt collection to commemorate those he has faced and a box of armbands from every time he led his nation as captain. A lifetime of memories, of heroic displays against teams that should have put up a cricket score against the minnows of Andorra but didn't – couldn't – given the intensity and passion that stood in their way.

It must be hard to pick a stand-out moment amongst 20 plus years of such experiences. Lima shook his head emphatically. 'I have been so proud to represent my country, to lead my country on the football field, to have played in amazing stadiums against amazing players. I have a great pride in having the most international appearances, the most goals, having played football all across Europe. But the best moment I have had in football? That was when we beat Hungary 1-0 in the World Cup Qualifiers in 2017.'

The defeat of a Hungarian team so much higher in the FIFA world rankings is Andorra's greatest footballing achievement (a 1-0 win over Macedonia back in 2004 remains their only other competitive victory), no doubt made all the sweeter for Ildefons that it was his centre back partner Marc Rebés who scored the goal. The result is also testament to the professionalism and sporting dedication of Lima and his fellow players.

To come from a country with a fraction of the resources of the majority around them, to take them on and come away with respectable results is a measure of the passion and desire that these players exude. It is not simply a case of turning up and taking the experience. Every game is an opportunity. And that focus and singularity of thought that is the preserve of the dedicated athlete enables them to compete and, on the rarest of occasions, come out on top.

That that victory is the highlight explains all you need to know about Ildefons, and those other minnow players the continent over, who compete in the face of seemingly impossible odds. They are winners. They have that winning mentality needed to reach and then compete at the elite level, even if they rarely come out on top. But when that win comes, a lifetime of hard work bears fruit.

Four draws in their six recent UEFA Nations League matches suggests that Andorra are not that far behind a cluster of nations with far greater infrastructure. That potential must be a real draw, even for the weary legs of Lima. Time will tell.

And there may yet be more European adventures for Ildefons, even with possible international retirement looming, as his current teammates put on one hell of a comeback beneath ever-strengthening floodlights. These lights dissolve the huddle of Ildefons and Koldo – international captain and manager, holders of more than 200 international caps between them – into shadow behind the goal.

A sucker punch double from Inter's Genís Soldevila and Mateo Rodríguez before half-time turned the game on its head, and caused the commentator to nearly pass out, so little time there was between one 'gooooooooooaaaaaaaaaall' and the next for him to catch his breath.

The second half turned into a tense affair beneath darkening skies, the valley beyond twinkling in the night from the lights in Andorra la Vella and precarious, isolated hamlets scaling the lower slopes of the mountains.

For Inter, a first genuine chance of top-flight silverware; for Sant Julià, a first league title in more than a decade made every tackle that bit sharper, every decision against them that bit more exasperating. When a poorly timed challenge ended up in a mass melee between all 20 outfield players, a player from each side found themselves taking an early bath, disappearing down a hastily extended players' tunnel.

Titles, European campaigns, both of which will leave little mark beyond the confines of the Pyrenees, were fought over with a fervour reminiscent of a desperate last-minute Champions League final comeback. From one end of the footballing scale to the other, the tone, the meaning of victory is no different, its importance imperceptible. This had Coke writhing in agony on the touchlines, made even worse by the need to quickly nip across to the second pitch, where Inter Club d'Escaldes B were lining up for a Segona Divisió fixture.

His position as media officer necessitated a fleeting visit to take the odd picture of the reserves, before a rush to the other side of the stand to catch up on the excruciatingly slow and agonisingly tense finale of the first teams' match. Every Sant Julià attack had him weaving and bobbing, as if attempting to avoid the jabs from some unseen boxing bout. The exhalation of breath at a near miss like the landing of a blow to the stomach.

Ultimately, the anguish would prove to be worthwhile for Coke, as the final whistle precipitated a one-man pitch invasion, with him hugging the Inter players before taking a few shots of a jubilant team celebrating. Ildefons, protecting his injury, decided against vaulting the perimeter barrier like Coke, preferring to simply applaud from the touchline before slipping away into the darkness.

As the celebrations died down and both sets of players made for the tunnel, the stand emptied and drained away into the night, an exhausted commentator and cameraman began to pack up. The eight-hour top-flight marathon was over.

Adolfo Baines, Inter Club manager, lingered by the touchline deep in thought. The satisfaction of a big win already fading, he was looking ahead. He knew that to break the recent domination of FC Santa Coloma and Sant Julià, it would take more than one big result. Fully aware that third place was nowhere in the Andorran League, they would have to overtake one of them to realise the team's and Adolfo's ambitions of European football, both to claim the title. Even in Andorra, top-flight management is a 24/7 occupation, or affliction. But it was one the affable Spaniard was relishing.

'I was an assistant coach for a club side in Algeria before here,' he said, nodding at the pitch. 'A long way to go to start your coaching career. But you have to take the opportunity when it arises, as they are not easy to come by. But I wanted to be head coach, so when I get the call saying, "We want you here in Andorra," I am on the plane!

'Inter Club d'Escaldes may be an amateur team, but we have very good players. They work hard, like professionals, and the aim is to qualify for Europe. Do that and the prize money from UEFA will make us professional. We will become a stronger club with better players again. Then we can aim for titles, the cup, to progress further through the qualifying rounds in Europe. Anything is possible with hard work. And it will be hard. Santa Coloma, Sant Julià, they are good teams. Traditionally Inter have been at the foot of the table, or in the Segona Divisió, so this is a new experience for everyone at the club.'

To hear someone so fluent in English is a rarity in Andorra. Catalan is the language here in the mountains. If not that then Spanish and French, and a little Portuguese. There is little benefit to knowing English. Like the principality itself, the league is populated by more non-Andorran players than Andorran. A large contingent hail from Spain, as well as a smattering from Argentina, Uruguay and Chile. Those outside the Spanish-speaking diaspora need to learn it – and fast – to get anywhere in Andorran football.

Adolfo's English is a by-product of a career as a goalkeeper that took in spells in the Spanish second and third tiers with Getafe, Gimnàstic de Tarragona, CD Badajoz and Tenerife, a short stint in Portugal, before a final season as a player in England with MK Dons, then a League Two side.

'What an amazing experience,' he beamed, 'to play in England. Though it didn't start so well. I got sent off in my first game against Bury before half-time!'

He went on to play 22 times, including a third-round League Cup tie against Premier League Tottenham Hotspur.

'Football is a passion everywhere. But in Britain? It is unlike anywhere else, I think. Truly a religion for the people. I couldn't believe that even in the fourth division, the children were coming to games in MK Dons shirts. Such passion. In Spain, at lower league games you will often see Real, Barcelona shirts on the kids. Not there!

'There is passion in Andorra for football. It just looks a little different. And that is great. I have been lucky to see it in a few different countries in my career. And I am excited to be here on this adventure in Andorra. It is a great league. Lots of great players. I am proud to be a manager here.'

It is a pride that is replicated in the players. Whether homegrown like Ildefons, or from one of Andorra's ex-pat communities, or from further afield, there is a pride to feature in such a technical, competitive league. A league that offers up European competition for the more successful.

Miguel Ángel Luque, Nicolae Vasile and Walter Fernández step out from the Sant Julià dressing room with looks befitting a team that have just lost their unbeaten record. All three dressed in club tracksuits, they appear smaller, frailer than out on the pitch – where blistering speed and crunching tackles accompanied a deft touch on the ball. A low centre of gravity enabling wicked feints and changes in direction and momentum, their stature raised beneath the floodlights. Now, despite sporting healthy sun tans, these 20-somethings appear gaunt and drained, faded by exhaustion and defeat. Though animation in the shape of a smile returns across Nicolae's face as he shakes my hand.

'You speak English! Oh my God! It has been such a long time since I have been able to speak English. My Catalan and Spanish are OK, and no one here speaks much of anything else!'

Born in Bucharest in 1995, Vasile started out with Rapid Bucharest, playing more than 60 games over three seasons before they were declared bankrupt in 2016. Without a team, he found himself a contract at Finnish second tier side Palloseura Kemi Kings, followed by a season in Spain with third division Arandina.

Two appearances for Sant Julià in the Europa League this season accompany his 11 under-19 caps and one under-21 cap for Romania. Like Ildefons, Adolfo and his teammates have careers to be proud of and go some way to prove that the Primera Divisió is a league of genuine substance. However, like the Highland League, Liechtenstein and the Faroes, it is at the end of a footballing path less travelled.

Where Nicolae, Ildefons and Adolfo's careers offer up some exotic names of teams not so well known, Miguel and Walter's CVs read like a schoolchild's dream. Miguel began in Villarreal's third team in the third tier, before a season and 21 appearances for Barcelona's reserves in the second tier. He appeared as an unused substitute twice for Almeria in La Liga the following season before 13 appearances and three goals for Atlético Madrid's B team. He then played for Puskás Akadémia in Hungary's top-flight, that fateful last Rapid Bucharest season with Nicolae, and at Lokomotiv Plovdiv in Bulgaria's First league, before joining Sant Julià in time to help them to runners up spot in his first season and Super Cup winners in his second. Seven under-19 caps for Spain help to underline the quality of the man.

Teammate Walter Fernández also started at Barcelona before breaking into first team football with second tier Gimnàstic de Tarragona, playing 40 plus times. He then played Europa League football during a 33-game stint at Fehérvár (formerly Videoton until a name change in 2018) in Hungary, before spells with Lokeren in Belgium, Petrolul Ploieşti of Romania, Xanthi and Panthrakikos in Greece, before returning home for a ten-game spell at second tier side Extremadura. He has won the Hungarian League Cup once, the Hungarian Super Cup twice, as well as the Andorran Supercup. Standing quietly among the Andorran Pyrenees, the efforts of the Segona Divisió echoing about a near empty centre d'Entrenament, this trio represent all that is great about the Andorran League.

There may not be the history of other European leagues, that extend back to the late 19th century. There may not be a fervent supporter culture, with flares, chants and the rest of it. But there is genuine quality, both on and off. Clubs are run with a passion and dedication that sees them ready for European campaigns. Supporters, friends and families create as laidback and welcoming an environment in the stands and along the touchlines of Andorran football as you could find anywhere in world football. And players like Tomás Lanzini of Encamp, national hero Ildefons Lima of Inter and this trio from Sant Julià produce attractive football that keeps anyone staying to watch four back to back Primera Divisió fixtures fully engaged.

Despite defeat that day, Sant Julià should have nothing to fear. Only FC Santa Coloma seemed capable of being genuine title contenders, with Inter a few too many points behind for first place. Beat Santa Coloma in what is called in Andorra 'El Classic', and the title should be theirs. Vasile, Fernandez and Luque nod, encouraged by my appraisal.

'Really?' Miguel said. 'I hope so. We have worked so hard this season. The aim was always the title and European football.'

'The club haven't won the league for ten years,' Nicolae added, 'so it would be great to bring the cup back to Sant Julià. Did you know that these guys used to play for Barcelona?' he said, embarrassing his colleagues. 'They are really good!'

'Miguel here has played for Barca, Atlético Madrid, Villarreal,' Walter said in broken English, attempting to draw attention away from himself. Miguel nodded and looked at the pitch beneath his feet for a moment, suitably embarrassed.

'And now I am here,' he said in an attempt at self-deprecation, looking across at the Segona Divisió match. Barcelona and Madrid, it is not. But at the same time, football in Andorra is not the hopeless, pointless entity that the wider footballing community imagine.

'It is a good league here,' Miguel said, 'a good standard with some talented players. Hopefully we can qualify for Europe and prove that against other nations. It is different, the league, for sure,' he said, nodding at the stand. Amicable support and neutral pitches had not been the norm across his career thus far. 'But it is a league we would love to win, to repay Sant Julià for bringing us here on professional contracts,' he added. 'They are good people, a good club. A title, another season of European football. To have that would be what they deserved.'

'We just need to get the job done,' Nicolae added. 'A first defeat in the league, that hurt today. It was a bad feeling. We need to finish what we started. See where it takes us.' And with that, a few warm hand-shakes and a wave, the trio slipped away into the night, leaving those few good people from Sant Julià to finish up packing away another Primera Divisió fixture.

Guillermo Burgos – goalkeeping coach, ex-Sant Julià goalie, Andorra Women's National team coach – helps Andres Boga, kit-man and committee member collect everything together. Hailing from Chile, Burgos speaks little English, but enough to ask me to wait by the exit, where after a few minutes he and Andres return with a Sant Julià shirt.

'For you to remember,' he said, handing over the shirt and point-ing around him at the glittering lights in the darkness – all that is visible of his adopted home.

Shirt or no shirt, Andorra, its football league and the people that populate it are an unforgettable melting pot of nationalities, ideas and passion. A league barely 25 years old, with teams not much older again – teams often without home grounds to call their own, or a vocal fanbase behind them, they make the Andorran Premier League a unique and vital experience.

A population where Andorrans are outnumbered by ex-pat communities is also reflected in the league's constitution. National team players are boosted by the competition with solid professionals from Spain, Argentina, France and beyond, all of whom take the opportunity afforded them in Andorra with the utmost respect. Titles, European campaigns – Andorra gives back as much as it receives from those who come to play here.

This is real football. Talent, skill, passion, excitement – Andorra has it all. A small, but glittering gem in the European football landscape. It is a gem that finds itself at the very end of a footballing road less travelled, a road that snakes between vast shadowy mountains, past the ancient Sant Julià and its tall, narrow streets – the last outpost before Spain. The road recedes into the darkness as if it had never been there as I make my way back to La Seu d'Urgell.

But for those who do take that road, whether for an international fixture at the breathtaking national stadium, or a European qualifying tie at the equally beautiful Estadi Comunal, or just another round of Primera Divisió fixtures at the Centre d'Entrenament, it is an experience that will reveal a love for the game as powerful and unshakeable as anywhere else. It's a unique experience that won't be forgotten in a hurry.

CHAPTER SEVEN

Highland No More – Cove Rangers

I HAD SEEN that haunted look once before. Worn by the die-hard supporters of Cowdenbeath on a bitterly cold March afternoon as they filed into Central Park, the home of the Blue Brazil. Shrinking behind collars, hats and scarves that sleet-ravaged day, there was that look, peering out as they leant into the wind huddled in pockets of threes and fours on *their* spot of exposed terrace, like urban penguins facing down some Antarctic storm blown all the way up to Fife. Penguins with the weight of the footballing world on their shoulders, because Cowdenbeath had found themselves cut adrift at the foot of League Two.

A 2-2 draw with Stenhousemuir that icy Saturday did nothing to ease the inevitability that the Blue Brazil were destined for last spot and a dreaded relegation play-off with the champion of either the Lowland or Highland League. It was a simple matter of maths and time before it was confirmed – a two-legged tie against a team with momentum to burn – in order to maintain their status as worst professional team in Scotland.

Away trips to Albion Rovers and Peterhead, once undertaken with a weary sense of duty, now took on the appeal of away days at Camp Nou and San Siro – so fearful was the drop down into non-league. For a team sporting more than a century of Scottish League history – much of it far from the very basement of the professional game in Scotland – the thought of trips to Civil Service Strollers, to Gala Fairydean Rovers was too much to bear for the proud supporters of Cowdenbeath. Especially given that the only team to be relegated through this play-off system since its introduction in 2014, East Stirlingshire, have never threatened to return.

But as the skies darkened overhead and numbed faces made for home on the final whistle, dispersing among the amassed stock cars and stock car racers waiting outside for their turn on the slick race-track that circumnavigated the pitch, all was not completely lost. An improved run, including a first win since September, showed that there was, at the very least, some fight left in Cowdenbeath.

As it turned out, that fight, both sporting and physical saw them come out on top of a fractious play-off tie with 2017/18 Highland League champions, Cove Rangers. The Wee Rangers from Aberdeen finished the second leg with just the nine players after two were sent off for their part in a mass brawl in the dying minutes. It had been a very close shave, for both the Blue Brazil and Cove. And both were determined to put things right the following season.

For Cowdenbeath, that produced a year of recovery in mid-table, where the highs and lows of promotion and relegation were avoided. The die-hard terrace penguins of Central Park could bemoan long mid-week away trips to Stranraer and Elgin, safe in the knowl-edge that no one was going to try to take that glorious right away from them.

For Cove, a long Highland League season would yield just the one defeat, a 1-0 loss away to third placed Fraserburgh. Ninety-three points gained over a 34-game campaign saw a second successive Highland League title come to Cove Bay, on the southern outskirts of Aberdeen. In the play-off with Lowland League champions East Kilbride, the Wee Rangers came out on top 5-1 on aggregate, setting up a second crack at breaking into the pro leagues.

Formed in 1922, Cove Rangers played more than 60 seasons in the local amateur leagues around Aberdeen, before being admitted into the Highland League in 1986. Their first Highland silverware came in 1995, winning the League Cup. But it would take a further six seasons before they claimed the first of seven Highland League titles in 2001.

Coming from a city of some 200,000 people (four times larger than the Highland capital of Inverness) and with Aberdeen FC firmly entrenched as one of Scotland's best sides, Cove Rangers grew among a community with football at its very core. No surprise then that such a large catchment area for players and footballing pedigree began to translate into trophies in an ever-growing trophy cabinet. Four Highland League titles and three Highland League cups between 2013 and 2019 have helped compliment numerous Aberdeenshire Cup and Shield successes in the 21st century.

Ambition on the pitch has been matched with ambition off it at Cove. In 2015, when Allan Park, their home for 67 years, was deemed not to meet the minimum requirements of the Scottish professional Football League, they built Balmoral Stadium – a ground that did. Though a wrench having to leave Allan Park, named after the local farmer who sold them the land to build it in 1948, entry into the newly formed pyramid system could only be achieved by leaving generations of memories behind. Memories including Scottish Cup ties against league opposition, and a record crowd of 2,100 to witness the winning of the Highland League title in 2009 with a 3-1 victory over Deveronvale.

Defeat at Cowdenbeath in 2018 had been Cove's second attempt at promotion. A 4-1 aggregate loss to Edinburgh City in the 2015 Highland/Lowland league play-off had preceded it. And with the 2019 demolition of East Kilbride complete, the hope in Cove Bay was that it would be a case of third time lucky for the Wee Rangers. Though ultimately, luck would have nothing to do with it.

Berwick Rangers are Scottish football's self-inflicted and most welcome anomaly. Hailing from a town less than three miles south of the Scottish border, Berwick's rejection by the North Northumberland Football League, and therefore English football in 1951, was met with open arms by the Scottish Football League. And so began 68 years of a football team from England playing within the professional ranks of Scotland.

A club with both the English and Scottish lions on its crest, the Scottish Saltire and English St George's cross on official club scarves, and where players are sent off in Scotland but punished by the English FA, Berwick Rangers are a glorious contradiction. With support on the terraces hailing from both sides of the border, they are a club that bucks the traditional trend of sporting enmity between the two nations. They are a club like no other. They are a club in dire straits.

A slow slide down League Two over recent years resulted in a terrible 2018/19 season. Just five wins all year and a goal difference of minus 64, Berwick found themselves cut adrift come the final reckoning, a good eight points behind ninth placed Albion Rovers. It would be their turn to face down the dreaded relegation play-off. Despite a new management team being installed to try and breathe a little life into a side that hadn't scored a goal for eight weeks, or won a match in six months, they crumbled in the first leg in Cove, a 4-0 defeat all but sealing their fate. They would be joining East Stirlingshire in the Lowland league, a league that only one side has managed to escape in five years. And still they had to prepare for the second leg, at home, where their fate would be rubber-stamped in front of their own crowd. As if any more salt could possibly be poured into such a deep wound.

I had seen that haunted look before, but this time it was worse – much, much worse. Brave faces and forced laughter among stewards and club officials at the players entrance of Shielfield Park, the home of Berwick Rangers, stuck in their throats. Knowing their fate, this was an exercise in torture, plain and simple. This ultimately meaningless fixture had to be fulfilled. The 400 or so jubilant Cove supporters that were on their way would have to be accommodated.

But in a quiet moment, those brave faces would slip. A look of confusion, horror, abject sorrow at what was about to befall their beloved little club washed out their faces. An old man beneath a flat cap, swamped in a high vis jacket many sizes too big opened a gate and looked out at the few early assembled supporters waiting to come in, himself waiting to watch his club fall away into potential oblivion. The hurt was writ large across his face.

From the walk from the train station into Berwick you would have no clue that such a traumatic event was about to be inflicted upon the town's football-loving brethren. To all intents and purposes, it was just another bustling Saturday in this pretty little market town. Nestled beneath large grassy banks of fortification that had, for more than 400 years, attempted to repel both Scottish and English advances (Berwick having been controlled by both royal houses throughout the Middle Ages), it cut a tranquil weekend scene.

Families on the lookout for a bargain bustled between market stalls, children lingering at the fresh doughnut stand, their hints instinctively ignored until heartfelt pleas and whines focused their parents' attention. Others took advantage of Berwick's position overlooking both the North Sea and the mouth to the River Tweed to meander along coastal paths or turn inland on a peaceful towpath past the Berwick Amateur Rowing Club clubhouse, and on toward a majestic viaduct connecting east coast rail services. Across the river, they would see the very tops of four sets of floodlights poking above a largely residential scene, marking out the parameters of the town's very own sporting tragedy, at least to those in the know.

In the Berwick Rangers club bar, their supporters rubbed shoulders with a biker gang who had booked the field surrounding the ground for a rally; no one thinking when the booking had been taken that Berwick would be hosting a fixture this late into May. Broad-shouldered bikers with gnarled beards and jackets covered with MC patches waited patiently to be served alongside old timers in Berwick scarves, dwarfed among these man-mountains decked out in oil-stained denims and tattoos. Never judge a book by its cover, though, as seats were given up for the elderly, doors held open to ease their journey with trays of beer destined for equally deflated friends. Possibly aware that this day was a horrendous one for those draped in the black and gold of Berwick, a little courtesy was the least they could do to try to ease the pain. Impossible.

As turnstiles opened and silent queues began to file through, many paused to pick up a programme, a collector's full-stop in a set spanning seven decades. Morbid memento secured, generations of Berwick support made their way to the seat they had always sat in or their spot on the terrace, looking across at the large industrial unit behind the club. Rows of large, dulled metallic silos towered above the main stand. Their dormant weekend state was a fittingly bleak backdrop for those assembled, most of whom looking like they had just paid £12 in order to watch their beloved pet being put down over an excruciating 90-minute period. Sporting glassy 1,000-yard stares they looked out across a pitch that had only ever known better times than this. And by better, read mid-table obscurity in Scottish football's fourth tier. Much, much better than this.

But for the assembled, their pain was about to be made worse, as coach after coach of Cove Rangers supporters began to squeeze between rows of Harley Davidsons, traffic barriers and pointing stewards. Safely stowed, doors opened to a wall of noise – songs ramping up with every Cove supporter stepping out into the light. They had been on a four-hour journey, fuelled by tins of lager and an almost unbearable expectation of the promised land had them all in heady spirits. The noise grew and grew, until a blue tide began to pour through the turnstiles of Shielfield Park.

It was as if there had been a double booking at a village hall, with guests for a wake and a wedding reception colliding in a mess of conflicting emotion in the same cramped space. Jubilant Cove supporters in kilts, wearing large Saltire flags as capes, danced between the mourners not out of spite, but at the sheer joy of this being *their* moment. As the Cove 400 made their way to their allocation of main stand, passing the sombre home support already seated, renditions of 'Flower of Scotland' interspersed more traditional football chants celebrating the fact that Cove really were 'Highland Dynamite'.

The kilts, Saltire and the national anthem, so it turned out, were the response to a number of young Berwick lads who had brought St George's flags up to Cove the week before in an act of provocation that wholly misjudged Berwick Rangers' standing within the Scottish game. It could not go unanswered – and it didn't.

Berwick's tenure in the Scottish professional leagues had never really been played out along xenophobic national lines. They had been accepted into the Scottish fold, and despite the odd blip (Stranraer had banned Berwick supporters from bringing in flags and scarves with a St George's Cross on them, even if they also sported the Saltire and the Scottish lion), they were seen as a part of the Scottish football family but from England.

Alec, an elderly Clyde fan, had summed up the experience of a trip down to Berwick perfectly a few years earlier when asked what it was like to have to come to England to see his team play: 'Aye it's alright. We're happy to come. And after all, it's not every day you get to see your team play in Europe!'

That a small group of young Berwick lads had got it so completely wrong, especially in a time where their team didn't need their opponents to be fired up any further, just compounded what had already been a disastrous season. As they unfurled them once again for this home leg, they seemed completely unaware of the fabric of the support around them, half of whom had come from north of the border to support their ailing team. The flags were a symbol, albeit hoisted by an unthinking tiny minority, of all that was going wrong at Berwick Rangers, an identity fogged by mismanagement, lacking in direction.

For Cove, direction wasn't an issue. They knew where they were going and where they had come from. They were proud Highland League champions, having traversed up to the far north of Wick to silence Barmy Army, the Highland capital of Inverness to face down founding members Clachnacuddin, the far west and Sam Lee's reborn Fort William (where a home win by eleven goals to nil was followed up by a spirited Fort William display at Claggan Park in keeping the score down to six – a decent feat against a Cove team who had narrowly lost 2-1 to Premier League Hearts in the Scottish League Cup groups stages, as well as beating League One Raith Rovers 2-0 in the same competition). Cove had overcome competition from the other big Aberdeenshire teams, subduing the incessant drums of the Chuff Chuffs in Inverurie and perennial big hitters, Formartine. They had also faced down the coastal powerhouses of Forres and Fraserburgh, Cammy Keith of Keith, the Cairngorm clubs in Strathspey Thistle and Rothes and their closest league rivals in Brora. They had taken them all on and come out on top.

Now it was their turn to follow in Peterhead and Elgin's footsteps, in Ross County and Inverness Caledonian Thistle (a club formed by the merger of two Highland League founder members Inverness Thistle and Caledonian in 1994 to take up a vacant spot in the SPFL) and represent the Highland League in the professional ranks.

A few Cove lads began to erect a large banner with 'Believe' printed across it in Cove blue, the club's crest in one corner, while another group began in on a wonderfully eccentric song and dance. The groups ringleader wove through the Cove support with a plastic flowerpot in one hand, while his cohorts built up a crescendo of 'ooh's until their captain placed it on the head of a fellow fan. With that, everyone began jumping up and down, belting out a chant full of in-jokes and Cove legend, while the supporter blinded by flowerpot tried to join in without tumbling over the seats in front of him. And so it went on, for ten minutes or so, until the flowerpot was confiscated by a policeman from the English Northumberland Constabulary, provoking a round of boos, then another rendition of 'Flower of Scotland'. Another Berwick anomaly – an English police force maintaining order at a Scottish football match.

As the Cove players came out to begin their warm-ups, the roar from the travelling support no doubt echoed through the corridors beneath the main stand, into the home dressing room. Their role as lambs to the slaughter already confirmed, the Berwick players took much longer to make their way out into the impossible environment they had created for themselves, where they would be stripped of their status as Scottish Professional Football League players in front of more than 1,000 of their own supporters. They were outgunned, pinned down and on the referee's whistle at 3.00pm, they did the only thing they could – they went over the top to face their fate.

Taking the game to their visitors, Berwick huffed and puffed for a while, trying for a goal to spark the unlikeliest of comebacks. It didn't come. Not long after, a scrambled Cove effort was deemed to have crossed the line by the linesman. 5-0 on aggregate. Game over. At least Berwick didn't give up – they were, after all, contractually obliged not to – though with the stuffing knocked out of them, they began to pose less of a threat as the minutes ticked by.

A ball-boy behind the Cove goal watched the play up the far end from his little stool. Having not been required to fetch the ball more than once all half, he stood up from his hunched position, stretched, then did the floss dance move a couple of times for no good reason before sitting back down. He wouldn't stand up again all half, which had been made even worse for Berwick with their captain Ross Brown being sent off with a minute to go, having hauled Cove striker Mitchel Megginson down when clean through on goal.

The decision wasn't met with derision from the home support as Brown trudged off. It didn't make a difference. The fixture had been such a foregone conclusion, even before the killer fifth goal early on, that doctors had given the green light for Cove joint manager John Sheran to attend, despite having had a heart attack only three weeks earlier. Falling ill the evening Cove had received the Highland League trophy, this trip to Berwick was considered so benign that it met the parameters of acceptable recuperation. He sat quietly in the stands, as relaxed as those on the away bench below, all smiles as he stood up for a half-time cup of tea on the referee's whistle.

At least there was a little respite from the misery for the Berwick support during the break, where a little gallows humour lightened the mood for a time.

'We're doomed!' piped up one old boy in the queue for the toilet, summoning up his very best *Dad's Army* impersonation.

'We were doomed long before today,' his friend chimed in. 'We've been doomed for months.'

'Years,' a third proffered. They all nodded before the first started in again.

'We're doomed!'

Others stood grumbling to one another, one muttering that Cove had a playing budget of £250,000, that it wasn't a fair fight. Anything to ease the pain of the reality that their team were getting hammered, plain and simple.

The home terrace fell quiet again during the second half, watching Cove deconstruct their ten men at will. The songs of the visiting support were only opposed by the revving of Harley engines from the field outside. An excruciating exercise.

With the comfortable score-line, there was even room for some sentimentality among the Cove ranks, as Eric Watson, a club stalwart with 12 years' playing service for Cove, came on for what would be his last ever appearance for the Wee Rangers. At the tender age of 36, and having never played up in the SPFL, all concerned knew that the club had finally outgrown him and that its new adventure would not be his. The away support roared its approval at his appearance. He would always remain a Cove legend. And in an attempt to cap his Cove career off with a goal, teammates in better scoring positions than him tried to pick him out for that cherry on the cake. Despite a few near misses, it didn't happen.

Across the pitch, at 5-0 down and down to ten men, the Berwick players put in the required effort demanded of a senior team. Frustrations and a misplaced pass played out in wild gesticulations. Hands on hips and the shaking of heads met every missed opportunity to install a little pride. But despite their best efforts given the situation, it was, nevertheless, a 45-minute exercise in humiliation. At the final whistle they were lucky to get away with just the 3-0 defeat, seven on aggregate.

Those home supporters who hadn't already drained away from the terraces after goals two and three stood motionless as the reality sunk in. Watching John Sheran, Eric Watson and the Cove players celebrating out on the pitch, weaving between fallen counterparts, who had sunk to their haunches, willing the ground to open and swallow them up, it was confirmed beyond all doubt. They were now a Lowland League football team. There would be no 69th season as a professional club.

Among those that remained, a young boy no more than eight or nine at the perimeter fence waved his Berwick scarf above his head with an enthusiasm that, in truth, didn't fit the scene. Too young to fully understand the fate his team had just befallen, he was, however, a symbol of Berwick Rangers' future. For this young lad, just setting out on his infatuation with the beautiful game, his love for his team was unconditional. Consumed by this life-long affliction already, even at such a tender age, he twirled his scarf with the pride and passion that it instils, no matter the gloom manifesting about him. That, if nothing else, can bring a little hope to a hopeless scene. That there are those prepared to persevere with their love for Berwick Rangers, who will fight to restore the good times of Scottish fourth division football back to Shielfield Park. One day.

For Cove and their delirious support spilling out onto the pitch to celebrate with their heroes, the future is a thing of endless opportunity. Why stop at League Two? A whole new world has just opened before them. Who knows where it will take them? The only thing they know for sure is that they are Highland no more. In name at least, if not spirit.

Because it is that spirit, of coming from the most northerly senior league in Britain – a league that is 'A small speck in the increasingly global world of football – a league with a special character, strong pride, and an integral part of the communities within which it is a part' – that has taken Cove up into the professional ranks.

They may be the vanguard of this remote division, but they are only a part of it. They typify the skill and ability within its ranks – the likes of Brora, Fraserbugh and Formartine only falling a short-ways behind their trailblazing path. And their passion to the cause is matched by all, from Fort William and Lossiemouth at the foot of the table, all the way up to Caithness and Wick Academy, via the Cairngorms of Rothes and Strathspey Thistle, the Moray Firth with Nairn County, Buckie Thistle and Deveronvale and the vast farm tracts north of Aberdeen in Turriff, Huntly and Inverurie. Cove's victory is the Highland League's victory. And the success, strength, and fortitude of the Highland League has enabled Cove to do what they do.

From top to bottom, the members of this highland division create something far greater than the sum of their parts. From Claggan Park to Cove, it is a vital mix of ability and community, entwined with unfathomable pride, passion and identity that makes the Highland League so special. It is this that enables it to thrive through wild winter storms, long away trips and a remote life among the far north of this beautiful, rugged country.

Pointless? Rubbish? A waste of time? Think on!

CHAPTER EIGHT

Europa No-hopers – La Fiorita, San Marino

SOMETHING SPECIAL WAS about to happen. You could feel the crackle of anticipation in the air. Outside, a young boy dressed in a football shirt much too big for him craned his neck, looking up expectantly at his mother chatting through the small window of the ticket office. He stood on tiptoes to try and see what is going on, see if his mother had secured those all-important tickets to the big match, his excitement ratcheting up as the clack of the turnstiles behind him signals that the stadium had finally opened; those with tickets already secured passing through them and up the steps beyond. Slipping from view and into the stand, the boy was desperate to join them. Because this was no ordinary match, this was a European night.

The flags of UEFA, the Europa League and the national flags of the two clubs involved hung limply in the withering humidity of a June heatwave, the odd breath of stifling air animating them just enough for the young boy to catch a glimpse of a strange flag from a far-away country. On an adjacent flagpole was the UEFA symbol, made so familiar from nights in front of the television watching the world's best competing in the latter stages of Europe's big two continental cups. The strange configuration of colour on the Andorran flag was tantalisingly obscured by the breathless evening, the boy's imagination filling in the gaps.

Through the turnstiles, his mother waited patiently while the boy queued to pick up a team-sheet and a programme; the familiar badge of his team, La Fiorita, joined on the cover by that of UE Engordany. Eyes widening, he scanned the strange crest, before looking over the exotic names among the opposition line-up.

His mother held his hand as they took the steps up into the stand, team-sheet and programme clutched in the other. At the top they turn right, disappearing into a vision of a pristine floodlit pitch, shimmering a brilliant emerald green. Those exotic Andorran names out on the pitch were warming up in a vibrant red kit never seen before by the boy. Taking it all in, they dissolve into the throng of excited bodies threading along the rows of seats, looking for theirs across the steep rake of the main stand.

Meanwhile, those still stood in line at the ticket office shift from one foot to the other, waiting for their turn at the front, for their European adventure to begin. The chatter of turnstiles began to step up a pace. Because something special is about to happen.

For those lucky enough to experience seeing their team playing in European competition, no matter if only during the qualifying rounds, it is a never to be forgotten experience. Everything about the match is elevated, just knowing that you are a part of something much, much bigger. Like non-league teams in England and Scotland revere being a part of their respective FA Cups, the weight of history and of prestige in participating in European competition is similarly generation-defining. A battling display or win against foreign opposition a thing of legend to be handed down to any who would listen – an 'I was there' moment, fading images forever set to adorn club-house walls. Always played mid-week, the experience takes on an added magic. Senses seem heightened beneath the halo of floodlights. The illuminated pitch was elevated to that of something almost supernatural, while the alien sights and sounds of chants never heard before, never to be understood, reverberate from the pocket of visiting support. Scarves containing unfamiliar club badges twirled above heads in a strangely pleasing, swirling vortex of chaos.

It is an occasion so overwhelming to those not blessed with regular European participation that the actual result of the game almost doesn't matter. That it happened is, for some, enough. No matter the club you support. It is something truly special. And as with the preliminary rounds of the FA Cup, the more you explore the early rounds of European competition, played mere weeks after the previous season's final has been resolved, the clearer it is to see. It seems fitting that, just as the first word on the Highland League came from its statistically weakest link in Fort William, these European minnow adventures should conclude in the location of the 'worst national football team' in the world.

San Marino, or the Most Serene Republic of San Marino as it is also known, is a 23.6 square mile enclave buried deep within the countryside of the Italian peninsula; one of only three countries worldwide to be completely surrounded by another single county – Vatican City and Lesotho being the other two. Its name derives from Saint Marinus, a stonemason who travelled to Rimini in 257 AD to help reconstruct its city walls after they were destroyed by Liburnian pirates. Fearing persecution after a series of sermons, Marinus fled Rimini and created an independent monastic community, building a church on top of Monte Titano, San Marino's highest point in 301 AD. And so, San Marino was born, with surrounding communities joining it up until 1463, since which point its borders have remained unchanged.

San Marino's quiet existence among the Apennine mountains since the 1st century AD means that it lays claim to be the world's oldest sovereign state still in existence, and the oldest constitutional republic. Largely unaffected by the world beyond its borders, San Marino has always done things slightly different. Its government – a unitary parliamentary diarchic directorial republic – has two heads of state and government, known as the Captains Regent. In 1945, it was also the first country in the world to have a democratically elected communist government and then, in 1957, the first democratically deselected communist government.

Remaining neutral throughout the two great wars of the 20th century it did, however, write to the British government in September 1940, after *The New York Times* had reported that San Marino had declared war on the United Kingdom. A message was quickly transmitted stating that they had, in fact, done no such thing.

Despite their neutrality, it couldn't escape the war entirely, and San Marino was bombed by the RAF in June 1944, believing that it had been overrun by German forces. It had not, though it did succumb briefly in September of that year, before allies liberated it again in the Battle of San Marino.

While one of the oldest states in the world, San Marino is a relative newcomer to the international football scene. Despite a San Marino Football Federation being formed back in 1931, it didn't establish a national side until 1986, with its first competitive fixture coming four years later: a 4-0 home defeat to Switzerland at the start of the Euro 1992 qualifying campaign.

With a population of just 33,000, competing at international level is always going to be hard for countries like San Marino. But while other international minnows have recorded memorable victories during European and World Cup qualifying campaigns, San Marino have struck out all but three times in over 160 attempts. 0-0 draws with Turkey in 1993 and Estonia in 2014, and a 1-1 draw with Latvia in 2001 are the sum-total of their competitive endeavours. A 13-0 home defeat to Germany and a further four losses by ten goals have helped root San Marino to the foot of the FIFA world rankings along with basement bedfellows the Turks and Caicos Islands, Anguilla and Tonga.

Dead last – the world's worst – is a position San Marino have held for nine consecutive months. A 1-0 friendly win (only the third clean sheet achieved by San Marino in their near 30-year existence) over Liechtenstein back in 2004 remains the only ever international victory for the republic.

Andy Selva, scorer of that historic goal, remains San Marino's all-time appearance record-holder with 74 caps. He is also the nation's record goalscorer with eight international strikes. The only San Marino player to have scored more than two international goals (strikes against Belgium on three separate occasions, and singles against Austria, Bosnia, Wales and Slovakia across a ten-year period complimenting that historic goal against Liechtenstein), his club career took in spells in Italy with SPAL 1907, Padova, Sassuolo and Verona amongst others, before returning to see out his playing days in San Marino with La Fiorita. Retiring in 2017, he remains the country's most successful export.

Indeed, without Selva, San Marino have embarked on a two-year international goalscoring drought. Mirko Palazzi's September 2017 strike in a 5-1 loss away to Azerbaijan was the last opportunity to celebrate. (A goal on home soil has been an even more precious commodity for the supporters of the national team. One was last scored back in September 2013, with a first half Alessandro Della Valle equaliser startling Poland into action, who finally ran out winners by five goals to one.)

However, despite losing their talisman in Selva, the national team did put on a strong show in the UEFA Nations League, where a 5-0 defeat to Belarus was the only blot on an otherwise respectable series of narrow defeats to the Belarussians in the return match, and home and away ties with Luxembourg and Moldova. At the very least, something to build on.

Whether San Marino really are deserving of their tag as worst team in the world is a matter for debate. Playing in one of the toughest confederations in the world, FIFA's complicated points system seems a little harsh. How can you truly correlate heavy Sammarinese defeats to world champions with narrower Tongan losses to the likes of Samoa and the Solomon Islands? Whatever their position, whatever the tag attributed them, the Sammarinese continue their love affair with their team. It is, after all, about more than just winning. It's about celebrating an identity, a people. A performance full of heart and spirit worth cheering to the rafters. Indeed, narrow international defeats to a population of just 33,000, from a country 23 miles squared, is victory in its own right.

Servicing the San Marino national team is a domestic system remarkably similar to their minnow colleagues, Andorra. San Marino Calcio were formed by the San Marino Football Federation in 1960. Predating both the domestic Sammarinese football league and a national side by 25 years, San Marino Calcio joined the Italian league system and were a de facto national team representing the republic. Playing in light blue shirts, the colour adopted by the national team in 1986, San Marino Calcio reached Serie C2, the then fourth tier of Italian football in 1988. Consolidating themselves among the lower reaches of the professional leagues, the Titani reached Serie C1 and Italy's third tier for the first time in 2005.

Currently back in the fourth tier, the club has only five Sammarinese players on its books, its mission statement to represent the republic diluted when the club was sold to entrepreneurs in the late 1980s. Now mostly populated by Italians, it is still the only professional football club in San Marino, and an aspirational carrot for any players from the republic wanting to make it into the professional ranks.

Competing with the Titani for the footballing affections of the republic is the Campionato Sammarinese di Calcio, an amateur football league founded in 1985. Providing regular competition to its 15 teams (before it there was only the annual Coppa Titano and whatever friendly matches could be arranged), the Campionato enabled a greater opportunity for the development of players in all corners of the tiny country. Unable to rely solely on San Marino Calcio to fill the squad of their newly formed national team, the Campionato remains the heartbeat of Sammarinese football, and the backbone of the national side.

Arranged into two groups, or Girones, the top three sides from each group compete in an end of season play-off to determine the champion and a lucrative spot in the Champions League preliminary round. As in Andorra, the £240,000 reward for competing in Europe is an enormous amount of money for an amateur side. It can enable it to become less amateur, offering contracts and, albeit humble, salaries to its best players.

Joining the champions in Europe are the play-off runners up, and the Coppa Titano winners, both of whom enter the Europa League at its preliminary round. For Sammarinese clubs, whose national league is ranked 55th out of the 55 UEFA member leagues, you must start right at the very beginning, mere weeks after the previous year's finals have been concluded.

Since being admitted into European competition in 2000, there has been only one Sammarinese victory in Europe. Tre Penne came close when they defeated Shirak of Armenia 1-0 in a Champions League home leg in 2013. However, a 3-0 defeat in the return match halted progression. It wouldn't be until 2018 and a 3-0 Tre Fiori home win over Bala Town of Wales, followed by a 1-0 loss in Rhyl, that saw a team from San Marino advance in European competition.

Though the list of defeats among Sammarinese teams competing in Europe is long, interspersed with the odd draw, many ties remained, at the very least, competitive. Heavy defeats that should be the norm when teams from an amateur league take on sides from the professional ranks around Europe are thinner on the ground than you might expect. The pride in representing your club, your country on an international stage can do much to level the playing field.

For me, the earliest rounds of European qualifying – those balmy late June and early July fixtures between a long list of obscure clubs from around the continent, some with tongue-twisting names seemingly devoid of vowels, others sporting the names of towns never heard of before – are the pinnacle of the entire competition. The magic of

European football nights seems stronger among those who have had to fight the hardest to reach it. Who will come and go without most of the continent even realising that they were a part of this great footballing carnival? Shorn of television cameras and vast crowds, trumpeting anthems and rolling advertising hoardings, the real essence of European football is laid bare, the celebration of a successful season just gone. This is an opportunity to test yourself against continental opposition, to show those that visit what your club is all about, how much it means to those in the stands.

The games may come and go in almost complete anonymity to the larger European footballing community, their endeavours discarded in the footnotes of the competitions. Forgotten in favour of great battles in the latter stages between the likes of Barcelona, Juventus, Bayern Munich, Liverpool and the other giants of the game. But these grand European nights, broadcast to millions from Kazakhstan to the Faroe Islands, Iceland to Israel, stand on the shoulders of the passion of the qualifying rounds, and the reverence clubs at that stage have for the competition.

The spine-tingling renditions of 'You'll Never Walk Alone', the vast wall of colour and noise cascading down from the nose-bleed seats high above the pitch at Camp Nou. The bank of flares – ignited in unison out of the dark to create a chaotic, hellish scene – stretching across the tribunes to inspire the home side, intimidate the opposition. Thousands of voices in song, hailing their heroes, roaring a goal with a deafening fervour – these passions are built on what went before, the foundations laid by these early qualifying rounds.

Volunteers sweep the stands, hoisting flags, tending the pitch, getting kiosks ready. Others stack piles of change in small ticket offices in readiness for what they hope will be a sizeable flourish before kick-off. Signs are placed on seats for visiting UEFA dignitaries, stewards checking turnstiles, programme sellers with armfuls of stock waiting beyond, ready to dispense these mementos celebrating the night *their* team play in Europe. Supporters milling expectantly outside, chattering excitedly to one another, desperate for the gates to open. The atmosphere is electric, charged with the excitement and the pride of seeing your team competing in such a prestigious competition. The crowds may be small. It may not be Anfield, or Camp Nou. But the meaning, the glory in making it this far and the pride in knowing that you belong here on this stage is palpable in the air, on the faces of those present.

And from here the tournament is built, growing in ever grander waves as the rounds go by. But no matter how far you go into the tournament, you will never find a greater pride, a greater sense of occasion than at the very beginning – those halcyon summer days of late June, early July.

Representing San Marino in Europe that 2019/20 season were champions Tre Penne, the first Sammarinese team to win a fixture in European competition. Their Champions League campaign is over, however, a mere 24 days after the previous season's final has concluded. A 1-0 defeat to Santa Coloma of Andorra on 25 June relegated them into the second qualifying round of the Europa League. There they hope to be joined by Coppa Titano winners, Tre Fiori, and play off runners up La Fiorita, who have preliminary round fixtures against KI Klaksvík of the Faroe Islands, and UE Engordany of Andorra respectively.

Between these three teams, the story of Sammarinese club football in Europe plays itself out. Tre Penne, champions of San Marino four times and runners up on three occasions suffered a 13-3 aggregate defeat to HŠK Zrinjski Mostar of Bosnia and Herzegovina on its first ever European adventure in 2010. This was followed by 9-1 and 11-0 defeats to FK Rad of Serbia and F91 Dudelange of Luxembourg. But narrow defeats to the champions of Armenia, Wales and Andorra in recent seasons represents a steady improvement.

Tre Fiori, national champions seven times and Coppa Titano holders – the only club side to ever win a European tie by beating Bala Town of Wales 3-1 in the Europa League – have put in impressive performances elsewhere. Losing on the away goals rule to Sant Julià of Andorra, and running Maltese champions Valletta close, they have also been on the receiving end of a chastening European adventure. Their reward for defeating Bala Town: a 10-0 aggregate defeat to Slovenian side Rudar Velenje.

La Fiorita, Sammarinese champions five times and runners up in the latest edition, came close to becoming the first team from San Marino to progress in a Champions League fixture when they lost 1-0 on aggregate to Northern Irish champions Linfield in 2017. Among solid displays against opposition from Hungary, Malta and Gibraltar have come 8-0 defeats to Levadia Tallinn of Estonia and a 9-0 loss at the feet of Spartaks Jūrmala of Latvia.

Heroic displays stand shoulder to shoulder with more realistic outcomes when amateur takes on professional. That both stand in equal numbers is a sign of how playing for your club, your nation in Europe, can inspire and elevate you to greater things, relatively speaking. It is a marker as to how much it means to take part in the greatest show in European club football.

As with Andorra, the 15 clubs within the Sammarinese league don't necessarily have their own pitch. Available land among the rolling agriculture and Apennine mountains that dominate the 23 square miles of San Marino is at a premium. Like in Andorra, the San Marino Football Federation allocate pitches for every league fixture, meaning that on some occasions, the 'home' side may have to travel further than the 'away' team to that week's ground. Another glorious peculiarity of life among Europe's minnows. When it comes to European fixtures, however, there is only one venue: San Marino Stadium in Serravalle, home to the national team and San Marino Calcio.

With both Tre Fiori and La Fiorita drawn at home for the first leg of their Europa League adventure, and all fixtures needing to be played on the same day, it was Tre Fiori who ceded home advantage, instead travelling to the Faroes on the opening day. It would be, by default, La Fiorita who would offer me a first taste of Sammarinese football.

La Fiorita, or Società Polisportiva La Fiorita 1967 as they are formally known, come from the small community of Montegiardino on the southern borders of the country. With a population of 967, La Fiorita were originally formed in 1936 to compete in the inaugural Coppa Titano but were disbanded as competition was suspended at the outbreak of war across the continent in 1939.

As peace descended across Europe once more in 1945, La Fiorita remained dormant. Players contented themselves with scratch games between themselves in the town square, while the Coppa Titano returned in an erratic fashion. Sometimes only played every three or four years, La Fiorita only reformed when it became an annual event once more in the late '6os.[3] Played over a few rounds to accommodate the 15 Sammarinese clubs, those few matches constituted an entire season of competitive football until the formation of the Campionato Sammarinese di Calcio in 1985.

With regular football and championships created by the fledgling San Marino Football Federation, La Fiorita flourished, winning their first ever trophies in the Super Coppa and the Coppa Titano in 1986, followed by the Campionato Sammarinese in 1987. A second title would follow in 1990; however, it would be another 17 years before the next piece of silverware made its way to Montegiardino, and another Super Coppa trophy in 2007.

It wouldn't be until 2012 that La Fiorita became a regular force in Sammarinese club football, winning three titles, four Coppa Titanos and two Super Coppas between 2012 and 2018, making them regulars in the opening rounds of European competition. A runners-up spot in the Campionato in 2019 meant an eighth consecutive European campaign and another shot at that elusive first victory on the continental stage.

Coming painfully close in 2017 with a first ever draw in Europe at home to Linfield of Northern Ireland, a result that followed a narrow 1-0 defeat in Belfast, it would be Andorran cup winners, UE Engordany who would stand in their way this season of that all-important (at least to one small community at the southernmost boundaries of this most serene of all republics) first win.

After those sun-drenched Primera Divisió marathon of four games in one day, months earlier in Andorra la Vella, it would be

---

3 Of the 15 Sammarinese clubs, only four predate the '6os, when the promise of more regular competition transformed the gatherings of local players in town squares into more formal entities. Tre Penne formed in 1956, while Tre Fiori and San Giovanni were founded in 1949 and 1948 respectively. It is only AC Libertas who survived the outbreak of World War II. They are the only football club in San Marino to predate the formation of the San Marino Football Federation in 1931, having been founded three years earlier in Borgo Maggiore, a community nestled at the foot of Monte Titano. Winners of that inaugural Coppa Titano in 1937, they have gone on to win it a further ten times, the last being in 2014. A solitary Campionato Sammarinese di Calcio came in 1996, before clubs from San Marino took part in European qualifying.

Nicolae Vasile and Joel Méndez's Sant Julià who would go on to pip Adolfo Baines and Ildefons Lima's Inter Club d'Escaldes to the runners up spot in the league, and that all-important spot in Europe. As expected, Santa Coloma jogged to the title, but what wasn't expected was Engordany's 2-0 win over the champions in the Copa Constitució final: their first ever cup success. And with it came only a second ever adventure in European cup competition.

Ominously for La Fiorita, Engordany's first taste of European football (after a runner-up spot in the Primera Divisió the season before) and their first ever European victory came at the expense of fellow Sammarinese side Folgore. A 2-1 preliminary round win at the Estadi Comunal in Andorra la Vella was followed by a 1-1 draw at the San Marino Stadium, setting up a chastening 10-1 aggregate defeat to Kairat of Kazakhstan in the first qualifying round.

But that was then, and this is now. A new season, and a new European campaign means hope springs eternal. Like Engordany, La Fiorita have experienced heavy defeats in Europe. They conceded seven goals in Tallinn, Estonia back in 2014; the same number as Engordany lost by in Almaty, home to Kazakhstan Premier League Kairat – a city further east than Afghanistan and Mumbai in India.

A goal conceded for every 2,000 kilometres of a 15,000-kilometre round trip seems poor reward for their endeavours. But for Engordany, La Fiorita and all the other teams at the very bottom of the European pile, the chance to represent your club, your country on the international stage will mean accepting tough nights and red-eye flights to and from all and any points on the continent. For Engordany, the familiarity of a trip back to San Marino would have been most welcome after last season's far-flung exploits. What wasn't, however, was the heatwave that had engulfed most of Europe.

Bologna airport shimmered in a stifling heat haze. The air conditioning of the terminal gave way with the swoosh of an automatic door to a morning already creeping towards 40 degrees Celsius. A relentless sun bleached the world outside to a withering palate of yellow and white, blanching colour, reducing it to the washed-out state of a yet to be fully developed polaroid picture or some grainy image of Mars or Venus from a rover mission; life beyond the terminal doors seemingly just as unlikely to be able to exist as on those distant worlds.

But somehow, life was carrying on. Hire cars were being rented. Taxi drivers leant against walls in the shade, reluctant to move when potential passengers began to gather at their vehicle. Bus drivers idled, the passengers inside looking forlornly out the window, willing them to drive on so as a little air could begin to circulate from dropped windows.

Beyond the city, the road to San Marino wound along the agricultural spine of Italy's peninsula. Enormous sweeping vineyards as far as the eye could see, dusty olive groves, huge fields of sunflowers, all in various stages of readiness to provide the produce so closely associated with Italy. Turnings to Florence, the world famous Imola race circuit, Cesena and the coastal town of Rimini hinted at the rich history, culture and beauty awaiting beyond. Lost behind a wall of shimmering heat, these roads dissolved quickly into a blur that suggested sightseeing was not an option today. Or any other day while this unseasonably hot spell persisted.

Unless you are used to the journey, it is very hard to know when you have actually arrived in San Marino. A signpost off the motorway points the way, but the actual moment of entering the republic isn't recorded by a border post like in Andorra or a sign as in Liechtenstein. Indeed, the road signs for San Marino, the capital, suggest to the first-time visitor that you still haven't reached San Marino, the country, after you have, in fact, crossed its borders. These borders contain large tracts of farmland spread across the rolling hills of the Apennines, small communities of shuttered terracotta-coloured houses interconnected by ribbons of winding road and, seemingly, no people.

In the midday sun, San Marino is deserted. Pavements are empty. Shops are closed. No surprise as, after less than a minute walking around the ghost town of Serravalle, I felt myself beginning to flag. My desire to explore was tempered by the fear of passing out, fading away there and then in the sun-scorched gutter, only to be discovered hours later after the heatwave-induced siesta had ended.

Seeking refuge in a small airconditioned shopping mall, I found San Marino, or at the very least, the Sammarinese: clusters of people sipping cool drinks and chatting around benches, luxuriating in the fresh breeze, waiting out the very worst of the heat. Exploring indefinitely postponed, I did the next best thing, spreading out a map of the republic bought in a little book shop adjacent to the cool drinks stall. From it, the topography of San Marino revealed itself.

As the car had climbed and dipped across the hillsides to Serravalle, Monte Titano had appeared as an apparition in the middle distance, no more than ten kilometres further on, the signposts had advised. The birthplace of San Marino, it is a modest mountain standing 739 metres tall, but with a sheer, rocky façade presented to the rest of the world, it would have been a perfect refuge for Saint Marinus and a safe haven for a fledgling country to grow.

On each of the three peaks of Monte Titano stands a tower, three citadels that have come to symbolise the country they look out on. They appear on the national flag and crest and on most club badges of the 15 football teams that are dotted about their feet. Guaita, built in the 11th century, was joined by De La Fratta in the 13th and Montale in the 14th. The three flowers of San Marino, protectors of this tiny enclave and visible from every corner of the republic.

A republic whose true size appeared deceptive across the expanse of the map that draped over the edges of the bench. Despite Serravalle being located in the north of the country, and Monte Titano – and the capital San Marino, which clings to a series of switchbacks on the slopes of the mountain's far side – appearing at the southern edges of the map, there are only the ten kilometres between the two. Being able to look out a shopping mall window and see from one end of the country to the other, even on such a hazy day, really does bring into sharp focus just how small San Marino is, as well as the size of the sporting battle faced when taking on opposition from countries a hundred or a thousand times bigger.

Poring over the map, Montegiardino – the home of SP La Fiorita 1967 on the southern border – was only a few kilometres further on from the country's focal point, looking back at its capital that is, by quirk of fate, not even the largest town in the country. As with Vaduz in Liechtenstein being smaller than the neighbouring town of Schaan, San Marino in San Marino is usurped by both Borgo Maggiore and Serravalle in size. Its precipitous location on the slopes of Monte Titano are not ideal for expansion. Unlike Vaduz, however, the capital city of San Marino (population: 4,500) has also had to cede the location of the national football stadium to one of its larger neighbours – Serravalle (population: 9,500) – flat ground in the capital being at a premium.

No matter the desire to explore the three flowers of San Marino and the capital city nestled beneath them, the short walk in Serravalle from shopping mall to national stadium put paid to that. Fortified with a large bottle of water and the certainty that San Marino Stadium was less than a kilometre away, it quickly became a war of wills: the heat from the roads and pavement rising in relentless waves, feeling hotter than the stifling, lung-burning air above. The water bottle quickly emptied as the floodlights came into view. Crickets chirped among scorched grass at the roadside, which looked like it could combust at any moment, small basking lizards skittering for safety as I wandered on, the odd look from passers-by in cars confirming my worst fears: that this was no place to be walking.

Finding a spot of shade in the lee of a stadium wall, the tantalising sights and sounds of a sprinkler dowsing the pitch beyond, the ridiculous sight of a runner putting in a burst of speed on another circuit of the pitch only served to make my throat tighten further. This was no time to explore and absorb the magic of a never before seen football ground, no matter how much I wanted to. Beating a retreat was the only option, waiting for the evening beneath the shade of an olive tree on a hillside overlooking Monte Titano, sitting absolutely still, catching the faintest of breezes while watching the three towers beyond. The slightest of movements to pick up a replenished water bottle sent beads of sweat tumbling across my brow.

Beneath the setting sun of a late June evening, temperatures plunged to a balmy 37 degrees and San Marino slowly began to come to life. Pizzerias grew animated with the chatter of friends, cigarette smoke billowing out from under terrace umbrellas. And from somewhere beyond, a tantalising, unexpected sound could be heard: the crack of ball meeting bat, an unmistakeable resonance made familiar to me by classic baseball films such as *Bull Durham* and *Field of Dreams*. And just as in *Field of Dreams*, following those siren sounds between narrow streets of apartments that were also coming to life with the clatter of opening shutters and dinner plates being stacked, there came into view the most unlikely of sights: a purpose-built baseball stadium.

Streets thinned, finally revealing a neat Olympic complex, where pitchers threw to batters who cracked slower than game speed tosses high up and out across the baseball diamond. Fielders jogged to retrieve them, occasionally picking up speed to catch a flying ball in their mitt. The odd home run sailed up and out of the stadium, over the fence and scoreboard, the batter pausing in the shade of the bleachers that rose up behind the batting plate to watch its trajectory.

Home to the San Marino Baseball Club, a professional team competing in Italy's top-flight, these players being put through their paces have competed, with some success, in European baseball's equivalent of the Champions and Europa League. Hailing from a tiny micro-state doesn't necessarily mean that you will always be bottom of the sporting pile.

Balls sailed far and wide, all the while the smell of chlorine drifted from the sports complex next door, where there was an azure blue Olympic-sized swimming pool that looked too tempting for words. Surrounded by rooms and halls containing the Sammarinese boxing, badminton, Taekwondo and who knows what other sports associations, swimmers of differing abilities glided up and back while a pair of synchronised swimmers honed a routine. Sporting opportunity is not in short supply here. The dream of becoming an athlete, representing your nation, is a realistic one in San Marino, given the right amount of hard work and dedication.

The idyllic sounds of baseball practice and the rhythmic splashing of powerful freestyle strokes disappeared as a tannoy system sparked into life, crackling once, before music filled the air. Beyond the baseball ground and the sports complex, the San Marino stadium was coming to life. Something special was about to happen.

Floodlights burnt up into a brilliant blue sky, the relentless evening sun not yet ready to fall behind Monte Titano; the oblong phalanx of bulbs in each corner of the stadium added to the brilliant glare of a sun scorched day. Rebel rousing anthems echoed from the PA system, pulsing in time with the sprinklers that chugged a steady path across the pitch, while a young boy, hands grasped to the railings outside attempted to get as good a view as he could.

There is something primal, almost religious in the emotion of catching sight of a football stadium. To the lover of the game, the football ground holds the key to all the magic of the experience. All the sights and sounds of match day contained within are so familiar, so fundamental that they can send you back decades to people and places long since lost. Moments of skill and endeavour, passages of symbiotic play that send a surge of adrenalin racing through you. The smell of tobacco smoke, the clack of turnstiles, the roar of the crowd, the bustle outside. It is home to a tangle of intangible emotions and unwritten, unspoken ritual. It is simply home, even though you may have never set eyes on it before, so familiar are the timeless dimensions marked out in white; the two goals, four sets of floodlights, all set behind exterior walls, towering stands and terraces.

They draw you like moths to a flame, a siren song to opportunity, that maybe this day, this season might be *our* season. You can't help but be consumed by them, whether they are yours or not. The fact that they are someone's – that they mean as much to those you have never met and never will meet, as yours does to you – is reason enough to pause for a time to take it all in. It is this magic that compels this young boy to press himself against the gates of San Marino Stadium, his oversized La Fiorita shirt billowing around his knees.

In truth, we all become little children once more at that first sight of the football ground, familiar or not. In older age, we somehow restrain ourselves from pressing up against the gates, hard though it may be. And in that boy, I see myself, peering through the gates at Bootham Crescent, the home of York City, one summer holiday long, long ago and catching a glimpse of the compact box-shaped stands between cracks in the turnstile gates. A sliver of green pitch, floodlights rising above the cramped streets that hemmed it in, holiday money spent on bundles of the previous season's programmes, the previous season's shirt. They are treasures from a precious, albeit modest and largely anonymous institution destined to linger at the foot of the football ladder.

Watching that boy, I remember pressing up against the gates of the national stadium in Luxembourg, having convinced my parents to take a short detour en-route to another holiday, in order to spend a few moments wondering at it. Or at an aborted attempt to track down a lower league ground somewhere in Spain, an hour walking dusty back streets resulting in nothing more than an exasperated family. It was all worth it, feeling the same awe as at a snatched glance of my footballing homes, at the Dell in Southampton, at the stand in Salisbury as my grandparents car drove by – even better if it was on a non-match day, where I could have these magical places all to myself, for a moment at least.

It doesn't matter the size. If the football ground matters to some, then it is as precious as the grandest cathedral that the sport has to offer. Which is why the San Marino stadium, the pinnacle of Sammarinese football, was as deserving of this little boy's awe as anywhere else in the footballing universe. And as he disappeared into the stand, craning his neck to catch that first glimpse, I couldn't help but recall the little Kosovan girl on a storm-tossed October night in the Faroe Islands, excitedly running up and down rows of seats, waiting for the heroes of her national team to come out to warm up. For both of them, their respective nights at two distant points on the European footballing map will no doubt form the foundations for a lifetime of dedication. These two moments might be one of the first that they will each recall, relive with their children and their children's children while taking them to their first game. The night their love ignited.

Despite the setting sun and the late hour, there was little respite from the heat in the stand; four members of the medical team on duty took up the offer of a programme with no intention of reading it, instead fashioning them into fans, closing their eyes as the self-propelled breeze washed across them.

San Marino Stadium is small and functional, though immaculately maintained. One main stand looks across the pitch at a smaller block of seating that is only opened to accommodate visiting national team supporters. Behind one goal stands a fence, the other an expanse of grass, across which red-faced ball-boys raced to retrieve wayward balls from Engordany's warm-up session, the heat of the day tempering their initial enthusiasm.

As kick-off approached, the main stand remained conspicuously empty, the majority preferring to linger by the kiosks near the turnstiles with their seemingly endless supply of beer, pizza slices, ice cream and bottles of water.

La Fiorita players looked up from their warm-up to see if they could spot loved ones among the rows of seats that stretched beneath a beautiful wooden vaulted roof. Among them, number 16 and La Fiorita captain Danilo Rinaldi smiled and waved at the little boy who had been pressed against the gate earlier. The boy jumped up and down, waving frantically next to his mother, the number 16 on his oversized replica shirt suggesting that this night will take on extra resonance for him, being the night that he got to see his daddy play in Europe.

Rinaldi, born in Argentina but a naturalised Sammarinese courtesy of his grandfather, is one of two San Marino internationals in the La Fiorita side. Having left Argentina back in 2008, after a season playing for La Emilia in the fourth tier of Argentinian football, Rinaldi has gone on to represent San Marino 40 times. His lone international strike to date came in a home friendly defeat to Malta back in 2012, and like the majority of his playing days for club and country, it came at a time when his son would have either not been born or was an infant. At 33 years of age, and with the best years of his playing career behind him, the opportunity to play on such a stage in front of a son old enough to remember the occasion must be a precious gift.

He was not the only La Fiorita player making the most of the moment. Damiano Tommasi, former Italian international, Serie A winner with Roma, who played all four of Italy's matches at the 2002 FIFA World Cup finals, warmed up alongside Rinaldi. Having played more than 260 times for Roma in Italy's top-flight, and 25 times for his country, Tommasi went on to play in La Liga in Spain for Levante, before a short nine-game stint at QPR in England. His career finally came to an end in 2009 at the age of 35 after a year in China with Tianjin TEDA. Or he thought his career had come to an end.

In 2015, after six years out of the game came the opportunity to sign for La Fiorita for their Europa League matches against Vaduz of Liechtenstein. Two appearances, and two defeats, 5-0 and 5-1, were tempered with a Tommasi goal in the away leg – the first and only goal scored by La Fiorita in European competition. Four years later and the offer came again.

So, at the tender age of 45, ten years after retirement, the opportunity to put the boots on once more in competitive action had proven too tempting to turn down, and Tommasi found himself warming up on that stifling night in Serravalle. Though this time he would start on the bench.

As the players came out for kick-off and the stand quickly filled, the heat tempered even the exuberance of the handful of Engordany supporters who had made the long trip. Jumping up and down and cheering as the Andorran players applauded their effort, the exertion in the clawing heat had them quickly settle back down into their seats. Even at nearly 9.00pm, the heatwave was still on top.

But despite the heat, the game began with probing runs and passes, testing the fortitude of each defence. And while Engordany shaded possession and technical ability, passing the ball neatly about the park with ease, the team from the worst league in Europe, the worst footballing nation in the world, held their own. Midfielder Andrea Bracaletti closed down space, snapped into tackles, and drove forward, before whipping wicked crosses into the Engordany penalty area. Danilo Rinaldi threatened to cause damage on the end of those crosses, holding up balls until the cavalry arrived, chasing down lost causes, just in case.

Just as at Claggan Park, Fort William, more than ten months earlier, the outward perception of others means nothing once that white line has been crossed. Pride, desire, a professionalism from those whose pay packet would suggest otherwise can close most gaps in ability or attitude. It is how San Marino survive in international football, looking for strong performances over points. Their pride in representing their country and their people inspires them to near superhuman effort.

Just as Odmar Færø and his Faroes' side strive for small steps forward and positives from every game, so too do the Sammarinese. And in La Fiorita's performance, the San Marino faithful had plenty to feel positive about. A scrambled Aarón Sánchez goal for Engordany midway through the first half provided the difference between the two sides at half-time.

As the stand drained away for the ice cream and cool drinks of the kiosks below, darkness crept across San Marino. The three towers of Monte Titano dissolved into the night, a lone beacon on top of each marking their position among the blinking lights of Serravalle and Borgo Maggiore. They were all made stronger as the floodlights of the baseball stadium in the distance cut out, practice complete for the day.

Among the growing darkness, the heat became more oppressive, claustrophobic even. The fresher air of night was not forthcoming, leaving a breathless pressure cooker of sweltering heat caught up beneath the floodlights. A cloud of gnats and what seemed like a dense fog of steam hung suspended above the pitch. A sticky pall of thick heat blanketed everything and everyone, turning air to soup, draining the energy of player and supporter alike.

With the second half came an unsurprising reduction in tempo, the stifling humidity draining legs and minds. Passes became a little more slack in their precision. Runs to chase them down faltered on heavy legs, pulling up long before they would have in the first half, shirts clinging to torsos like a second skin. Neither side was used to playing in temperatures in the high thirties at 10.00pm. Time for the cavalry in Damiano Tommasi and La Fiorita's second San Marino international – the 28 times capped Adolfo Hirsch.

Ten years after retirement, Tommasi could still pick out a pass, a pass no one else on the pitch had the vision to see. With nearly his first touch, he found a cross-pitch, defence-splitting pass to Bracaletti, whose driven cross caused chaos in the Engordany defence, scrambling it away as if their lives depended on it. Their European footballing lives most definitely did.

Despite the injection of Tommasi, ultimately it would be the heatwave that would win out. Hirsch's energy in midfield, that saw him flitting about the pitch like the swarms of gnats above, soon drained away. A frantic 20-minute cameo burned him out, so as, at the final whistle, his hands dropped to his knees in an attempt to suck more arid air into his heaving lungs.

In the face of a narrow defeat, there was little despair from the La Fiorita camp. There was, after all, a second leg in Andorra the following week. The dream was still alive as they took the applause of the crowd at a well-fought match; Rinaldi's son still waving at his dad frantically, clutching his programme with his dad in it for dear life. A treasure for all time.

Despite defeat, the evening had been a success – in igniting young children's imaginations, the future of Sammarinese football. In representing their club and country in Europe with pride and valour, and coming away with just the one goal loss against a team from a nation 71 places higher in the FIFA world rankings than San Marino, it had been an exercise in dispelling the throwaway tag of being from the worst footballing nation in the world. It had been a small-time celebration of identity and belonging among a round of largely anonymous fixtures, ignored by the vast majority of football fans the continent over.

No matter how obscure, how marginalised this fixture, like the six other preliminary round ties, it mattered. Its meaning was etched into the memories of players and supporters alike. Pennants and photographs proudly would be displayed on clubhouse walls, forever celebrating the time their team played in European football.

From the hill above Serravalle, the floodlights of San Marino Stadium still burned up into the night a good hour after the final whistle. Surrounded by the lights of the town, it burned brighter still, a modern-day sporting epicentre to the republic by night, just as the three flowers of Monte Titano were the spiritual centre by day.

An irrelevance to many, an inconvenience to others, to those that know, who care to look, football in San Marino is just as passionate, adored and revered as anywhere else – from Barcelona to Buckie Thistle – no matter its lowly ranking. Because, as we all know, football is simply bigger than that.

The following week, at the Estadi Comunal in Andorra la Vella, it would be another tale of so near yet so far for La Fiorita. An early Engordany goal by Nikola Zugić gave the visitors a mountain to climb, needing at least two away goals where they had only ever scored one in their previous 16 European matches. To add insult to injury, when Adolfo Hirsch believed he had scored one of those two goals, doubling La Fiorita's all-time European tally midway through the second half, it was later agonisingly recorded by the referee, UEFA and the history books as an own goal by Engordany keeper Jesús Coca, leaving Damiano Tommasi, for another year at least, as the only La Fiorita player to have ever scored in Europe.

It is such fine margins that separate Sammarinese football from their European minnow bedfellows. Where the similarly minute populations of Liechtenstein and Gibraltar have recorded competitive national team victories, San Marino have fallen just shy, that proven goalscorer remaining elusive, that moment of magic thundering back off the post rather than nestling in the back of the net. Fine margins. A competitive Nations League campaign suggests as much. But with every defeat, every competitive European campaign at club level, they get closer. How long until that first ever competitive victory? Only time will tell. It is not through a lack of passion or endeavour, that is for sure.

For Engordany, a 2-1 win at home and a 3-1 aggregate victory saw them progress for the second year running, this time needing a mere 9,000 kilometre round-trip to face and lose 6-0 to Dinamo Tbilisi of Georgia in the first qualifying round.

Just the 1,500 kilometres per goal conceded this time, and another tough lesson in European football. But like their preliminary bedfellows, a wonderful adventure and test against clubs and players with far greater resources. A test that they will strive to qualify for next year. Because hope springs eternal. And for the minnow institutions of La Fiorita and Engordany, maybe next year could be *their* year.

And if it isn't, it won't be through a lack of desire and passion, which is on display in spades down among the clubs in the preliminary round. Because there is no club across Europe, no matter its size or bulging trophy cabinet, that can lay claim to more of either commodity.

CHAPTER NINE

From Barcelona to Buckie Thistle – Buckie Thistle

AFTER A LONG, hot, football-free summer, the day of the new season's fixtures being released is a dizzying affair. A crisp, pristine sheet of paper, on which the dates and opponents for the upcoming season scroll down, maps out your destiny for the following nine and a half months. Away trips are pencilled in, Boxing and New Year's Days, bank holidays arranged around its contents.

Though published online and updated weekly, that initial, hastily procured sheet of paper endures, holding as it does that first surge of expectancy, that blind faith that this year, above all others, could be *your* team's year. Unfolded and perused countless times before being tucked safely away in a wallet, or a favoured pocket, its folds become threadbare over time, ultimately failing as its overuse reduces it to a kind of sporting paper doily, a frail spider's web of segments. Dates and names become obscured, disintegrating like the hopes and dreams of that expectant summers' day do with the reality of poor refereeing decisions and even poorer defending once the season begins. Draws and defeats sully the optimism with which that sheet was first received, until one particularly rain-sodden post-match view when it fails com-pletely. Dissolving into a wet, shredded, unreadable pulp, the sheet is consigned to a bin during your trudge off the terraces – a metaphor for those dreams of an unlikely league title or, at the very least, an improvement on last season. It is the hope that kills you.

But on those long, lazy days of summer, that first glimpse of a fresh set of fixtures represents a hope for something better. We cannot help but dream. Even those who, on the face of it, should have been battered into submission by the season just gone. People like Sam Lees and his fellow Fort William committee members and supporters.

Having met Sam at Claggan Park in the early weeks of the 2018/19 season, little did he or I realise that that 1-1 draw against Strathspey

Thistle would constitute one of only two positive results for the Fort all year. A 3-3 draw at home to Clachnacuddin in November would be the only other time that Fort William failed to lose. Finishing the season on -7 points, and with a goal difference of -224, Fort William became the first senior team in Britain to finish with a minus points tally – and the pub quiz answer that they didn't want to be.

Not having won a league game for two years and four months (a 2-1 victory over Strathspey Thistle on 12 April 2017 being the last, one of three victories that season that saw the Fort finish two points above the Strathy Jags in second last place), you would imagine Sam and his fellow band of volunteers, who had kept Fort William afloat against all the odds the summer before, would be on their knees after such a traumatic season and a learning curve as steep as Ben Nevis itself. After all, Sam and the committee had only a matter of weeks to prepare for the season, with five players and no manager. Defeats in double figures and the low teens were not uncommon, and that lost player registration form resulting in a nine-point deduction had them on course for a hiding to nothing barely a month into the season.

Better all that, however, than no club to support at all. And it was that thought that had Sam in a typically stoic, glass half full attitude (that had steered Fort William through the seemingly impossible waters of last season), when looking back on it.

'From my own personal point of view, it's been a 50/50 season,' said Sam of a campaign in which his team conceded 245 goals in 34 games. 'We have made a lot of improvements off the park with the clubhouse and as a committee. Also, as the season went on, I started to see some of the boys become a lot better at Highland League level, and I feel they can play well if we give them the right backing.

'There has been massive upheaval – the changing of management and club secretary, which is a massive off-field role. It's been harder than I expected, but nevertheless a very worthwhile cause in my opinion.

'As for next season,' he went on, 'we obviously need to strengthen quite a bit, and I feel we can manage that but not to the extent where we won't be fighting at the bottom of the league. But I hope the heavy defeats won't continue with such regularity. I can see us being on the end of a few big scores still. Maybe twice or three times over the season.

'I'm hopeful for a couple of wins, to get that monkey off our back. The longer it goes on the harder it seems to break that. I'd love to see us properly competing in games against the bigger sides too!

'We have a long way to go and we are just at the beginning. Getting through last season has been nothing short of amazing given the knocks we've taken. But interest in the club is at an all-time high, and results changing for the better will only help that.'

Whatever the destiny of Sam's beloved Fort William, there is something beautiful and timeless in the knowledge that, as the Highland League and countless others around the world begins to grind back into life after a summer being mothballed, Sam and his counterparts are there and will always be there. They volunteer far more time than they can spare for *their* club, no matter the results out on the pitch.

It is easy to imagine Sam with a broom, a pot of paint, making good his position by the entrance gates to Claggan Park, sweeping the little ticket booth, giving it a fresh coat of amber and black paint in readiness for the new season, a season where he would continue to welcome all through that narrow cut in a sweeping bank of tall firs. His face is the first seen by those entering the Highland League's very own Narnia, the majestic Ben Nevis towering behind him beyond the far goal. It is easy to imagine because similar acts of selfless dedication are playing out across the Highland League in preparation of the first game of the season.

Beneath the balmy summer sun of late July-early August, kits are being washed and dried at Dudgeon Park, home of Brora Rangers. Clothes horses litter the players' tunnel, while towels are draped across the seats of the small main stand. There is no such luxury as tumble dryers in the Highland League.

At Mackessack Park, Rothes, four old men wander beneath the hot sun, painting lines on the immaculate pitch, checking the nets, sweeping the terraces, scrubbing clean the seats in the stand. The rich, sweet smell of cut grass and the sit-on mower not yet stowed away in its shed suggest that they have been at it all day. Nevertheless, sounds of laughter echo about this compact little ground in the Spey Valley, lined by tall oak trees, a steel reclamation yard and low lying, moss-covered walls. Clearly no labour is too much when it is a labour of love. The only witnesses to their efforts on this idyllic day are the fog of gnats lingering among the lowest boughs of the old oaks.

To the north, sprinklers hiss and skitter across the pitch at Grant Park, Lossiemouth. Gulls squawk and drift on the warm currents above the home of the 1940 Central Highland Emergency War League winners, before coasting out to the beach and yellow sands across the way. Summer holidays are in full swing along the Moray Firth, complete with ice creams and windbreakers, buckets and spades and short, sharp dips in the chill water. From the hush of an empty football ground, you can just hear the squeals of those braving the water, the animated shouts and chatter of scores of children at play. The smell of suntan lotion and fish and chips linger in the air. This is a far cry from the wind-battered days of winter, where Grant Park often rivals Harmsworth Park up in Wick as a venue for debilitating gales and boomerang goal-kicks.

Along the Moray Firth coast, small, picturesque fishing towns and villages huddle around the protective arm of their harbour. The briny smell of seaweed is ripe on the air at low tide, while fishing boats idle dockside among large stacks of lobster and crab pots, bobbing on sparkling waters dotted with jellyfish and schools of minnows. Vast tranches of kelp undulate on sandy sea-beds below, twisting on the currents.

Beyond, thick-walled fishermen's cottages weave and tangle about a network of narrow alleyways and roads that seem too small for modern day motoring. From Lossiemouth to Banff and Macduff, via Findochty, Portknockie, Cullen, Portsoy and Whitehills, a vision of a century-old existence plays out, all with the harbour at its heartbeat.

Among it all sits Deveronvale Football Club. Looking out at a swathe of sandy beach and open sea that suggests this is another venue that is no stranger to wild winter Highland League football, Deveronvale's Princess Royal Park ground sits in perfect neutrality between the two communities of Banff and Macduff that it serves. Named after the river Deveron that splits the two, the Vale's preparations for the new season are almost complete.

The club's minibus sits outside ready for the long trip up to Wick for the first away game of the season, while the chatter inside the function room in the bowels of a neat, modern stand betrays the excitement for the footballing year ahead. High up, on the side of the stand, looking out at the car park below is a large Christmas decoration. Somewhere within, a corresponding switch is waiting to illuminate this festive scene of Santa and an elf. It could be taken down every year, but in an institution run by volunteers, there are bigger and more pressing jobs. So, it sits dulled, biding its time... For some unlucky volunteer, a more pressing job will be to clear the carpet of feathers, and possibly worse, that litters the Princess Royal Park's playing surface. Whatever happened here, it wasn't pretty, and the circling gulls above screech a lament to what looks to be a fallen comrade or two below.

Deveronvale are, however, clearly not the only club to suffer from the interference of gulls. Bellslea Park, Fraserburgh is the last Highland League port of call on the Moray Firth coast. Indeed, all roads end at Fraserburgh. Beyond it lies the North Sea, wild fishing grounds, off-shore oil rig platforms and, ultimately, Norway.

Its football club sits beneath the shadow of a large, austere, neo-gothic church that looms over the far corner flag and a pitch littered with makeshift scarecrows. Upturned buckets on large metal stakes join a more sophisticated set-up of a bird-shaped kite, swirling and swooping about the centre circle on a flimsy pole. Beyond the old main stand, lined with wooden benches not too dissimilar to the pews that pack the church looming over its shoulder, lies the reason for such deterrents.

While every small village and town before it looks out on harbours dotted with small, two- or three-man fishing boats, Fraserburgh harbour is a vision of industrial scale fishing. Large vessels that could stay out for days, weeks if needed, thrum and idle alongside support ships for the oil rigs out in the North Sea. Their wheelhouses just visible on a rising tide from the far side of Bellslea Park, their offcuts and fishing waste must be rich pickings for the clouds of impatient gulls that follow the ships back to port. And when the fishing boats sit dockside, a freshly seeded football pitch could provide a handy alternative food source. But thanks to these deterrents, not today.

The lush Bellslea Park turf basked in the hot sun, mown and tended to near perfection. More bowling green than football pitch, it was ready for the long season that was about to begin. A season that would, for me, begin at another of the Moray coast's Highland League towns – Buckie.

Situated halfway between Lossiemouth and Banff, the earliest mention of the settlement of Buckie came in 1362 when 'the lands of Rove Bucky in le Awne were leased to the Vicar of Fordyce'.[4] This was at a time when much of the region lay under the vast Forest of Awne that stretched down towards the Speyside communities of the Cairngorms.

Possibly due to the forest, Buckie found itself spreading along the coast rather than developing out, creating distinct communities within a community with Nether Buckie, Cluny Harbour, Seatown and Buckpool spreading out either side of Buckie itself. Cluny Harbour was constructed by Robert Louis Stevenson's family business, who had built the Noss Head Lighthouse north of Wick, though no record exists of whether Robert ever visited while the work was taking place and, if he did, whether he enjoyed the experience more than his time in 'breezy, breezy' Wick.

Like the rest of the Moray coast, Buckie has always relied on fishing and its port to keep its economy in rude health. Indeed, in 1913, Buckie had the largest steam drifter fleet in all of Scotland. However, as the fishing industry went into decline during the 20th century, Buckie, like every fishing community, scrambled to adapt and survive. And while the fishing fleet is a mere fraction of what it once was, fish processing is still a major employer in the town. Fish factories and smoke houses are dotted along the harbour road, servicing the catch fresh off the boats. Employees winding down after their shift pause in the sun, still kitted out in hair nets and large aprons, chatting with colleagues before getting changed and slipping away into the town.

With a reduced customer base, the Buckie shipyard beyond the smoke houses has moved away from solely making and repairing the fishing fleet. Its main operation these days is repairing and refitting RNLI lifeboats for most of its UK fleet.

As with every small community along the Scottish coast, the downturn in fishing was offset somewhat by the booming offshore oil industry. A significant number of Buckie's 8,000 population find work in this way, though the town missed the opportunity for a greater involvement when the development of Cluny Harbour to

---

4 From *Buckie and District*, Dr Cramond, 1936. Retrieved from www.buckieherirtage.org.

accommodate supply vessels failed to materialise. Buckie's loss was Wick and Fraserburgh's gain.

Buckie, like most of the coastal communities of northern Scotland, is a close-knit town where people are welcomed into shops and cafés by their first name. Like those around it, Buckie is an old town of old, heavy-set buildings, constructed in the same mould as the Granite City of Aberdeen. On a warm summer's day, the old shops of Buckie's main strip gleam along the coast as far as the eye can see – a drag racer's dream. But in the storms of winter, rain will stain everything a slick soup of brown and black, facing down the bleak weather with an appropriate moodscape.

Steep steps that lead down to the harbour road offer a little sanctuary for most of the town from the North Sea winter swell. However, there can be no escaping the gales and driving rain. Like Wick, Buckie and the communities of the Moray coast, the Highland League is no place for those not hardy enough to face down a North Sea winter, something that feels a world away this balmy August afternoon of shimmering seas and glinting windows, lazing in deckchairs in front gardens, looking out at a glassy dead calm. This is a far cry from the concerned glances out of those same front room windows during storm season, watching the fishing boats lurch and drop from view among the churning waves, struggling to reach the safety of the harbour.

A small café just off the main strip was doing decent business, tourists and locals mingling over cups of tea and sandwiches, while a book on a shelf of local interest titles reminded me of my notorious connection to this small corner of Scotland.

Peterhead: The Inside Story of Scotland's Toughest Prison by Robert Jeffrey tells the story of Peterhead Prison – a short hop further down the coast from Fraserburgh and home for an undetermined number of years to my great grandfather, the bigamist Samuel Alexander Omand. Known as the 'Hate Factory', Peterhead Prison became a brutal, cold and windswept institution, having been built in the late 19th century initially to house prisoners working on the construction of Peterhead Harbour.

That bigamy could find you in such a hell may seem a little harsh now but, in the 1940s – during the war effort – the rule of law, in conjunction with the morality of the Presbyterian Kirk of Scotland, found Samuel in contempt of both legal statutes and the word of God. To Peterhead with you.

While feeling a degree of sympathy for any human being finding themselves in such terrifying conditions, the damage caused and the effect it had on my grandmother, sending her out on a tumultuous life, had me buy the book. Some morbid curiosity to learn just how bad my great grandfather got the better of me, possibly as well as a desire to close a chapter of my family's history long after all protagonists and those affected by Samuel's actions had passed out of the sphere of catharsis.

Outside, the odd flash of green and white began to slip past the window, leaning into the incline that rose up and away from the seafront. Hooped shirts and scarves made for Victoria Park beyond, the home of Buckie Thistle, a characterful ground celebrating its centenary year. As if following a siren song, it was impossible not to pay up in the café and join the procession, the anticipation of a new season adding an extra spring in the step of three or four generations of Thistle supporters that made their way to the park.

As with every other side in the Highland League, the history of Buckie Thistle is a rich vein of stories, often handed down from one generation to the next on walks to and from the ground, helping to convert the recipients to a lifetime supporting the Jags.

Formed in 1889, though the exact date has been lost to the fog of time, Buckie Thistle played in the Banff and District League for 20 years, before being accepted into the Highland League in 1909. Some say that the green and white hoops came from Glasgow Celtic, who donated a strip to the fledgling club. However, the prevailing theory as to the colour scheme comes from when Thistle absorbed another local club into its fold in 1908 – Buckie Wednesday – who wore green and white hooped shirts. The strip is a mostly forgotten nod to Wednesday, whose colours, if nothing else, remain.

In 1916, Thistle goalkeeper and Canadian International Alex 'Charlie' Davidson, Buckie's first ever Highland League keeper, lost his life during World War I, killed in an offensive at Ancre, the Great War affecting even the smallest of far-flung communities like Buckie. Thistle would lose one of their own in World War II as well, when George Cormack was killed at Anzio in 1944.

Among such sadness also came triumph, with 11 Highland League titles won, the first in 1920, the last in 2017. Complimenting that, eight Highland League Cups have been paraded around Victoria Park between 1954 and 2012.

An even greater source of anecdote and pride shared on walks up to the ground derives from a Scottish Cup fourth round replay at Hampden Park in October 1954. A 2-1 victory over Queen's Park not only sent the Jags into the fifth round but also into the record books. That win was the first and only time that a non-league club has won a competitive match against a professional team at the national stadium, the names of goal scorers Alex Stewart and Willie Cowie forever etched into the fabric of the town and the club. Their names now echo across conversations down the decades, snatched retellings of that glory day wafting through café doors and shop frontages, followed, no doubt, by even more animated tales of when Scottish Cup holders Falkirk came to town to defend their crown in 1958. At 1-1, Thistle had what the home support believed to be a legitimate goal chalked off, only for Falkirk to go up the other end and score what would be the winner. More than 60 years on and the decision still rankles.

It is not only the great and the controversial that fuel the oral history of Buckie on walks up from the town, sat in the stand at Victoria Park, in the queue for the tea hut or leant against the perimeter fence around the pitch. Every supporter the length and breadth of the nation finds themselves, as a perverse badge of honour and dedication, basking in being there at the club's lowest point – through thin and thin as it is described the country over.

For the Jags, that nadir came in the 1969/70 season, in the middle of a 52-year spell without a league title, when Thistle failed a single win all season, conceding 146 goals in the process. To say 'I was there' for the great title seasons or cup exploits only rings whole when accompanied by tales of humbling defeats far from home, an unblemished attendance record during that long, long season of 69/70. It is an important tale to be told to the younger kin – it can never just be about triumph and victory. The love of a team goes way beyond that.

Victoria Park sits looking down at the town and the North Sea. The back to the main stand, which spills out into a road hugging right up against it, acts as a windbreak on a wild day. Protecting the middle third of the pitch from the worst of the winter storms, the goalmouths get no such luck. It is easy to imagine huddled keepers cursing their positional choice, trying to stand firm among bitter gales, supporters pinned to the back of the covered terracing on the far side of the pitch, faces raw from the freezing easterlies.

That day, however, a flag fluttered lazily on a flagpole above the main stand. A steward wandered from the players' entrance, stepping out into the road to stand in the sun for a few moments before returning to his voluntary position. Laughter and screams from children playing on a set of swings and a roundabout in the play park came from across the way. Those supporters decked in shirts and scarves who had just walked up from town stopped to chat with a few club officials stood by the turnstiles. It was a scene of timeless familiarity, a routine more than 100 years old.

Though having never set eyes on it before, it felt like I had because of the little unspoken rituals that play out the same up and down the country: turning up at a certain time, paying through a specific turnstile, taking up a spot in the stand or on the terracing. Why? It's where we always go. It's what we always do. My parents first took me to this spot. Their parents took them. And I stand here too, with my children, grandchildren. Unspoken rituals knitted deep into the unconscious.

It was hard not to think back to my own Victoria Park, former home to Salisbury FC, my grandfather's team. It all came back as if it were yesterday, those sights and sounds, routines, familiar faces. It was a refuge from the outside world for a short 90 minutes or so. It also was *the* world, in its importance and meaning. And though my Victoria Park no longer hosts Salisbury, it feels comforting, despite being more than 600 miles from home, that this Victoria Park is still going strong. One hundred years not out. Here's to the next 100. It may not be Barcelona or Camp Nou but Buckie Thistle and Victoria Park – to those who call it theirs – is every bit as important. And they would rather be nowhere else.

Through the narrow turnstile, Victoria Park was a vision of devotion. Painted perimeter walls, tea huts, terrace barriers and toilet blocks gleamed a brilliant white. It had been a busy off-season for someone. At the centre of it all, the pitch basked in the sun a resplendent emerald green, while the unforgettable smell of deep heat emanated from the changing rooms somewhere within the bowels of the stand. Mingling with the rich smell of freshly painted and varnished old wooden stairs that lead up to the rows of benches sheltering beneath the vaulted corrugated roof of the main stand, it is a footballing scent for all time.

From the images littering the match programme celebrating 100 years of Victoria Park, it looked like the stand had hardly changed during its long service taking care of Buckie's support. A team photo taken in front of it back in 1939 could have been taken last year, but for the dated hair styles and heavy-looking kit. How many times those old stairs had been treated, varnished, painted a vibrant yellow and green over the years no one could surely know. That they had seen every kick of every game, possibly right back to 1919, does not seem outlandish – a small-time monument to the Jags and all who believe in it.

Like the stories told on the way to the ground, there are countless tales echoing about Victoria Park and other grounds of a similar stature. Like the folk songs of the Faroe Islands kept Faroese culture alive when the written language had been supressed, these tales of people and events, past and present, when overheard help create a joyous patchwork of the Jags' history. From the fallen heroes of Alex Davidson and George Cormack lost at war to the great cup games, title wins and that infamous low of the 1969/70 season, stories also mingle with the seemingly banal: the selfless, often thankless people behind the scenes who do what they do to enable a game of football to take place. People like Sandra Paterson, who volunteered to help out in the tea hut for the club's centenary celebration match against Celtic some 30 years ago, who has been ever present since. Thirty years' voluntary service, without fail, every game. In the tea hut or up in the boardroom, Sandra has worked it all. She is one name plucked from a pool of similarly selfless and anonymous characters who drive this small-town institution forward.

Others range from the old woman barely tall enough to see out over the counter of the tea hut, smiling and remarking 'Aye, you're sweet enough as it is' whenever someone turns down the offer of sugar in their brew, to the two women tending the club shop, proudly displaying replica kits, scarves and pennants, welcoming all and sundry into their cramped but immaculate domain; from the barman pulling pints in the clubhouse behind the goal to the two old-timers from the supporter's club next door, sweeping the floor to their portacabin home, displaying photos of games long gone on the walls and nabbing anyone who strays too close, asking in a gentle but an accusatory tone as to why their latest prey hasn't already signed up for the supporter's club.

And as the players came out for their warm-ups and attention began to turn pitch-side, none of it could happen without the man on the turnstile, Sandra in the boardroom, those in the tea hut, club shop, bar, supporter's club, the groundsman, the small army of painters who had given Victoria Park a fresh coat for the season ahead: people who quietly went about their voluntary way, joining those who went before them. The ghosts of dedication past are captured among the crowds in sepia-tinged photographs within the pages of the match programme.

Buckie Thistle and those who dedicate much of their time to Victoria Park are by no means the exception. Every club in the Highland League relies on a similarly enthusiastic bunch to operate. And every club has its own rich history littered with success, failure and a tangle of glorious foibles that have become institution. None more so than Buckie's opponents, Strathspey Thistle.

Formed in 1993 to offer winter football to the players of the Strathspey and Badenoch Welfare League that ran through the summer months, the Strathy Jags were meant to play in yellow and red stripes. However, less than 48 hours before their first game in the Morayshire Junior League, their kit that had been bought from a company in Liverpool hadn't arrived. Their secretary flew down to collect them in time for the big game but picked up the wrong bag of kit. Upon opening it in the dressing room before the first match, the team discovered a blue strip instead. And Strathspey Thistle have worn blue ever since, the initial colour scheme abandoned, possibly to avoid the blushes of the club secretary.

A year is a long time in football, and the Strathspey Thistle team who turned out against Sam Lees' Fort William at Claggan Park a year earlier were not the Strathspey Thistle warming up in Buckie. Where Lees had noted that you never knew what Strathspey team would turn up on their travels, so erratic was their away form, there was no such concern now. A year of consolidation and rebuilding had created a consistent, stubborn team who, while never troubling the top half of the table, could more than hold their own against any Highland League opposition. A Buckie Thistle team with aspirations of the league title now that Cove had moved on warmed up with a focus that suggested this would be no walk in the park. And so it proved to be.

As the old timers from the supporter's club portacabin gingerly dragged plastic garden chairs pitch-side, somehow managing chair, walking stick and pint without calamity, a match of real intensity began. Early season promise at a year to remember meant both sides raced out of the blocks. Ripples of applause and shouts of encouragement rolled down the terracing, amplified about the stanchions of the stand, calling out players by their first name.

'Great run, Sam. Super cross, Scotty. Get in amongst them, Mark.'

They would, after all, stop being their heroes in green and white hoops and become friends, neighbours, work colleagues once more come a 4.45pm.

Beneath the relentless sun, a game of ebb and flow played out, though the home side boasted more of the latter than the former. Rows of supporters by the tea hut looked on, hands shielded their eyes from the glare, while the latest customer smiled at being called sweet enough by the diminutive tea urn operative.

It was an idyllic scene of bright sunshine and long shadows, effervescent football played with skill and intensity. Captivating to all present bar a couple of young children who, having been the mascots that led the team out, played chase in their brand new Buckie kits between the transfixed supporters. And at half-time, as both sets of players trudged back into the shade of the dressing rooms, it felt a spectacle far greater than the goalless score-line suggested.

As the supporter's club old-timers abandoned their seats, making for their post inside the portacabin door, and the queues to the tea hut grew, and as more filed back into the clubhouse for a quick pint, while others stretched in the main stand and gingerly made their way down the timeless wooden steps for a 15-minute wander, I found myself transported back to that cold, wet, fruitless book-signing more than 18 months earlier – to that man so dismissive of the Highland League: 'Don't bother. It's awful. Terrible. Not worth the trouble.' Never had I felt so glad in ignoring another's advice.

Over five long trips north, covering 14 towns and grounds of the Highland League, watching six matches featuring ten different teams, I had found nothing but joy among Britain's most northerly senior football league. The passion among the stands and boardrooms of the Highland League were matched only by the endeavour and guile out on the pitch. Skill, drama, blood and thunder encounters any given Saturday litter the Highlands from Wick in the far north to Fort William in the west, Inverurie in the east to Forres and Buckie along the Moray coast. Maybe one day someone might drag that man from the book-signing to a game at Brora or Clachnacuddin, Fraserburgh or Nairn, and what he would witness might possibly change his opinion. It is a pity he wasn't present for the second half at Buckie and 45 minutes that he would surely have had to concede were well worth the trouble.

From the restart Buckie went for the kill, with devilish slide rule passes splitting the Strathy Jags' backline and wing play twisting and turning the visiting full backs inside out. It came as no real surprise when Scott Adams finished off another move of neat passing play to produce an opening Buckie goal. But better was to come a few minutes later, taking the breath of the amassed Buckie supporters away for a moment before they recovered enough to roar their approval. The tricky striker Sam Robertson controlled a high ball on his chest, shielding it from his marker, controlling it as it dropped to the floor. A body feint and he lost his man just long enough to take a touch and rifle the ball into the bottom corner of the goal from a good few yards outside the penalty area. A moment of sheer brilliance to match that of darts lover Marc Macgregor's last-minute equaliser for Wick; Jamie Michie's spectacular free kick and less than spectacular cartwheel celebration for Inverurie Locos; and Alan Kerr's long-range lob for Fort William that just grazed the wrong side of the bar. The Highland League will be littered with stupendous moments just like these, this and every season.

Robertson's strike was worthy of winning any game and converting any cynic of the Highland League's worth. However, it very nearly wasn't enough, as going two goals down stung Strathspey Thistle into action in a desperate attempt to rescue something from the game. One shot fizzed narrowly over the bar, before a second crashed against it; the two-goal cushion and energy-sapping heat slowed the Buckie tempo enough to bring a murmur of discontent from the old-timers of the supporters' club. Their warnings went unheeded, however, and when a glanced header nestled into the back of the Buckie net in injury time, the most unlikely of comebacks was cut short by the shrill whistle of the referee calling time on a riveting watch.

To the Buckie and Strathspey supporters who saw life as a glass half full, the first 80 minutes for Buckie and last ten for Strathspey had those who had just witnessed the match buoyed for the season ahead. For their glass-half-empty compatriots, the last ten minutes for Buckie and first 80 for the Strathy Jags of this season-opener had them fearing for a year of disappointment. Such is life that supporters could leave a game with so many opposing thoughts on the same match, fuelling animated conversations back down into town; the sun on their backs, calm seas ahead, the shriek of gulls coasting on balmy trade winds above for company.

And with that, as they turned a corner and slipped from sight, after one last lingering glance in the rear-view mirror of my hire car at that old main stand, slowly draining of occupants who gingerly took its steep steps down, Victoria Park, the Highland League and my adventure among it was over. First the floodlights, then the town of Buckie faded away. And with every mile, the wild beauty of the Cairngorms slowly dissolved into Scotland's central belt and the country's more established footballing institutions regarded the world over. The Highland League was gone, as if it had never been there, though the people I had met, the communities I had explored, the grounds I had visited and matches I had watched had ensured that, for me, the Highland League would never be forgotten.

Exploring football's roads less travelled has taught me many things: that passion and meaning cannot be quantified by numbers in attendance and the capacity of a football stadium. It has shown the dedication and self-sacrifice that many willingly offer to maintain and service their community football club, a club that has been, in most instances, at the heartbeat of their community for well over a century. It has taught me that no matter where you go, from the Faroe Islands to San Marino, Fort William to Wick Academy, beauty truly is in the eye of the beholder.

To some, those clubs and countries well off the beaten path are an insignificance or an annoyance in World Cup and European qualifying campaigns – a waste of time and effort when you can watch Barcelona and the rest of the world's best every week on your television. To some it is of no matter whether they thrive or die; the thought of passing up Camp Nou, Barcelona for Victoria Park, Buckie is worthy of sectioning.

However, these experiences among the Highland League, the lower reaches of the Nations League, Europa League and Andorra's unique Primera Divisió sing to the soul in the same way as a swaying, baying 80,000-strong crowd at some of Europe's grand footballing cathedrals. Belonging, coming from a long line who have belonged before you, allowing the identity of your team to become your identity; finding brothers and sisters, friends for life; finding meaning, passion, pride and belief in any team, big or small, is a profound, life changing experience. That it can exist at Ibrox, Celtic Park and Anfield means it can exist at Claggan Park, at Tórsvøllur Stadium and Harlaw Park.

By ignoring the small-time – those that exist on the roads less travelled – you are also denying yourself a larger world of fascinating cultures and people, of unique footballing passions and outlooks. It is a precious thing being able to explore foreign lands and far-away places through the universal language of football, finding someone to chat to at a gale force Harmsworth Park in Wick having never been there before. Building friendships and bridges, understanding and empathy – it is what football can do. It can hold towns like Wick together, embrace 'lost causes' such as Fort William, it can create a vibrant sporting platform for communities to strive and thrive in. A platform such as the Highland Football League, which far from being a waste of time, is a small sporting body for all time.

And the last word on these adventures on football's roads less travelled must be from the Highland League. There were 18 teams when I started, now reduced to 17 following Cove Rangers' promotion to the Scottish professional football league in May 2019. An application by Inverness Caledonian Thistle's Colts team to take that vacated slot was rejected by the league in the off-season. However, Caley Thistle still found a way to play its part, loaning nine Colts team players to Fort William for the 2019/20 season, a move that, at the time of writing, still hadn't yielded a victory in the league, although a 5-2 North of Scotland Cup win over Nairn County on 31 July 2019 saw a first win of any kind for more than two years at Claggan Park. One can only imagine the scenes, complete with Sam Lees bear hugging every Fort player off the pitch.

Small victories in the grand scheme of things but seismic for a club like Fort William, who just want to create a team for the local community to enjoy and embrace. It is what all 17 Highland League teams aim to do, though those with loftier ambitions hope to follow Cove up into the professional leagues before too long.

And while we have the Highland League, a league 'with a special character, a sound commitment to the game, exceptional skill, strong pride and an integral part of the communities within which it is a part', we have the true soul of football at our disposal. And from Barcelona to Buckie Thistle, that really is the most important thing.

Acknowledgements

THANK YOU TO Gavin MacDougall of Luath Press for his continued faith in stories from the fringes of the footballing world and to this book's editor, Maia Gentle, for her patience, her insight and for throwing her energies into the pages you now hold.

I am forever indebted to the people I met on my travels, who gave up their time to help me better understand their little corner of the footballing world. To Sam Lees of Fort William, and Hannis Egholm and Odmar Færø (who got his move to Norway and now plays for HamKam in the second tier OBOS-ligaen) of the Faroe Islands. To the Chuff Chuffs of Inverurie, and Alan Hendry and Blair Duncan of Wick. To Andres Rueda Boga, Guillermo Burgos Viguera, Nicolae Vasile, Miguel Ángel Luque and Walter Fernández of Saint Juliá, Andorra. To their rivals in Coke González, Ildefons Lima (who still shows no sign or retiring from international football) and Adolfo Baines of Inter Club d'Escaldes.

To the young son of Danilo Rinaldi of SP La Fiorita, San Marino, and the young Kosovan girl supporting her team all the way out in the Faroes – both of whom reminded me in their joyous actions of what it feels like to fall under the spell of this beautiful game. To everyone in every crowd, no matter how big or small across my travels – thank you. Thank you for doing what you do and being the people that you are. The privilege truly was all mine.

Thank you to Andy Poole of Ape Publications and Jon Lyons from *Late Tackle Magazine*, and Duncan Mckay from *A View from the Terrace* for all your help and encouragement.

Thank you to Marge and Charlie Truckle, who influence and inspire me even now.

Thank you to Mum, Sam, George, Nicky and Nick for always being there.

Finally, thank you to Deb and Ellie: Deb for your patience, understanding and encouragement when watching me shoot off, yet again, on another football adventure; Ellie, for your companionship on long days of writing and knowing when I needed a break – by curling up on my notes, standing on the laptop or attempting to climb up the curtains only to get stuck. Life really is a beautiful game with you two in it.

Some other books published by **LUATH PRESS**

Another Bloody Saturday

Mat Guy

ISBN: 9781910745724 HBK £8.99

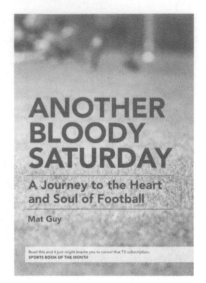

Why do people head out on windswept Saturday afternoons and wet Wednesday evenings watch lower and non-league teams play when they could watch Premier League football from the comfort of their living rooms?

Does an international match between two countries that technically don't exist have any meaning?

Why do some people go to so much trouble volunteering to support clubs which run on a shoestring budget and are lucky to get even a glimpse of the limelight?

Over the course of a season, Mat Guy set out to explore the less glamorous side of the beautiful game, travelling the backwaters of football across the length and breadth of the country – and beyond. He watched Bangor as they were cheerfully thrashed by Reykjavik's UMF Stjarnan, was absolutely won over by the women's game, and found a new team to love in Accrington Stanley.

From Glasgow to Northern Cyprus, Bhutan to the Faroe Islands, Mat discovered the same hope, sense of community, and love of the game that first led him to a life in the stands at Salisbury FC's Victoria Park, where his own passion for football was formed.

Minnows United

Mat Guy

ISBN: 9781912147069 PBK £14.99

Following his first book, *Another Bloody Saturday: A Journey to the Heart and Soul of Football*, Mat Guy continues his exploration of the 'beautiful game' in Minnows United; an ode to the unsung heroes of football matches taking place out of the limelight, all over the world.

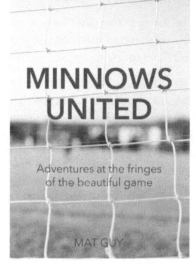

MINNOWS UNITED

Adventures at the fringes of the beautiful game

MAT GUY

From little known teams within the UK, to teams representing countries that, to most of the world, don't even exist, Mat Guy travels to remote parts of the globe to experience football not only on the fringes of the pitch, but on the fringes of the world. On his travels, he watches matches in Iceland, interviews members of the Tibetan Women's Football team, explores the impact of football in war-torn Palestine and explores the unsung heroes in the football clubs present throughout the length of the UK.

What he finds is countries transcending the game itself and instead building communities, lifelines and friendship with football at the centre.

Should've Gone tae Specsavers, Ref!

Allan Morrison
ISBN: 9781908373731 PBK £7.99

The referee. You can't have a game without one. The most hated man (or woman) in football but you have to invite one to every game.

Enjoy a laugh at the antics and wicked humour of Scottish referee Big Erchie, a powerhouse at five foot five, and a top grade referee who strikes fear into the hearts of managers and players alike as he stringently applies the laws of the game.

But Big Erchie is burdened with a terrible secret... He's a Stirling Albion supporter.

Stramash

Daniel Gray

ISBN: 9781906817664 PBK £9.99

Fatigued by bloated big-game football and bored of a samey big cities, Daniel Gray went in search of small town Scotland and its teams. At the time when the Scottish club game is drifting towards its lowest ebb once more, Stramash singularly falls to wring its hands and address the state of the game, preferring instead to focus on Bobby Mann's waistline. Part travelogue, part history and part mistakenly spilling ketchup on the face of a small child, Stramash takes an uplifting look at the country's nether regions. Using the excuse of a match to visit places from Dumfries to Dingwall, Gray surveys Scotland's towns and teams in their present state. Stramash accomplishes the feats of visiting Dumfries without mentioning Robert Burns, being positive about Cumbernauld and linking Elgin City to Lenin. It is as fond look at Scotland as you've never seen it before.

Luath Press Limited

committed to publishing well written books worth reading

LUATH PRESS takes its name from Robert Burns, whose little collie Luath (*Gael.*, swift or nimble) tripped up Jean Armour at a wedding and gave him the chance to speak to the woman who was to be his wife and the abiding love of his life. Burns called one of the 'Twa Dogs' Luath after Cuchullin's hunting dog in Ossian's *Fingal*. Luath Press was established in 1981 in the heart of Burns country, and is now based a few steps up the road from Burns' first lodgings on Edinburgh's Royal Mile. Luath offers you distinctive writing with a hint of unexpected pleasures.

Most bookshops in the UK, the US, Canada, Australia, New Zealand and parts of Europe, either carry our books in stock or can order them for you. To order direct from us, please send a £sterling cheque, postal order, international money order or your credit card details (number, address of cardholder and expiry date) to us at the address below. Please add post and packing as follows: UK – £1.00 per delivery address; overseas surface mail – £2.50 per delivery address; overseas airmail – £3.50 for the first book to each delivery address, plus £1.00 for each additional book by airmail to the same address. If your order is a gift, we will happily enclose your card or message at no extra charge.

Luath Press Limited
543/2 Castlehill
The Royal Mile
Edinburgh EH1 2ND
Scotland
Telephone: +44 (0)131 225 4326 (24 hours)
email: sales@luath. co.uk
Website: www. luath.co.uk